P9-DGQ-485

THE FAREWELL TO LINCOLN

THE FAREWELL

VICTOR SEARCHER

TO LINCOLN

ABINGDON PRESS

NEW YORK — NASHVILLE

THE FAREWELL TO LINCOLN

Copyright © 1965 by Victor Searcher

All rights in this book are reserved.

Library of Congress Catalog Card Number: 65-11517

SET UP, PRINTED, AND BOUND BY THE
PARTHENON PRESS, AT NASHVILLE,
TENNESSEE, UNITED STATES OF AMERICA

+57.5%
.94

IN MEMORY OF MY FATHER,
a patient and kindly man

94139

EMORY AND HENRY LIBRARY

AUTHOR'S NOTE

The narrative in the following pages is authentic. No incidents are invented. No conversations are contrived. All is solid fact based on careful evaluation of first-hand sources and is the result of thorough-going research at the Library of Congress, National Archives, National Library of Medicine, Smithsonian Institution, and other sources. Sources are documented, page by page, in an appendix.

V. S.

Washington, D.C.

CONTENTS

PART I

JUBILATION AND DESPAIR

1

UNRESTRAINED joy coursed throughout the Union when Lee surrendered to Grant. Determined men in blue led by a dogged commanding general finally had prevailed. No more would that valiant, fantastic Army of Northern Virginia hold the people of the North in mortal terror.

When the news came through, the federal states were in the midst of celebrating the fall of the Confederate capital. That long-sought achievement had set off a spree of major proportions the week before. The two great victories, coming so close together and virtually ending hostilities, were almost too much to bear after forty-seven and a half months of unbelievable bloodletting in the greatest civil conflict the world had experienced. Wherever the Stars and Stripes was flying jubilation reigned.

In Washington the news of Richmond's capitulation relieved all government employees from further duty for the day; and soon they were parading Pennsylvania Avenue, bands playing, banners flying. Merchants, mechanics, clerks, and other working people joined the celebration. Stores and shops shut down. Streets throbbed with excitement. Everybody shook the hand of everybody else at the wonderful news.

The third of April, 1865, was a memorable day for Washingtonians. With Richmond safe in Union hands they could breathe easy; no more would they be menaced by gray-clad troops. To celebrate there were "processions, serenades, general suspension of business, and pithy speeches by Secretaries Seward and Stanton."

Secretary of State William H. Seward was at the War Department when the Richmond news arrived, and Secretary of War Edwin M. Stanton insisted he speak first. Seward stepped to the front of the veranda and gave an impromptu talk in his inimitable manner. Stanton followed with remarks that were Lincolnian in inspirational brevity. "In this great hour of triumph," he began, "my heart as well as yours is penetrated with gratitude to the Almighty God for His deliverance of this nation." He said they should all give thanks to the President (cheers), to the army and navy and their great commanders (cheers), and to "the gallant officers and men who periled their lives and drenched the soil with their blood" (ovation). He concluded by asking them to "beseech Him to teach us how to be humble in the midst of triumph and to be just in the hour of victory."

The little war dynamo then did an unusual thing. He introduced to the assembly the telegraph operator who had taken the dispatch announcing the fall of Richmond. He was fourteen-year-old William E. Kettles of Burlington, Vermont. The enthusiastic throng gave Willie a rousing cheer mingled with cries of "Speech," "Have him speak." Willie demurred. He said he could not speak, he "felt so."

Salutes were ordered by War and Navy Departments. Eight hundred times the guns fired from a battery stationed in Franklin Park near Stanton's home on K Street; five hundred times they boomed for the Richmond victory and three hundred for Petersburg. That evening the city was lighted by "the rocket's red glare." Principal thoroughfares dazzled with blue lights. Saloons were jammed; wassail flowed freely. Day shifts of police stayed on duty all night to assist in coping with overexuberance, but only those who made trouble were arrested. The occasion obviously called for all-out celebration.

The Negro population in their demonstrations surpassed the most ardent of the whites. They had special reasons. A very special reason was that Negro infantry, a portion of General G. A. Draper's brigade of the Twenty-fifth Corps, Army of the James, was among the first to enter Richmond and was so reported in the daily papers.

President Lincoln's part in the march of events was unusual. For some time past his friends and the press had been commenting on his haggard appearance and how the war had worn him down. He was thirty pounds underweight. Horace Greeley, after an interview, reported Lincoln's face looked "care-ploughed, tempest-tossed and weather-beaten." To secure relief from the unrelenting pressures of executive business, at the invitation of Commanding General Ulysses S. Grant, he went down the Potomac and up the James River to the general's headquarters at City Point (now Hopewell), Virginia.

On the chartered passenger steamer "River Queen" he arrived Friday evening, March 24, accompanied by Mrs. Lincoln, son Tad, and

several of the White House staff. Awakened early next morning by
the thunder of a nearby battle he went to Fort Stedman attended
by General Grant, reaching the scene after a jolting journey on the
hastily built military railway and then on horseback.

From an eminence that offered a broad view of where the
struggle had ended only an hour before, Lincoln scanned the field
of battle where gray valiants tried to break through lines of blue
and draw them away from Lee in order to give Lee time and space
to junction with Johnston in Carolina. The Confederates had failed;
they could not break with Grant's bulldog grip. The cost had been
high on both sides.

Union troopers soon spied the President's lanky frame and tall
hat silhouetted against the soft spring sky. Like electricity coursing
a copper wire, cheers flowed along the lines. Captured Confederates,
amazed at the uproar, learned that yonder was the Commander-
in-Chief of the United States of America, President Abraham Lincoln. To the yankee boys it was the thrill of a lifetime and they
made the most of it.

Shout after shout and cheer upon cheer echoed as the President
rode over to review Crawford's division, which would soon be
engaged in the bloody business. That evening Lincoln returned to
City Point, declined supper, went directly to his quarters on the
boat, and retired early. The experience he had undergone that day
had been a moving one and he was a sensitive person.

The bright spring weather held next day, Sunday. The President
boarded the "Mary Martin" and speeded downstream to review the
Union flotilla, then turned upstream to within six miles of the Confederate capital. Here General Philip H. Sheridan and his men were
assembling after their successes in the Shenandoah Valley. "Little
Phil" came aboard and the President greeted him: "When this peculiar war began, I thought a cavalryman should be at least six

feet four high, but I've changed my mind—five feet four will do
in a pinch."

Next evening General William Tecumseh Sherman paid an unexpected visit. He had come from Goldsboro, North Carolina, where
his victorious "bummers" were getting supplies after slashing their
way from Atlanta to the sea and from Savannah to Bentonville
where they had whipped Johnston. "Uncle Billy" wanted to find
out what to do next. He had cut the Confederacy clean in two.
There was nothing left but Lee.

In the aftercabin of an unarmed side-wheeler temporarily serving as executive mansion two top generals, Grant and Sherman, and
a top admiral, David D. Porter, conferred with The President Who
Was but Did Not Want to Be a Dictator. From him The Military
Three wanted to know what to do when the fighting ended. The
President Who Held the Country in the Palm of His Hand wanted
to know first: Could not further fighting be avoided? Was there
not enough bloodshed already? Must it keep on?

The Mighty Militarists shook their collective heads. Grant said
the decision would be controlled by events and Lee would determine the event. Sherman felt he would have another fight near
Raleigh. The admiral foresaw further sinkings to maintain the chok-
ing grip the Union navy had on southern ports. That the finish
was near was agreed by these four Americans in whose hands the
fate of the nation rested, but whose thoughts and ambitions were
furthest from despotism and dictatorship.

The President Who Was a Peaceful Man said all he wanted of us
(Sherman speaking) was to defeat the opposing armies and get the
men back to their homes, their shops, their farms. "He assured me
he was all ready for the civil re-organization of affairs in the South
as soon as the war was over," the war-is-hell general related in his
memoirs; "and he distinctly authorized me to assure Governor
Vance and the people of North Carolina that as soon as the rebel

armies laid down their arms and resumed their civil pursuits they would at once be guaranteed all their rights as citizens of our common country."

Sherman persisted; what about Jefferson Davis and others like him? Should they be allowed to escape too? Lincoln replied he was hardly at liberty to speak his mind fully but he was reminded of a story.

The story Lincoln told he would repeat on several occasions when like inquiries were put to him. He had another just as apropos, the pet raccoon tale. Of both there are a number of versions, each differing with the narrator but all making the President's position plain. Related by General Grant, here is Lincoln's "unbeknownst" story.

His position, Lincoln said, was like that of a certain Irishman (giving the name) he knew in Springfield who was very popular with the people. Unfortunately he had acquired the habit of drinking strong liquor to excess and his friends could see the habit growing on him. These friends determined to save him and to do this they drew up and signed a pledge to abstain from all alcoholic beverages. They asked him to join and he consented. He had been so long out of the use of plain water that he resorted to soda water as a substitute. This soon grew distasteful to him. Holding the glass behind him, he said, "Doctor, couldn't you drop in a bit of brandy unbeknownst to me?"

With that presidential procedure in mind Grant left for the fighting front. Sherman returned to Goldsboro. Mrs. Lincoln went back to Washington. Lincoln and Tad remained at City Point. "Having no great deal to do here," he wired Grant next day, "I am sending the substance of your dispatches to the Secretary of War." Stanton forwarded them to the press and the nation's newspaper readers were startled by a headline: "The President's Dispatches!" Telling the latest war news, just as a war correspondent would,

they were modestly signed "A. Lincoln." A New York journal
avowed the presidential work was so good they would offer him a
job when he left office.

When Petersburg fell Grant wired Lincoln to come, and the
President responded with alacrity, riding the bumpy railroad, taking Tad with him and meeting Robert, a captain, en route. "I have
had a sneaking idea for some days you intended to do something
like this," he greeted his hard-driving commanding general. He
toured the fallen stronghold, ran into an old Whig friend, and then
returned to army headquarters at City Point. News awaited him
that the Confederate capital had capitulated. He telegraphed Stanton, "It is certain that Richmond is in our hands and I think I will
go up there tomorrow."

Never in the annals of the world did the head of a mighty nation
and conqueror of an armed rebellion enter the capital of defeated insurgents in such simplicity as Lincoln did when he *walked* into
Richmond. He reached the city by the James River and came
ashore in a barge rowed by a dozen sailors. Not a soul greeted
him as he landed a block from notorious Libby Prison. Twelve
seamen formed the only escort as he, chief of a million-man armed
force, tramped the smoky unpoliced streets of the rebel city evacu-
ated a few hours before. Beside him walked his youngest son, his
personal bodyguard who held Taddie's hand, Admiral Porter, and
three junior staff officers.

"Nothing could have been easier than the destruction of the entire party," related Captain John S. Barnes, who was charged by
the Navy Department with the President's safe conduct. Barnes
had followed in a gig from his gunboat "The Bat," acting as naval
escort, but was unable to catch up when Lincoln landed. A crowd
seemed to spring out of the ground and he became much alarmed.
He supposed federal troops were in full possession of the city and a
proper escort would be on hand. Instead, to his horror, he saw the

President hustled and elbowed along without any regard, "While I was packed closely and had to drift along."

At length a lone federal cavalryman patiently guarding a street corner and wondering what all the commotion was about was sent bug-eyed to headquarters for reinforcements. The long uphill climb on the warm humid day through the shouting, singing throng of adulatory Negroes and astonished whites finally brought the perspiring President to the Confederate Executive Mansion.

Seating himself at the big desk he requested a glass of water, then went sight-seeing with twenty-nine-year-old Major General Godfrey Weitzel. The young general, in command of the Twenty-fifth Army Corps occupying Richmond, asked for the President's instructions regarding conquered soldiers and civilians in the city. Replied Lincoln, "If I were in your place, general, I'd let 'em up easy; let 'em up easy."

That afternoon, again in the office of the escaped head of the rebellion, Lincoln interviewed a former justice of the Supreme Court who had resigned when war began to become Assistant Secretary of War in the rebel cabinet. John A. Campbell of Alabama remained in Richmond when other Conferedate officials fled. Lincoln suggested to him that members of the Virginia Legislature reconvene and withdraw Virginia's troops from the fighting front.

What Lincoln was suggesting to Judge Campbell was not undeserved kindness to rebel leaders as some of his political enemies made it appear; rather, he was endeavoring to exercise his political powers to make it possible for Virginia soldiers to cease their resistance to federal authority.

Johnny Reb was not fighting to destroy the Union nor to save the slaves; in his mind he was battling damyankees to protect his home and loved ones from invasion and to preserve his freedom— "states rights" he called it. Lincoln reasoned that if the Virginia Legislature which had voted the state into the war could be reas-

sembled and vote the state out of it, General Lee and his formid-
able fighters would be withdrawn. That would practically end the
Confederacy. Lincoln's personal presence in Richmond added considerable force to the proposal since Union governments were already operating in Arkansas, Louisiana, and Tennessee. With the
Confederate capital occupied and Davis fleeing into the unknown
why keep on dying for a lost cause?

Lincoln informed Grant of his action: "I do not think it very
probable anything will come of this, but I have thought it best to
notify you so that if you should see signs you may understand
them. From your recent dispatches, it seems that you are pretty
effectually withdrawing Virginia troops from opposition to the
Government. Nothing I have done, or probably shall do, is to delay,
hinder or interfere with your work." Lincoln, by going to Richmond, risked his life if by that risk he could halt further effusion
of American blood.

With the rebel capital now being occupied and with Lee out in
the open, Grant "pressed the thing." The President returned to City
Point and anxiously awaited the outcome on the "River Queen."
Mrs. Lincoln brought back a party of friends from Washington
that included the young man who had married a granddaughter of
General Lafayette, Marquis Charles Adolphe de Pineton de Chambrun. The literate marquis, attached to the French embassy, was
keenly interested in events swirling around the head of the American
government. He accompanied the President on visits to nearby
hospitals and expressed astonishment at the fortitude displayed
by the American soldier. Most of the wounded with whom Lincoln
shook hands were from the Fifth Corps, the gallant troops that
had borne the brunt of recent fighting around Five Forks.

Among the patients was a twenty-four-year-old captain who
had been noticed for bravery in action but who was reaching the
end of his mortal strength. At his bedside sat two friends, one

holding his hand, the other reading from the Bible in a low voice. Lincoln walked over and gently clasped the young captain's free hand in his. The reading continued. The others of the party grouped around the President.

Presently the dying youth, comforted by the inspiring words, half opened his eyes and noticed the President of the United States standing at his side, holding his hand. A faint smile fluttered over his lips. Then his pulse stopped beating. Tenderly Lincoln put down the lifeless extremity of the young soldier he had helped guide into eternity; just as a young soldier-doctor would hold his hand a few days hence when he too would pass to the other shore.

A telegram arrived from Washington advising that the Secretary of State had been thrown from a carriage and was seriously hurt. Lincoln decided he could stay away no longer. He had hoped to be on hand when the fighting ceased so that he might help restore the people of this strife-torn region to the Union of States. Disembarking at the Sixth Street Wharf on the evening of Palm Sunday, April 9, he went directly to the injured Seward and comforted him with news of the impending end of the war. Later, at the White House, his fondest hope was realized when he received Grant's telegram announcing the surrender at Appomattox.

Again guns boomed, bands played, people marched, business stopped, and headlines screamed. The End! Peace! Surrender of Lee and His Whole Army! The Glorious News! Washington Wild with Joy! A Grand Salute to Be Fired in Every Part of the Union! Rejoicings of the People! Popular Demonstrations at the Executive Mansion! The President's Speech!

Early Monday morning popular demonstrations started at the President's House. Engaged with the Cabinet at the time Lincoln did not respond at first. The third demonstration he could not ignore, there was such an outpouring of exuberant people. Appearing at his familiar window, the center second-story one, he received a tumultuous greeting of waving hats, swinging umbrellas, fluttering handkerchiefs. When quiet was restored, he began: "I am very greatly rejoiced that an occasion has occurred so pleasurable that the people cannot restrain themselves." (Cheers.) "I suppose arrangements are being made for a general demonstration tonight or tomorrow night." (Cries of "We can't wait.") "I shall have to respond. But I shall have nothing to say if I dribble it all out before." (Laughter.) "I see you have a band of music with you; I propose for closing up that you have them play an air or tune called 'Dixie.' I have always thought it the best tune I ever heard. . . ."

The band evoked the stirring march, the President remaining at the window and at its conclusion proposing "three good rousing cheers for Lieutenant General Grant and all under his command." The audience responded with a will. He then suggested "three more cheers for our gallant navy," and the happy crowd roared as heartily as before. Lincoln bowed and retired. The band struck up "Hail, Columbia!" and the people dispersed.

The trip to the fighting front, though short, had done Lincoln a deal of good despite deep lines still furrowing his face. His two secretaries, John Nicolay and John Hay, avowed he had enjoyed ten days "of the most satisfactory relaxation in which he had been able to indulge during his entire Presidential service."

The war had been pure agony to him. Many were the nights he had been unable to sleep and many were the days he was so exhausted he had to lie down. After one such sleepless night he remarked to his early morning caller, the Speaker of the House: "How willingly I would exchange places with the soldier who sleeps on the ground in the Army of the Potomac!" To sick Owen Lovejoy, congressman from Illinois, he said on one of his many visits, "This war is eating my life out. I have a strong impression that I shall not live to see the end." He paced the deck of the "River Queen" all night long, his bodyguard related. To Noah Brooks, the White House correspondent of the *Sacramento* (Calif.) *Union,* slated to be his second-term private secretary, Lincoln confided he had a tired spot down inside that rest alone could not cure.

Of the many manifestations celebrating newfound peace the grand illumination of the city was most noteworthy. The White House was a magnificent sight, its windows radiant with light from an array of candles along each sill. Flags flying from every part of the mansion made a veritable riot of patriotism in color. Windows and doorways were adorned with evergreen and all the portico lights were beaming. Never had the President's House offered such a handsome spectacle.

Its blaze of glory was matched at the other end of the avenue by the Capitol. Five tiers of gas lights made the noble structure appear to be in flames from base to dome, giving the "Lady of the Capitol" a fiery pedestal visible for miles. Streets of the city were rivers of light. Showers of emeralds and sapphires and diamonds cascading from fountains of fireworks crowned the breathtaking scene.

Across the Potomac River General Lee's former home now used as an army hospital, setting majestically atop the river bluff, was outlined against dark foliage and low-hanging clouds, the brightest spot on the Virginia shore. A large lamp suspended from a tall flagstaff sparkled like a guiding star—like a beacon poised between heaven and earth telling thousands of heroes asleep in surrounding graves, whose souls looked down from other stars, that they had not died in vain.

Over Washington floated strains of martial music; drums, bugles, fifes, trumpets, and glockenspiels paraded the fiery streets and serenaded phosphorescent buildings. Mingled with military tunes, deep-throated singing arose from thousands of voices lifted in thanksgiving. The ex-slaves and freedmen of the District of Columbia poured their jubilation into the misty evening, chorusing "The Year of the Jubilee," "Hallelujah," "Old Hundred," and kindred songs that made the heart beat stronger and the eyes moisten. It was a generation worth living in. The Republic had been saved from the curse and shame of human slavery.

Tuesday evening the President was ready with his promised speech. The mass of people surrounding the Executive Mansion let loose a roar of approbation as he came to the well-known second-story window. Their deep roar was such as men make when they feel their own voice too small to give adequate relief to pent-up emotions. It was a scene of the wildest enthusiasm. Manuscript in hand, the President waited for the demonstration to subside. When he could make himself heard, he opened his remarks with the most cheerful sentence he had been able to utter during his entire term of office. "We are met this evening, not in sorrow, but in gladness of heart," he began.

To make clear that the cheers and applause with which his words were being interrupted were not for him alone, he told the assembly: "I myself was near the front and had the high pleasure of transmitting much of the good news to you; but no part of the honor for plan or execution is mine. To General Grant, his skillful officers and brave men, all belongs. . . ."

Launching into the much-debated question of how to restore the Union he said, "We all agree that the seceded states, so called, are out of their proper relation with the Union; and that the sole object of the government, civil and military, in regard to those States is to get them into that proper practical relation." This could be done, he proposed, without deciding or even considering whether those states had ever been out of the Union. "Let us all join," he urged, "in doing the acts necessary to restoring the relations . . . and each forever after innocently indulge his own opinions whether in doing the acts he brought the States from without into the Union; or only gave them proper assistance, they never having been out of it."

This was Lincoln's first step toward reuniting the nation—an earnest plea to act with comity and forbearance. He explained how the reconstruction program was operating in three Southern states. Long and detailed his explanation was hardly the kind of speech expected by people vibrant with victory. But this was the opportune moment, he evidently felt, to expound the problems of peace that lay ahead. The responsibility of a restored nation was the concern of every citizen. The audience listened respectfully; and an eyewitness reported it was a "silent, intent and perhaps surprised multitude."

The subject was very much on the President's mind. Next day an influential Montgomery, Alabama, citizen, William J. Bibb, called on him. Bibb was one of many pro-Unionists in the South bottled up by the war. His mission to Washington had been to find a way to dispose of his cotton; but now with the war almost over he wanted to know what would come next. "My desire is to restore the Union," Lincoln told him. "I do not intend to hurt the hair of a single man in the South if it can be avoided." Before the interview ended, Lincoln told Bibb he would "pardon Jeff. Davis himself if he asks for it."

Two days later at the Friday Cabinet meeting, Lincoln reiterated his stand on amnesty. He said—reported by the diary-keeping Secretary of the Navy—that it was the great pending question, that they must all work for harmony and reunion.

Secretary Gideon Welles recorded another subject very much on the President's mind that morning. Lincoln had inquired for news from General Sherman. Finding none, he said he had no doubt it would be coming soon and would be favorable. He had a

dream the night before, he explained, such as he always had when
great events portended; had had the same dream preceding Sumter,
Bull Run, Antietam, Gettysburg, and others. "I inquired," Welles
recorded, "what this remarkable dream could be." The President
replied that he "seemed to be in some singular, indescribable vessel
moving with great rapidity toward an indefinite shore."

Something weighing down Lincoln's mind was also noted by
Ward Hill Lamon, the trusted friend whom Lincoln had appointed
marshal of the District of Columbia. At the White House on an
evening during the week Lincoln had sat silent and absorbed, taking little part in the general conversation. Mrs. Lincoln commented
on his want of spirit. This seemed to arouse him.

He proceeded to enumerate, surprisingly, references in the Bible
to supernatural visitations and to descriptions of visions and dreams.
He looked so sober Mrs. Lincoln exclaimed, "You frighten me.
What is the matter?"

"About ten days ago," answered the President, "I retired very
late. I had been waiting for important dispatches from the front.
I could not have been long in bed when I fell into slumber, for
I was very weary. I soon began to dream. There seemed to be a
death-like stillness about me. Then I heard subdued sobs as if a
number of people were weeping."

He said in his dream he left his bed and went downstairs, going
from room to room, but could not locate the mourners though the
sobbing continued. It was light in all the rooms and he recognized
every object. Still the people were invisible. He determined to find
out what was going on and kept on until he reached the East
Room, which he entered.

"There I met with a sickening surprise," he continued. "Before
me was a catafalque on which rested a corpse wrapped in funeral
vestments. Around it were stationed soldiers who were acting as
guards; and there was a throng of people, some gazing mournfully

upon the corpse whose face was covered, others weeping pitifully.

" 'Who is dead in the White House?' I inquired of one of the soldiers. 'The President,' was his answer; 'he was killed by an assassin.' Then came a loud burst of grief from the crowd which awoke me from my dream. I slept no more that night; and although it was only a dream I have been strangely annoyed by it ever since."

"That is horrid!" exclaimed Mrs. Lincoln. "I wish you had not told it. I am glad I do not believe in dreams or I should be in terror from this time forth."

"Well, it is only a dream, Mary," the President responded. "Let us say no more about it and try to forget it."

To help her harried husband forget his dream and give him relief from the pressing problems of peace, Mary suggested a theater party. She knew he loved to go to the theater; it provided him with much-needed relaxation. At Ford's new playhouse on Tenth Street, Laura Keene was making a final appearance in the English farce, *Our American Cousin*. It was a comedy-drama, the only one in town, and would offer an evening of entertainment for him.

There the Lincolns went Friday night.

2

OVERNIGHT the unrestrained joy turned to deep sorrow. Never had a people been plunged so precipitately from heights of exultation to depths of despair. The hysteria that dark conspiracy generates took hold of the populace and feelings of revulsion, suspicion, and apprehension gripped their minds. Fear seized residents of the capital city and the night of the murder became a night of terror along the Potomac.

Awakened by the long roll beating in camps and forts around the city, Washington householders locked doors and windows and sat up all night, frightened at the sound of hooves pounding the roads. They wondered: Were rebels attacking the heads of government in a last desperate attempt? Were they lurking about, ready to strike at will? Whom would they hit next? Ten thousand rumors were afloat.

Agitated citizens debouched into the streets and milled about the fateful theater, shouting "Burn the place!" Word came that the Secretary of State also had been assassinated and they hastened to his residence on Lafayette Square to find it nearly true. He had been slashed across the throat while lying helpless in bed. Son Frederick, who was Acting Secretary since his father had been hurt in a carriage accident, was severely stabbed and his life despaired of. Another son and two domestics in the house were wounded in the assassination attempt. The intense excitement flew across the square to the crowd gathered in front of the White House where the stricken President was expected to be.

The wild night was made wilder by unverified reports that General Grant had been struck down en route to Philadelphia, that Vice-President Andrew Johnson was another victim, and that the entire Cabinet had been marked for destruction. The murderous deeds, so sudden and so concerted, put the people in an ugly mood. Men wept and cursed in the same breath; being certain the rebels meant to paralyze the nation by striking down "its head, its heart, and its arms." Such a night of unseen fright seldom dominated any city let alone the seat of American government. The news spread like a raging prairie fire.

Secretary of War Stanton was notified at his home of the assault on Seward and hurried there. Here he learned of the attack on the President and hastened to the Petersen house. Setting up headquarters in the back parlor, he issued orders with such rapidity and sureness that his assistants were amazed. Malicious criticism has been leveled at his high-handedness but the energetic secretary displayed cool judgment and directed the course of law and order when most needed. With him was the chief justice of the District Supreme Court, Judge David Cartter, who conducted a court of inquiry and interviewed witnesses. Using a soldier stenographer to take down testimony, by morning he had evidence of the alleged culprits; a remarkable performance considering the confusion.

The unconscious President was carried across the street from Ford's Theater to the house of William Petersen, a tailor who took in roomers.* Carried to the first-floor rear bedroom of a soldier in the Thirteenth Massachusetts Volunteers, he was laid cater-cornered on the too-short bedstead attended by several army surgeons who had responded to the call for a doctor.

First to reach him had been twenty-three-year-old Charles A. Leale, M.D., of New York who was sitting in the dress circle nearest the Presidential box and had leaped over the seats when he heard the shot and saw the assassin land on the stage. "O Doctor, is he dead?" cried out Mrs. Lincoln as he entered the box saying he was a United States army surgeon. "Can you save him? Will you take charge?" Replying he would do all that could be done, he turned to an usher guarding the doorway and asked that brandy and water be procured at once.

"It was owing to Dr. Leale's quick judgment in instantly placing the almost moribund President in a recumbent position the moment he saw him that Mr. Lincoln did not expire in the theater within ten minutes from the fatal syncope," attested Dr. Charles S. Taft, an army surgeon personally known to the Lincolns who had been in the audience also. When the family physician, Dr. Robert K. Stone, reached the bedside he took charge, and later Surgeon General Joseph K. Barnes. Both continued Leale's mode of treatment without change.

The minutes and hours dragged interminably through the night.

* Preserved today as it was then and open to the public.

As morning approached the President grew visibly weaker. At times the pulse could not be counted and respiratory intervals extended over long periods. Then he would resume breathing accompanied by guttural sounds. His vitality was extraordinary.

Below the Petersen house on Tenth Street at the headquarters of the metropolitan police the superintendent telegraphed all precincts to put every available man on duty. Using horses supplied by the army quartermaster, the men were mounted; and it was they, together with army cavalry and provost marshal soldiers ordered out by Stanton, whose constant hoofbeats alarmed residents.

Saloons, concert halls, beer gardens, and other places of entertainment were ordered shut down by the mayor, enforced by the police. The cast of players and employees of Ford's Theater were taken to jail for safekeeping and questioning. Ferryboats to Alexandria and other ports were halted; no ship was permitted to leave the Washington wharves. Incoming and outgoing trains were searched and passengers interrogated. The railroad station and freight yards were closely invested with the military. All traffic on roads into the city was halted: even milkmen, market gardeners, and farmers. No food supplies entered the beleaguered city this dark rainy morning. No person left the city without permission from the authorities. The federal capital was as tightly sealed as a fortress under siege.

The Union Light Guard, a cavalry regiment of picked men charged with guarding the person of the President, patrolled Tenth Street all night, screening those who entered the Petersen place. Sergeant Smith Stimmel, who four years before had cheered President-elect Lincoln when he passed through Columbus, said the scene before him was like a horrible nightmare. He had to pinch himself to make it real. That the great and good man he had come to know personally and whose life he had sworn to protect, had

been felled from behind and lay dying in that house, he could not
bring himself to believe.

Sergeant Stimmel did believe every word a bunkmate on the day
shift told him when he came off duty—about meeting another
cavalryman on patrol who, recognizing the uniform as the President's own, came up and cried out, the tears rolling down his face,
"He means more to me than he does to you"; and then turned the
horse around and said, as if to excuse the unsoldierly tears, "He
signed an order that saved me from being shot"; and rode away
sobbing.

Squads of soldiers guarded the homes of Cabinet members.
Sentries stood at the doorways of high government officials. The
Commissioner of Public Buildings, Benjamin B. French, returning
to the city Friday evening from a trip to Richmond, went directly
to bed after the long journey and awakened at sunrise to see a
sentry pacing in front of his house, the street lights still burning.
He rushed outside to be confronted with the awful news. "I
thought I should suffocate," he wrote his sister later, "it had such
an effect on me."

Jumping into his clothes he hurried to the President's bedside
to find him still alive but nearing the end. From there he took the
President's carriage and brought back Mrs. Gideon Welles to
comfort Mrs. Lincoln. He galloped to the White House and ordered
that all patriotic insignia be replaced by emblems of sorrow, then
went to the capitol to direct that federal buildings be attired in
suitable mourning. At the end of the long hectic day, Commissioner
French noted in his diary: "There is no doubt it was an organized
conspiracy."

Nothing less could explain the multiple attacks so perfectly
timed and so daringly executed. The synchronized acts must be
the work of those plotting to topple the government. It was a
conspiracy of desperate men; the same men who had broken up

the Union and had brought untold suffering to achieve political
power. They would stop at nothing, not even at behind-the-back
murder of the Head of State. They had vowed: "If we can't win,
neither can you!"

News media concurred and added to the dreadful dispatches
expostulary comments: "He was murdered, not that slavery might
live, but that it might bring down its most conspicuous enemy in
its fall." "The popular voice demands enforcement of the strictest
justice against all connected with the assassination and against
obdurate rebel leaders." "All circumstances show that the same
political fury and hate which lit the flames of the great rebellion
inspired these hellish deeds." "The most horrible crime ever committed on this globe was perpetrated by rebel emissaries. *The
foolish rebels have killed their best friend."*

The *Washington Morning Chronicle* cried out that nothing was
so calculated to exasperate the loyal millions since the firing on
Fort Sumter to cause them to demand vengeance for the authors of
the rebellion. "We may say that reason had culminated in the
murder of President Lincoln."

When was such a chapter of horrors ever written as of last night?
When did such stupendous crimes stain human nature in this land
before? So lamented the *Washington National Republican* and said,
"The heart grows sick and faint. The pen almost refuses to trace
the details of the tragedy."

Only a few hours ago the Stars and Stripes had proudly floated
from every dwelling and building. Each pane of glass had been
brilliantly lighted in the night. Bands of music had given forth
stirring patriotic tunes. Washington was happy. The Union was
happy. The war was won and it was all over.

Now the flags drooped at half staff. Windows were dark. Streets
were silent. The red-white-and-blue decorations had vanished, re-

placed by emblems of grief. The War Department was clothed in crape. The people were steeped in gloom.

"Our heart stands still as we take our pen to speak of the awful tragedy of last night," moaned the *Washington National Intelligencer,* regretting they had no words adequate to express their feelings. "He who yesterday was our good, gentle, wise, upright, affectionate President is no more! Not in all the records of crime did any surpass it except rebellion itself; of which it was one of the legitimate fruits. The deed will discourage and retard pacification and reconstruction which was the benevolent aim of the late President. *The assassins have murdered the peace!"*

In a special Sunday edition that contained so much material it sold for ten dollars a copy a few days later, and continues to be a prime source from which historians garner facts, the *New York Herald* asserted that for the first time in the history of "this democratic republican government" the tragic scenes of the Roman Empire and the French Revolution were enacted in America almost within sight of the last resting place of the Father of the Country. "We have read accounts of similar scenes in other nations," the *Herald* declared, "but they were never before brought home to our doors. It is not to be wondered at that the people were dumbfounded."

Murder for political purpose was not an Anglo-Saxon tradition, and least of all was it American. The heinous act was foreign to the liberty-loving people of the United States, nurtured as they are in human dignity. The Founders of the Republic had established the rights of the individual as the keystone of the American system, and their fundamental proposition was the greatest practical application of freedom in the history of mankind. Murder for any purpose is without warrant; for political profit it was unthinkable.

"The news of the assassination carried with it a sensation of horror and agony which no other event in our history has ever excited," expostulated the *New York Times,* and pointed to the universal sense of dismay and indignation that filled the public mind. "That a man so gentle, so kind, so free from every particle of malice, and whose every act has been marked by benevolence and goodwill, should become the victim of cold-blooded killing shocked the people beyond expression."

"He not only put forth no speech, no paper, no manifesto, that gave the least countenance to these calumnies," said Horace Greeley in the *New York Tribune,* "but he never, even in his most intimate and confidential moments, indicated a hope that evil should befall one of these enemies save as it should be necessary for the salvation of the country. . . . His very last utterance was conceived in this spirit and had no other purpose than to reconcile the North to the most gentle and magnanimous treatment of the discomfited insurgents. If ever a man," concluded Greeley, "made war in the Christian spirit, that man was Abraham Lincoln."

Emphasizing it was that which was infuriating so many Americans, the *Boston Transcript* said, "The horror of the deed was all the more deepened by the fact that its victim was the kindliest and most magnanimous of great magistrates and seemed to fall a martyr to his own goodness of heart." Maintaining there could be no doubt the crime had its motive in political fanaticism, they demonstrated the point by reprinting from a Southern newspaper an advertisement offering to assassinate President Lincoln, Vice-President Johnson, and Secretary of State Seward. That a newspaper should even carry such an announcement made this New England journal see red. "What associates the act with them," declared the *Transcript,* "is the brutality and hatred against the North with which they have filled the hearts of the Southern people." *

* The advertisement, which asked for one million dollars to assassinate the three federal heads of state, appeared December 1, 1864, in the *Selma* (Ala.) *Despatch.* Following Lincoln's death the perpetrator was tracked down. He claimed it was a joke. The circumstances indicated he was correct though not without some difficulty. He was finally pardoned by President Johnson.

In a special Sunday edition, the *Washington Evening Star* announced that developments showed conclusively the existence of a "deep-laid plot including the members of the Order of the Knights of the Golden Circle." The *Intelligencer* said the facts developed by the official investigation showed that there was an organized conspiracy, the object of which was the destruction of all the leading officers of the federal government. Stanton, as Secretary of War, had prosecuted hostilities with implacable energy and naturally assumed he was marked as a prime victim. Nevertheless in the dispatches he sent out of the Petersen back parlor he reiterated, "It was nothing but a Southern plot, a conspiracy deliberately planned and set afoot by the rebels."

Further credibility to that conclusion was given by the flight of Confederate officialdom from Richmond. Undisciplined guerrilla warfare was now to be expected. All rebel sympathizers were suspect. Mob violence became a serious threat as the Washington populace grew more excited. Masses of people surged from point to point as though burning to execute revenge upon someone connected with the crime. Crowds congregated on street corners, at hotels, at Ford's Theater, at the Seward house, at the Executive Mansion. Mutterings arose. Threats punctuated with expressions of sorrow were heard. Businesses shut down. Cavalry patrolled the streets. The entire police force was on duty and patrolmen walked their beats. The blow that struck down Abraham Lincoln threw the nation's capital—and the nation—into a turmoil of high excitement and deep emotion. Anything could happen.

A young Conferedate officer strode blithely along Pennsylvania Avenue in the full uniform of a rebel captain, seemingly unaware of the night's tragic events. When he reached the White House the angry mob gathered there demanded to know what he was doing. He answered he was on his way to the provost marshal's office on

Fourteenth Street. This did not satisfy the crowd and they demanded he remove the hated uniform. He protested he had no other clothes and no money to buy any. "Strip him!" came the cry, and hands reached out to pluck the clothes from his back. Denouncing the assassination of the President, he cried that he had sworn allegiance to the Union. The statement saved his life and he was allowed to proceed.

Any person under guard of the military immediately became the object of attention. It was fortunate that few gray uniforms were seen on the streets that day since the number of deserters and captured Confederates marching in the federal capital had grown enormously. Toward afternoon a rebel major general and aides taken in Virginia were brought in. Riding to the provost marshal's they passed numerous agitated groups who, seeing the graybacks under guard, assumed they were connected with the assassination. The procession burgeoned into a howling mob. Just as the prisoners were to enter the marshal's headquarters the mob made a determined rush, yelling, "Kill the assassins!" "Hang the rebels!" The guard managed to pass them inside. To disperse the angry crowd, a union general and a senator who happened to be nearby, made fervent pleas. Meanwhile the captured Confederates were spirited out a side door and hurried to Old Capitol Prison. It was a near thing.

The excitement continued unabated throughout the city. Anyone showing the slightest disrespect for the murdered President was manhandled forthwith. A wandering preacher spoke at an evening service in the Mission Church near Camp Fry. He made derogatory remarks about Lincoln and said that if the new President pursued the same course he would meet the same fate. He was at once set upon by soldiers in the congregation and only escaped serious injury by being arrested and carted off to jail.

Similar violence was reported from all parts of the country. This was the first great unexpected event to be broadcast by telegraph. Clicking brass keys carried the shocking news to population centers and to every wayside railroad station. War's end had been anticipated; that news was anticlimactic. But this intelligence fell upon the people as they sat down to breakfast, unheralded, undreamed of. Clemency had been brutally cut down in the national capital. Madness ruled the hour.

An old man in New Haven, Connecticut, Harvey Ford, was so affected that after appearing depressed all day, he dropped dead in the evening. A blacksmith in Brookfield, Massachusetts, expressed satisfaction at the event and, being given his choice of a coat of tar and feathers or departure from town, chose the latter. A man was thrown from a Brooklyn ferryboat into the East River for disloyal and offensive language, his life saved by a passing vessel.

A young man known as "Southern George" stood at the corner of Chatham and Pearl Streets in New York and loudly remarked that "Old Abe, the son of a bitch, is dead and he ought to have been killed long ago." Sergeant Walsh of the Sixth Precinct overheard the scurrilous remark, knocked him down, and hauled him to jail. In default of $1,000 bail Justice Dowling sentenced the recalcitrant to the penitentiary for six months.

Also sentenced by the justice to six months for uttering profane remarks were several others including the treasurer of a theater. A Fifteenth Precinct policeman, John Brady, made vulgar comments to fellow officers who turned him in and preferred charges. He resigned before the charges could be pressed.

A squad of patriotic young Unionists went to the Staten Island home of Mrs. John Tyler, widow of the former President, who was a Virginian. They obtained the rebel flag hanging in her front parlor concerning which many boasts had been made. The parlor was reputed to be the gathering place of secessionists. When the

squad arrived the ex-mayor of Savannah was present but kept quiet
and was not molested. The "captured" flag was turned over to
Major General John A. Dix, commander of the New York military
district. Other secessionists did not get off so easily; they were
beaten by Unionists infuriated at snide remarks about the honored
dead. Placards appeared around New York and Brooklyn proclaiming, "Death to the traitors!" "The Union, one and indivisible!"
"Strike early and often!"

The machinery and plant of an opposition newspaper in San
Francisco was destroyed so quickly by an angry mob that the
authorities were unable to prevent it. By that night all Montgomery
Street was under military control. The sudden outburst, it was
generally agreed, resulted from long pent-up grievances brought
to a head by the President's murder. A huge meeting of citizens
gathered next day, arranged for obsequies to be held, passed resolutions, and appointed committees to take action. "Before his death
peace was possible," read a resolution. "All the atmosphere was
filled with generous emotions and kind sympathy—but now peace
means subjugation or annihilation! God have mercy on the souls
of the rebel chiefs!" The resolution was cheered again and again.

At Westminster, Maryland, citizens angry at the disloyal character of a local newspaper, entered its plant on Main Street and
made common ruin of the type, machinery, and property, warning
the editor to stay away. This took place the night of the day
Lincoln died. A week later the editor returned. A delegation of
citizens, incensed at his return despite their warning, went to his
house and knocked on the door. He appeared with a gun in his
hands and fired, wounding several persons. The enraged people
killed him on the spot.

At Hagerstown, near the Antietam battlefield, a rebel sympathizer
went to the county jail and asked to be locked up as a protection
from citizens out to punish him for his apparent connection with

the presidential murder. Early in March he had confidentially told
a customer in his store that a hundred thousand dollars was being
raised to secure the President's death. Affidavits to this effect were
made by those who had heard his statements. He left the vicinity
for good.

At Buffalo, New York, a passerby, possibly a disgruntled office-
seeker, threw a handful of mud at former President Millard
Fillmore's unadorned house; and the incident was blown up in
news dispatches to say that an angry mob splashed ink and other
objects over his pretentious Niagara Square domicile because he
exhibited no emblems of mourning. Another mob, a real one, waited
on former President Franklin Pierce in Concord, New Hampshire.
Opposed to the Lincoln administration, Pierce had voiced remarks
to the effect that he could not commend a single act of the party
in power. The crowd demanded of him, "Where is your flag?" To
which the fourteenth President responded with asperity that it was
not necessary for him, a former President of the United States,
"to show my devotion by any special exhibition upon the demand
of any man or body of men."

At Swampscott, Massachusetts, George Stone was tarred and
feathered for cheering Lincoln's death; and Otis Wright, superintendent of the Middlesex Horse Railway narrowly escaped hanging
for the same reason.

The Baltimore City Council posted a reward of $10,000 for appre-
hension or arrest of the assassin, the feeling being that since the
culprit called the city his home, "our loyal people trust that one
who so dishonored the fair name of this community should meet
with speedy justice." To maintain peace and tranquillity they
resolved that "those who left the city to cooperate with the so-
called southern confederacy" should not be allowed to return and
that those already in the city should not be permitted to remain.
The *Baltimore Sun* posed the rhetorical question: "Men will nat-

urally ask themselves, is it possible that a Republic, born, nurtured and reared in an age of civilization and Christianity, can hold within its bosom men capable of the vilest crimes that blot and disgrace the pages of history?"

In Norfolk, then as now the Virginia city with the largest northern population, great numbers of paroled soldiers and officers from Lee's army milled about the streets, the officers carrying side arms, parading like conquering heroes. The news of Lincoln's demise "fell like a bursting shell" upon the community and "paralyzed everybody"—everybody except the commanding officer of the Department of Eastern Virginia who promptly ordered all Confederate military men not residents of Norfolk or Portsmouth to stay off the streets. If found on the streets, said his order, they would be taken into custody. They could wear their uniforms temporarily but must remove all insignia and buttons and within forty-eight hours must procure civilian dress. Otherwise they would be arrested and held "until their friends could dress them in a Christian garb." The general tightened security measures, replacing the Second U.S. Volunteers made up largely of Confederate deserters and refugees with the Thirteenth New York Artillery whose loyalty was unquestioned.

The result was no outbreak at America's largest naval base. "Southerners deplore the President's death and Unionists weep over it," said a telegraphic dispatch. Norfolk's main street was draped in black from end to end. No boats arrived or departed. There were no mail deliveries. The community stood still in sadness, and all was quiet along Hampton Roads.

Not so the Army of the Potomac. The impact on the boys in blue was terrific. The Sixth Corps report said that "astonishment and rage were depicted on every countenance"; and they demanded speedy justice be meted out to the "perpetrators of this diabolical act." A New York volunteer wrote his father a letter that was

widely quoted in news dispatches, saying they expected to stay in
camp only until General Grant ordered: "Sixth Corps! Take up
thy beds and walk! Crush Johnston as Lee was!" The veteran
soldier avowed, "We will take no prisoners!"

From the Fifth Corps the dispatch said, "The effect is indescribable." The corps had pulled into Farmville (Va.) on Sunday
afternoon and for the first time since taking Lee's surrender received rations and mail. They had shared their yankee food with
starving rebel troops and then had had to go hungry themselves.
They were in an ugly mood.

The Ninth Corps, at Burkesville Junction, reacted with indignation and horror. "The treatment of the rebels in our midst is
giving way to a scarcely suppressed vengeful feeling that 'as it is
meted to us so shall it be meted to them.'" The dispatch said that
forbearance of the men toward their former enemies was lost in
contemplating "the foul blow struck at the head of government and
safety of the nation."

Returning from Richmond, the publisher of the *Philadelphia
Press*, close friend of the President whom he had seen a few days
before, refused to credit the news. When he reached City Point the
tidings were confirmed in a newspaper from Washington. He handed
the paper to a blue-coated guard who looked at it and muttered,
"There's going to be trouble hereabouts." He was not far wrong.

Fortunately for both sides, noted a soldier in the Twentieth
Maine, the rebel army had been paroled before the assassination.
"With the intense feeling that existed when the news reached us,"
Private Theodore Gerrish wrote, "there would have been a conflict
of the most deadly character." A double guard was thrown around
the camp. The Twentieth Maine's heroic battle actions had brought
medals of honor to five of its most intrepid members. The regiment
was in the front line of the advance to Appomattox when a flag of
truce from Longstreet's lines stopped them. For their valor they

were accorded the place of honor in the surrender ceremonies. These "down-Easters" had fought at South Mountain, Antietam, Fredericksburg, and Gettysburg (extreme left at Little Round Top); had battled through the fire-and-brimstone of the Wilderness, Cold Harbor, Spottsylvania, Fort Stedman, Petersburg, Hatcher's Run, Five Forks; and then had shared their rations with starving Johnny Rebs at Appomattox. They were not to be trifled with.

Upon receiving the awful tidings, Private Bill Todd of Company B, Seventy-ninth Highlanders, New York Volunteers reported, "It was with considerable difficulty that our hotheaded comrades were prevented from coming to blows or even worse with hotheads of the other side." The regiment was engaged in shipping home surrendered rebel troops, some of whom they found unrepentant and obstreperous.

Adding fuel to the disturbing news were rumors that a conspiracy was afoot to destroy the government by murder, that the army was going to the capital city to take control of the government, that Grant would be made military dictator until order was restored and the rebellion put down once and for all.

To the deep feelings of the Ninety-sixth Illinois Regiment only one thought gave relief when the news hit them in the Tennessee mountains and that was revenge. These lean and rugged campaigners from Lake and Jo Daviess counties felt a personal loss such as comes only to those to whom the President of the United States means home. He was their man.

The Ninety-sixth had hit the summit of Lookout Mountain after having gone through Tullahoma, Chickamauga, Chattanooga, and then had followed the Battle Above the Clouds with smashing successes at Tunnel Hill, Resaca, New Hope Church, Kennesaw Mountain, and Atlanta; had turned around and decimated Hood at Franklin and Nashville; had cleaned up at Knoxville and Strawberry Plains and were now regrouping at Bull's Gap. To commemorate their successes they were holding a brigade ceremony at Lick Creek with a program of music by veteran bands, fine solos, and group singing. Thousands of husky soldiers, glad to be alive, glad to have served their country so well, glad to have given life to a reborn nation, lifted their voices in the familiar campfire songs: "When This Cruel War Is Over," "Tenting Tonight," "Tramp, Tramp, Tramp," "Battle Cry of Freedom," and ending with the soul-stirring "Praise God from Whom All Blessings Flow." It was an occasion long to be remembered.

Saturday dawned cold and cloudy. Despite the uncomfortable weather the men, elated at the prospects of going home, were constantly shouting and cheering, starting at any point and rolling from company to company until everyone was wild with the joy of peace. What came next arrived when the afternoon supply train pulled in. An officer hurried ahead and quietly gave to headquarters the words that had been flashed from Washington. Like lightning they were passed from man to man. An ominous hush fell. Men caught their breath, stood stock still, felt a pain tugging at the throat. The shock benumbed the mind and left but one compelling emotion: *revenge!*

These men were soldiers; good soldiers, battle tried and proved. Their grief was great and their sorrow deep. But their discipline was greater. And discipline prevailed. Camp was broken next morning and the units were hurried to Nashville for mustering out. The end had come; but what an end!

Would soldierly discipline carry the Union Army through the crisis? What about Sherman's tough "bummers"? How would they take it?

"Uncle Billy" sat on his horse in front of the Capitol at Raleigh, reviewing the troops as they tramped in. The natives took the occupation calmly. There were no "incidents." The streets were filled, and many spectators were paroled soldiers from Lee's forces.

Everyone knew the Confederacy was defunct with Richmond gone, Lee surrendered, Davis on the run. The Union men were bursting with jubilation at the thought of going home. Only General Johnston and his crew were left and they had licked him. "Uncle Billy" would take care of him in person; had, as a matter of fact, a date with Johnston the following day to discuss matters.

To keep the appointment Sherman was leaving early on a special train. As he boarded the car, the telegraph operator handed him a coded wire from Washington. The general read the operator's decoding, drew him aside, pledged him to secrecy. When he was seated opposite his old West Point classmate in the little farmhouse between the contending armies, Sherman handed Johnston the fateful telegram. As he read the message, sweat broke out on the Confederate general's forehead and he exclaimed, "This is the greatest possible calamity to the South!"

The question was whether their armies should be informed. Both dreaded the consequences. They decided to withhold the news until their negotiations were completed. Returning to Raleigh Sherman moved some units away from the city and waited until Monday to publish the official announcement.

"On the morning of the 18th of April while kneeling on the greensward around the breakfast dishes a newsboy came running into camp with a lot of Raleigh newspapers, shouting, 'All about the assassination! President Lincoln assassinated!'" So wrote Lieutenant John G. Janicke, Company G, Fourth Minnesota Infantry, of the fabulous Fifteenth Corps. He bought a copy; saw the black-bordered columns; scanned the dispatches. "We drop knives and forks and rise, grief-stricken, and in solemn silence leave our breakfast. Lieutenant Dooley is standing behind an oak tree, the tears falling from his eyes. Before I get through reading I am overcome with painful emotion," related Janicke. His newspaper got wet all through. The camp went into mourning.

Inevitably the reaction came. These men who, by their own hands had slashed the Confederacy in two and had marched for two thousand miles and had battled every inch of the way, now cried for vengeance. Curses filled the air. They gathered in angry knots and threatened to march on Raleigh and put it to the torch. Generals and colonels and majors and captains and lieutenants moved in with the bitter troops imploring, reasoning, begging, ordering them to their quarters. Gradually, reluctantly the men simmered down. Discipline won.

At Richmond federal officials in command of the city did not at once disclose the news but let it reach public and army gradually, hoping in this way to reduce the reaction. No out-of-town newspapers were allowed to reach the city Saturday. A famous war correspondent, George Alfred Townsend, reported it was almost midnight Saturday before the troops were informed of the assassination. "For sometime there was every indication of a terrible riot," he wrote, referring especially to the bluecoats guarding Libby Prison, Castle Thunder, Belle Isle, and other places that formerly held federal prisoners but were now filled with Johnny Rebs.

A special object of attention was the sadistic former turnkey of Libby Prison. A determined movement got under way to burst in and hang him. Vigorous action by the commanding general and provost marshal prevented the lynching. Reporter Townsend told about a paroled Confederate officer first hearing the news while dining at one of Richmond's famous hostelries, the Ballard House, and exclaiming he was "damned glad Lincoln was dead." The Negro waiters tossed him bodily into the street; and he disappeared, running for dear life.

Martial law was instituted to control the touchy situation. Came reports that Judge Campbell, Mayor Mayo, and paroled rebel officers were all being arrested on orders of General Grant. This proved to be erroneous, although many arrests were made of escaped criminals, deserters, and the like. The men from Lee's army were prohibited from walking the streets or assembling in groups. Timid citizens left town for fear of riots.

Not until Monday evening did the *Richmond Evening Whig* print the news in full and comment sadly, "The heaviest blow which has fallen the people of the South has descended. . . . God grant it may not rekindle excitement or inflame passions anew."

PART II

FAREWELL TO A LEADER

3

HARDLY had news of the President's death been telegraphed over the nation than wires began pouring into Washington requesting interment in Springfield and the remains returned by the same route he had come.

The vice-president of the Pennsylvania Railroad wired Secretary Stanton, "Do you wish any special arrangements by our route through to Illinois for the remains of the President? I will have done whatever you may deem needful." The president of the Erie Railroad "begged leave to tender the use of a special train for the friends and escort of our lamented President should his remains be brought via New York." Similar offers arrived from the railroads over which Lincoln had traveled on the inaugural journey.

Two and a half hours after the death of their esteemed townsman the Springfield City Council was meeting with the mayor, and at noon leading citizens gathered at the State House. Both gatherings voted resolutions expressing sympathy to the family. The citizens group elected as chairman Lincoln's former law partner, John T. Stuart, and appointed a committee to cooperate with the governor. The City Council elected a committee to proceed to Washington to escort the remains home, and named Judge Stuart to the group. The governor, Richard T. Oglesby, in Washington at the time, was telegraphed the council's action.

At the moment of receiving the wire he and Senator Richard Yates were holding a meeting of Illinois folks in the latter's rooms at the National Hotel. The group had elected the senator chairman, passed resolutions extending condolences to the bereaved family, and set up two commitees: one, that included the governor, the senator, General Grant, and other Illinois generals, to call on Mrs. Lincoln and secure her approval to remove the remains to Springfield; and the other, to carry out the arrangements so made.

Meanwhile, at nine o'clock, quartermaster soldiers filed into the Petersen house, placed the body in a pine box, wrapped the box in an American flag, and carried it to the waiting hearse. Mrs. Lincoln was in a state of tolerable composure, but when she entered the carriage and glanced at the theater opposite, she reacted bitterly: "O, that dreadful house! That dreadful house!" She was driven directly to the Executive Mansion. A mounted detail of Union Light Guard encircled the hearse as it slowly moved up Tenth Street to G and thence to the White House. A group of general officers walked behind in the heavy rain. The streets were solidly packed with people, who uncovered their heads despite the downpour, as the pitiful procession moved by. City-wide tolling of bells told of the trip.

The autopsy was performed not in the President's bedroom as so often misstated but in the guest room on the northwest corner. Present were the new President, the Surgeon General, family physician, several army surgeons, and a select group of general officers.* The postmortem confirmed Dr. Leale's early diagnosis and prognosis that "the wound is mortal; it is impossible for him to live." During the necropsy Mrs. Lincoln sent a messenger to request a lock of hair and Dr. Stone clipped a tuft from the region of the wound.

The autopsy over, an embalmer entered the chamber. President Johnson, the doctors, and the generals remained until the work was complete and the body dressed in the same suit he had worn at the Second Inauguration. The embalming technique was the finest obtainable, an important consideration in view of the long travel ahead.

Until the casket was made ready, the body was laid out on the undertaker's velvet-covered cooling board set on stools in the middle of the room. A guard of sentries was placed at the entrance. Sometime next day, the precise time not recorded, the sixteenth President of the United States, stiffened to the hardness of stone, was borne down to the East Room and placed in the handsome coffin where intimates were permitted to see him for the first time since his sudden end.

Mrs. Lincoln, prostrated with grief and often hysterical, had been comforted by Mrs. Gideon Welles at the Petersen house and was accompanied by her to the Executive Mansion. Both were under the

---

* Vice-President Andrew Johnson was administered the oath of office at the Kirkwood House by Chief Justice Chase in the presence of two Cabinet officers, five senators, the two Blairs, and a general. They had gathered in Johnson's rooms soon after 10 A.M., leaving an interval of about three hours between Presidents.

watchful care of Dr. Stone. Later Mrs. Welles was relieved by Elizabeth H. Keckley, seamstress and personal maid to Mrs. Lincoln, who had tried to enter the President's House three times that night but each time had been turned back by the extra military guard's failing to recognize her. Mrs. Keckley was born a slave. No other visitors were allowed in Mrs. Lincoln's bedroom except Robert who treated his mother with tender affection. He tried to comfort her in her great grief.*

At the foot of the bed crouched little Taddie. His grief at his father's death was as great as his mother's but her terrific outbursts of emotion and her hysterical crying awed the little boy into silence. At times he could stand it no longer and he would plead, "Don't cry so, Mama! Don't cry, Mama! You will make me cry too!" She could not bear to see her darling child in misery and would clasp him in her arms and calm herself with great effort. The two would sob together until the paroxysm passed.

Even today Mary Todd Lincoln is the most misunderstood person in the Lincoln epic. Seldom realized is the fact that her brother, three half-brothers, and three brothers-in-law wore the Confederate uniform. Of them only the youngest, George Todd, a physician in gray, survived the war. Yet by reason of her station Mary could not exhibit the slightest emotion for the loss of her loved ones who fought and died for the bonnie blue flag. The husband of her favorite half-sister Emilie, General Ben Hardin Helm, lost his life at Chickamauga. At Lincoln's personal invitation Emilie visited the White House, her presence there bitterly resented by Union politicians and the northern press. Disregarding the uproar, the President urged "Little Sister" Emilie—loveliest of the

---

* Dr. Anson G. Henry, an old Springfield friend and political associate of the late President who had been down to Richmond, returned as quickly as he could. Mary threw her arms around his neck and begged him to stay at the White House. He did, remaining until she left six weeks later, accompanying her to Chicago.

Todd sisters with her light brown hair, luminous eyes, peach-blow complexion, and slender figure—to stay on as a companion for Mary. So filled with pent-up grief was Mary that she burst out, "Kiss me, Emilie, and tell me that you love me! I seem to be the scapegoat for both North and South!" She was accused of being "the spy in the White House."

When Mrs. Lincoln came to her high station she was going through the menopause and the nervous system is often capricious. That must ever be borne in mind in judging her actions. As First Lady she was continually importuned by office seekers and social climbers. Unfortunately she yielded to pleas and thereby exposed herself to political attack. She was plagued by threatening letters. The press generally was hostile to her and frequently misrepresented her most innocent acts in an irresponsible manner. No woman lived under more trying circumstances as First Lady than did Mary Todd Lincoln.

On the fatal night she was sitting close to her husband, her hand in his, as they watched the play-acting. At the instant of the loudest laugh in the play the killer fired the lethal shot, having planned it that way. Thus Mary was made aware of the murder as much by his hand jerking from hers as by the sound of the weapon being fired. Her recall of the horrible moment she told Dr. Henry a few days later. The doctor wrote his wife in Oregon on the day of the White House ceremony (which he attended) that Mary described how "she sat close to him, leaning on his lap and looking into his face when the fatal shot was fired"; and that his last words had been in reply to her question, " 'What will Miss Harris think of my hanging on to you so?' " To which he had answered, " 'She won't think anything about it' and had accompanied his reply with an affectionate smile."

To have the father of one's children butchered from behind while sitting at his side is the greatest tragedy a loving wife can experience. Then to have a tug-of-war take place over the loved one's remains was cruel and heartless; yet such is the lot of public servants whose lives become public property.

Conflict had arisen between those who advocated interment in the national capital and those who said he belonged on the prairie from whence he had come. The controversy was heightened by items in New York papers promoting erection of a memorial where his remains would be enshrined. Nicolay and Hay in their biography make the point that "whenever a President dies whose personality, more than his office, has endeared him to the people, it is proposed that his body shall rest at Washington; but the better instincts of the country, no less than the natural feelings of the family, insist that his dust shall lie among his own neighbors and kin."

Could Mary have had her way she would have taken the first train to Springfield with her beloved spouse's body on it. When her cousin, General J. B. S. Todd, and Secretary Stanton, consulted her on Saturday afternoon she settled the matter at once. But the others did not give up.

"Resolved: that the family of Abraham Lincoln, late President of the United States, be earnestly requested to permit his remains to be deposited temporarily or until such time as Congress shall take action in relation thereto, in the vault of the Capitol in the City of Washington." This resolution the Commissioner of Public Buildings submitted to the Congressional Committee on Obsequies.

"The more I think about the suggestion made at our meeting last evening of depositing the remains of our beloved President in the rotunda of the Capitol," Commissioner French wrote the chairman of the standing committee on public grounds, "the more forcibly the propriety of so doing strikes me."

To have her husband's body lying under the Capitol of the Republic did not appeal to Mrs. Lincoln. Fresh in her memory were

his remarks as they were driving along the banks of the James
River near City Point. He had been so cheerful that day, she recalled. The war was coming to an end and his sojourn at Grant's
headquarters had visibly refreshed him. Their carriage took them
past an old country church. They stopped the driver and walked
together in the lovely tree-shaded graveyard. The day was ethereal,
presaging a beautiful summer. The old grave sites were blooming
with jonquils and iris and arbutus; and the trees and shrubbery
were trimmed in new green lace. The rural quiet and spiritual environment inspired a deep sense of peace. Lincoln had been moved
to say: "Mary, you are younger than myself. You will survive me.
When I am gone, lay my remains in some quiet place like this."

His words had chilled her heart then. Now they raced through
her mind. "A quiet place like this." Was that not the kind of place
where she too could be laid beside him? And would not that be
impossible in a public memorial? Mary was determined to be with
him to the end of time; for he had pledged her and had inscribed
in her wedding ring, "Love is eternal."

Though distraught and ill she had to make vital decisions. Three
times she had to say no and as many times had to give in. No, she
said to the remains being enshrined in New York City; no, to interment in Washington (the Congressional Cemetery was another
recommendation); and no again to his being deposited in the vault
under the Capitol rotunda.* She did accede to the procession to
follow the White House obsequies, and she yielded also to the
lying-in-state at the Capitol en route to the homeward-bound train.

When she agreed to Springfield interment, everyone took it for
granted the itinerary would approximate the inaugural route.
Secretary Stanton, to whom fell the duty of burying his Commander-in-Chief, appointed a committee to work out the return

* Originally prepared for George Washington, whose family had insisted he
be interred at Mount Vernon where he now lies.

trip. "His Excellency Governor John Brough and John W. Garrett, Esq. are requested to act as a committee of transportation of the remains of the late Abraham Lincoln from Washington to their final resting place," read his instructions. "They are authorized to arrange the time-tables with the respective railroad companies, and to do and regulate all things for the safe and appropriate transportation. They will cause notice of this appointment and their acceptance to be published for public information."

Brough of Ohio, self-made and a successful railroad president, had entered politics to beat the notorious peace-at-any-price agitator Vallandigham; and he had done so by the biggest majority ever received by a Buckeye gubernatorial candidate. He was also credited with being originator of the hundred-day troops that proved so successful in helping Grant to victory. Garrett, president of the Baltimore and Ohio Railroad, was a skillful business executive, and had cooperated fully with the federal government throughout the war, the consequence having been constant destruction of his road's property by Confederate raiders. To both men the Lincoln administration was grateful for services rendered; both were deserving of the honor now conferred upon them for the late President had held them in high esteem. They promptly acceded to the Secretary's request, accepted their appointment, and entered at once upon the discharge of their duties, announcing their recommendations in the newspapers as requested. The schedule:

Lve. Washington	8:00 A.M.	Friday, April 21
Arr. Baltimore	10:00 A.M.	same day
Lve. Baltimore	3:00 P.M.	same day
Arr. Harrisburg	8:20 P.M.	same day
Lve. Harrisburg	12:00 M.	Saturday, April 22
Arr. Philadelphia	6:30 P.M.	same day
Lve. Philadelphia	4:00 A.M.	Monday, April 24
Arr. New York	10:00 A.M.	same day
Lve. New York	4:00 P.M.	Tuesday, April 25

Arr. Albany	11:00 P.M. same day
Lve. Albany	4:00 P.M. Wednesday, April 26
Arr. Buffalo	7:00 A.M. Thursday, April 27
Lve. Buffalo	10:10 P.M. same day
Arr. Cleveland	7:00 A.M. Friday, April 28
Lve. Cleveland	12:00 M. same day
Arr. Columbus	7:30 A.M. Saturday, April 29
Lve. Columbus	8:00 P.M. same day
Arr. Indianapolis	7:00 A.M. Sunday, April 30
Lve. Indianapolis	12:00 M. same day
Arr. Chicago	11:00 A.M. Monday, May 1
Lve. Chicago	9:30 P.M. Tuesday, May 2
Arr. Springfield	8:00 A.M. Wednesday, May 3

The committee's recommendations were validated by the War Department's ordering that "for the purpose of said transportation the railroads over which said transportation is made be declared military roads, subject to the orders of the War Department; and the railroad and the locomotives and the cars engaged in said transportation be subject to the military control of Brigadier-General McCallum, superintendent of military railroad transportation; and all persons are required to conform to the rules, regulations, orders and directions he may give or prescribe for the transportation aforesaid; and all persons disobeying said order shall be deemed to have violated the military orders of the War Department and shall be dealt with accordingly."

The order specified that "no persons shall be allowed to be transported upon the cars constituting the funeral train save those who are specially authorized by the order of the War Department. The funeral train will not exceed nine cars, including baggage car and hearse car, which will proceed over the whole route from Washington to Springfield, Illinois."

As to the obsequies en route the order stated that "at various points where the remains are to be taken from the hearse car by

state and municipal authorities to receive public honors according
to the aforesaid program, the said authorities will make such arrangements as may be fitting and appropriate for the occasion under
the directions of the military commander of the division, department or district; but the remains will continue always under the
special charge of the officers and escort assigned by this Department." The order was signed by the Assistant Adjutant General
and approved by the Secretary of War.

Being the top government official in charge of Lincoln's burial and
being also of the so-called "radical" group working to keep the
federal government in Republican hands, Secretary Stanton was
denounced by political opponents for extending the trip to gain
political advantage. The alleged advantage was to keep the martyred
President in the public eye as long as possible to incite revengeful
reaction against the rebel South (who were presumably responsible
for the deed) so that he and fellow "radicals" would gain added
support for their reconstruction program.*

Throughout the war Stanton had been a special target for the
political opposition. Although many Republicans were former
Democrats (Chase and Blair in the Cabinet for example) what
made the opposition so bitter toward Stanton was that he had
discovered duplicity going on in Buchanan's Cabinet. He had been
responsible for revealing the design of the seceders to betray
Buchanan and take possession of the national capital by a *coup
d'etat* before March 4 and thus prevent accession of Lincoln and
the Republicans. Stanton, in making the plot known, had placed
country above party. Patriotic and courageous President Buchanan
(not many accord him those virtues but he had them nevertheless)

---

* Shelby M. Cullom, who had been elected congressman from Lincoln's
former district along with Lincoln's reelection, saw the extended obsequies as
a means of quieting public reaction. "No one knew but that there would be
a second and bloodier revolution," he wrote, "and it was thought the funeral
would serve to arouse the patriotism of the people, which it did."

dismissed the plotters and replaced them with patriots, among them Stanton whom he appointed Attorney General. That Stanton had helped to save the Republic and in doing so had placed himself in political, if not in mortal, jeopardy, registered with Lincoln. When he had to remove an incompetent Secretary of War he appointed the loyal, energetic, capable native of Steubenville, Ohio. Stanton's enemies succeeded in making him the villain of the Lincoln epic. That he was irascible and erratic did not endear him to his own associates and supporters.

How prejudiced the charges against him were was indicated by the Brough-Garrett report. The first paragraph stated that the routing of the train had been furnished them by the Illinois citizens committee. That committee, headed by Governor Oglesby and Senator Yates, included congressmen, army and navy officers, government employees, and other Illinoisans residing in Washington. Their recommendations concurred with, and likely were initiated by, the Springfield committee who had come to escort the remains home.

Meetings of citizens were being held in all principal cities of the loyal states to express their condolences and to arrange for the obsequies in their communities. Pressure exerted by these groups to have a cortege routed through their cities was unceasing and especially since the deceased himself had set an inescapable precedent by his inaugural journey. "As soon as it was announced that Mr. Lincoln was to be burried in Springfield, every town and city on the route begged that the train would halt within its limits and give the people the opportunity of testifying their grief and reverence," wrote the two private secretaries, who were in the best position to know.

Stanton and his colleagues did not originate and obviously could not manipulate the emotional forces that welled up from the hearts of millions of Americans and that were so powerful they could

Washington City, D.C.
April 18, 1865

Hon. Edwin M. Stanton,
Secretary of War.

Sir: Under your commission of this date we have the honor to report:

1. A committee of the citizens of the State of Illinois, appointed for the purpose of attending to the removal of the remains of the late President, has furnished us with the following route for the remains and escort, being with the exception of two points the route traversed by Mr. Lincoln from Springfield to Washington—Washington to Baltimore, thence to Harrisburg, Philadelphia, New York, Albany, Buffalo, Cleveland, Columbus, Indianapolis, Chicago to Springfield.

2. Over this route, under the counsels of the committee, we have prepared the following time-card, in all cases for the special train. [See separate schedule] The route from Columbus to Indianapolis is via the Columbus & Indianapolis Central Railway; and from Indianapolis to Chicago via Lafayette and Michigan City.

3. As to the running of these special trains which, in order to guard as far as practicable against accidents and detentions, we have reduced to about 20 miles per hour, we suggest the following regulations:

1. That the time of departure and arrival be observed as closely as possible.

2. That material detentions at way points be guarded against as much as possible so as not to increase the speed of the train.

3. That a pilot engine be kept ten minutes in advance of the train.

4. That the special train in all cases have the right of the road; and that all other trains be kept out of the way.

5. That the several railroad companies provide a sufficient number of coaches for the comfortable accommodation of the escort, and a special car for the remains; and that all these, together with the engines, be appropriately draped in mourning.

6. That where the running time of any train extends beyond, or commences at, midnight, not less than two sleeping cars be added and a greater number if the road can command them, sufficient for the accommodation of the escort.

7. That two officers of the U.S. Military Railway Service be detailed by you and despatched at once over the route to confer with the several railway officers and make all necessary preparations for carrying out these arrangements promptly and satisfactorily.

8. That this program and these regulations, if approved, be confirmed by an order of the War Department.

Respectfully submitted,
John Brough ⎫ Committee
John W. Garrett ⎭

not be denied. "The throngs pressing to see the body of the President is beyond all precedent," reported a local newsman on the White House lying-in-state. "It required waiting for not less than six hours to get in . . . and the line, four deep, extended for blocks." To satisfy overwhelming public demand an extra day was added for the lying-in-state at the Capitol. But this was not enough. Still they came. The railroad station was engulfed in a mass of people who stood reverently in mud and rain just to watch the train pull out. The Washington scene was a preview of the hurricane of grief sweeping the Union. The heart of America had been struck.

Under a war measure Congress passed and the President himself signed on January 31, 1862, the Secretary of War was charged with the operation of America's railroads. The law never had to be invoked against a loyal railway but it did give the government full authority to act in case of emergency. When military necessity required rail transportation an order from the War Department sufficed. It was as a military necessity that the last journey of the civilian head of United States armed forces was conducted.

Military operation or not Mrs. Lincoln held a dim view of it. The combined pleadings of personal friends and relatives (who had arrived to attend the obsequies) were needed to convince her the extended itinerary was in the public interest. She finally yielded, deploring the public exhibition of her deceased husband's person— a normal reaction for a woman who loved her spouse as dearly as Mary did. Her indecision had kept the operation in a state of suspense and not until the day before the scheduled departure was the War Department able to telegraph military district commanders along the homeward route and confirm their original instructions, that the schedule would be adhered to.

Mary's judgment regarding entombment in downtown Springfield was yet to be made but the subject was under consideration; it would be another major decision she would have to make. On the morning of departure Governor Oglesby received a telegram from the Illinois Secretary of State reading: "A national monument fund is on foot and a plot of ground six acres in extent in the heart of the city has been selected as the burial place of our lamented President."

Bedridden and grief-torn though she was, they would not let the widow alone in her bereavement; her husband was still considered public property.

4

A T SUNRISE on Wednesday the big guns in forts around the
seat of government thundered the tidings that this was the
day appointed for the nation to pay homage to the fallen Head of
State.

All over the Union memorial services were being held. By
common impulse the populace thronged to the churches which
were opened for the occasion. The press carried the announcement
of the Acting Secretary of State that the obsequies would take place
"at the Executive Mansion at 12M. on Wednesday the 19th inst. and

the various religious denominations throughout the country are invited to meet at their respective houses of worship at that hour."

The response was massive. "More people," declared Edward Everett Hale in Boston, "united in public worship of God in this land than ever united in such service before."

The Secretary of War ordered commanders of the sixteen military districts into which the country was divided to suspend all labor at their posts and on all public works under direction of the War Department. "The headquarters of every department, post, station, fort and arsenal will be draped in mourning for thirty days and appropriate funeral honors will be paid by every army and in every department and at every military post and at the Military Academy." General Grant further ordered that at dawn "thirteen guns will be fired and afterwards at intervals of thirty minutes between the rising and setting sun a single gun, and at the close of day a national salute of thirty-six guns." In addition, a twenty-one gun salvo at noon was ordered to salute the deceased Commander-in-Chief as the White House ceremonies began.

To the nation's capital all manner of Americans hastened to pay their last respects. Willard's Hotel had to decline four hundred telegraphic applications for beds despite having set up cots in all available suites and public rooms. Six thousand strangers spent Tuesday night in public buildings, parks, and vacant lots. A hundred thousand poured into Washington this day. Thirty thousand marched in the three-hour procession.

From the adjacent countryside rumbled hay wagons, dearborns, and buggies bulging with humanity. Plow horses clumped along unpaved streets carrying as many riders as their broad backs would accommodate. Military and naval men who could, slipped into the city from nearby camps and ships. Alexandria and Georgetown were depopulated. Baltimore, Philadelphia, and New York forwarded large delegations. Trains leaving Washington were as empty as those entering were overcrowded. All sections of the Union were represented at this in-gathering.

City Hall was the focal point for arriving civic delegations who were greeted by members of the Washington City Council.* The mayor also was on hand to greet corporate dignitaries and make sure their wants were cared for. He took special care of the Boston delegation headed by Mayor Frederick W. Lincoln of the collateral Lincoln family in Massachusetts. For those who had no transportation a long line of saddle horses and carriages stood ready, loaned for the occasion by civic-minded citizens.

The civil section of the procession was headed by the President's old friend and unofficial bodyguard, Marshal Ward Lamon. To assist him a hundred and seventy aides had been appointed. Their names appeared in the newspapers and it was immediately noted that secessionist sympathizers were included. This created an uproar. The list had been compiled while Lamon was in Richmond for the President. Upon the demand of a determined loyalist six names were stricken from the published list. A committee of citizens called upon Deputy Marshal Phillips, and he admitted the list had been based on the number of horses and carriages appointees could furnish. He acknowledged he had been remiss in not checking their loyalty and offered to resign. His resignation was accepted. That ended the commotion about the secessionist marshals in the Lincoln memorial procession.

By ten o'clock Lafayette Square was packed to capacity as the throng sought the cool shade of its beautiful trees. Windows of the Treasury and State Departments were bursting with spectators. Streets and sidewalks were dense with Americans of all kinds. In front of the Executive Mansion the military escort was formed into

---

* A mayoral form of government operated the District of Columbia from 1802 to 1871; changed in 1878 to the prevailing system of three commissioners appointed by the President.

line, extending along Pennsylvania Avenue from Fifteenth to beyond Seventeenth Street. The units were accompanied by bands
and drum corps. Flags were draped in black as were artillery cais-
sons, band instruments, and officers' swords. Drums were muffled.
Firearms were carried reversed.

Notwithstanding the thousands of strangers milling about the
streets more than a sabbath stillness prevailed. Everyone sensed
the solemnity of the occasion. Sometimes the cry of a fretting child
could be heard or the call of a street vendor hawking badges of
mourning or sometimes from Pennsylvania Avenue the clatter of
hooves and thump of deadened drums as the military moved into
formation. Otherwise it seemed as though everyone were holding
their collective breath. All who were here were united out of respect and veneration of the honored dead. The day's events demonstrated that the public heart was reverent and unselfish despite the
years of killing and plundering.

The ceremony at the White House was scheduled to begin at
noon. Arrangements were handled by the Treasury Department,
Assistant Secretary George Harrington in charge. The procedure
he devised worked well. To enter the Executive Mansion one had
to have a special pass. The pass could be obtained only from the
chairman of the designated group in an assigned room in the
Treasury Building. Each group assembled at the room prior to
walking over to the White House.

Harrington arranged a section for the press in the East Room,
an arrangement much appreciated by the historians of the moment.
They were seated in fifteen chairs, draped in black, across a recess
formed by closing the two main entrance doors from the hallway.
This position offered excellent vantage from which the scene could
be reported.

As its name denotes, the East Room is on the east side of the mansion and extends the full width. A correspondent who came early to paint word pictures said the beautiful chamber appeared to him much like the varnished interior of a large vault. The frescoed ceiling, purplish gray in tone, was decorated with the national shield, vases with flowers and assorted fruit, and from circular emblazonings of gilt hung chandeliers draped in deepest dye, the center chandelier having been removed to make space for the catafalque. The expanse of red-and-gold wallpaper around the room was interrupted by eight lofty mirrors margined in red damascene faced with black gauze. The mirrors were overlaid in white barege, a veil-like material which diffused the pink-stained sunlight coming through partly closed Venetian shutters. The tall windows, outlined in the same crimson drapery as the mirrors and edged with white lace curtains, revealed the lovely spring day outside, green grass, lilacs in bloom, and budding trees through whose graceful archways could be seen the bronze and marble statues breaking the blue horizon.

Furniture was veiled in black as were the marble mantels upon which stood wax candles in slender silver candlesticks. Only the flowered Brussels carpet remained unmasked by mourning, most of it obscured by a series of raised steps arranged on three sides of the chamber. This amphitheater offered a better view of the proceedings and accommodated more people. The steps were covered in black broadcloth and were marked off in thin white lines, each division reserved for the group indicated by a card placed therein. Size of the division was determined by the number of tickets allotted. Measured for standing room, the total space accommodated six hundred persons. The first step came within five feet of the principal feature of the room, the catafalque.

This ornate structure was positioned in front of the press section. Eleven feet in height, it was sixteen feet long and ten wide.

The platform supporting the dais was eighteen inches off the floor and was surfaced in black broadcloth fringed with festoons. The dais, or in plain words, the bier, upon which the casket rested was surmounted by an arched canopy the outside of which was black alpaca, the inside, fluted white satin. Alpaca festoons bordered the canopy and alpaca curtains hung at the sides, looped to the posts.

Ensconced in white satin upholstering lay the embalmed remains of the war President. He appeared as one having gone gently to sleep. The eyes were closed as in peaceful slumber and on the lips was the touch of a smile. At the north end of the bier stood a cross fashioned of white flowers; at the foot, the south end, rested an anchor of lilies of the valley and rosebuds, its flukes of calla lilies. A wreath of laurel and cedar dotted with camellias encircled the casket.

The upper lid was opened to reveal face and bust; the closed section was strewn with blossoms and sprigs of green that shed a pleasing incense over the somber scene. The odor was "fresh and healthy," a newsman reported, and the spectacle was sad but not oppressive, simple yet rich, worthy of the powerful nation the deceased had represented in his person.

Strange, however, to find the remains closely guarded by high military officers. Somehow this did not seem in character with A. Lincoln. It was not easy to reconcile that vast body of fighting men —the Union military forces were the greatest armed might gathered in the annals of the world up to that time—as having been welded into their enormous power by genial Father Abraham, the homely backwoodsman who told earthy jokes, recited Shakespeare, and often worked in carpet slippers. That he exercised the power for beneficent ends and succeeded in those ends made the military might acceptable, even if exceptional. These thoughts were forced upon the mind as one contemplated the round-the-clock guard of high military men.

At the edge of the coffin, dark, reticent General David Hunter rested a white-gauntleted hand as if in deep thought, pausing in his vigil over the corpse of the man he had accompanied from Springfield four years before; a journey he now would repeat in reverse. Other officers of the Guard of Honor—selected without reference to their previous association with the late President—included two generals and two staff captains, each wearing a white sash that ranged across the breast and around the waist. The upper left sleeve of their Union blue jacket was banded in crape in accordance with the Secretary of War's order that it be worn for six months by all officers. The two aides paced slowly to and fro; the generals did likewise at intervals. As they moved around the hushed twilit chamber their shadows crossed and recrossed the tall veiled mirrors and were reflected as vague shapes and formless images.

Entrance to the East Room was gained at the south end through the Green Room. This had been the course of the general public the day before when the remains were exposed to public viewing from nine-thirty in the morning until five in the evening. Admitted at the western entrance on Pennsylvania Avenue, they had come up the curved driveway to the main portico, thence into the grand entrance hall, from there to the Green Room, and into the East Room. Approaching the bier, they had divided into two lines and stepped to the platform, catching a full view of the familiar features as they passed along. Exiting through the north door into an entryway, they went through a window over a temporary bridge or staging to the driveway and out of the grounds.

The Executive Mansion and its approaches were guarded by a detachment of the Seventh Regiment, Veterans Reserve Corps, and the regular White House military guard, Company K, One Hundred

Fiftieth Regiment of the Pennsylvania Bucktail Brigade. Having
been on guard duty at the White House since 1862, the Bucktails
were encamped on the southeast White House grounds. The President's cavalry escort, the Union Light Guard, were also encamped
there.

Company K's captain, David V. Derrickson of Mercer, Pennsylvania, had been so well liked by the President he was frequently
invited to breakfast when the Lincolns were in summer residence
at Soldiers' Home. When Mrs. Lincoln and the boys were absent
at the seashore, and the President wanted company, Derrickson
would be invited to sleep in the big bed with him, attired in a
borrowed presidential nightgown. The captain was later detailed to
Meadville as provost marshal in his section of the state, but
Company K stayed on at the President's specific request.

Being so intimate with the head of the nation and his family,
the assassination hit these units with terrific impact. Only deep
sorrow and strict discipline diffused their fierce feelings of vengeance and kept them at their posts. They desperately wanted to
catch the murderers; they felt it was their responsibility as well as
their duty. But they were ordered to stay on the job while others
hunted for the culprits.

At the scheduled hour of eleven o'clock, the first accession in
force arrived in the East Room. These were the clergy. Sixty
representatives of all denominations had come from all sections
of the country, and the darkly attired, devout-looking men were
ushered to the division reserved for them at the south end of the
room. The four divines who would conduct the service were seated
in a row of draped chairs at the north end. A committee of New

York merchants and members of the Union League arrived next
and were placed opposite the clergy. Heads of bureaus, auditors
of the Treasury, chiefs of army and navy bureaus, officials of
government departments were located near the northeast corner.

Every few minutes more groups that had assembled in their
rooms at the Treasury reached the Green Room. Ushers took up
the printed passes and conducted the holders to the proper division.
In the northeast section were placed Senate and House officials,
Christian Commission and Sanitary Commission officers, and these
governors: Andrews of Massachusetts; Brough of Ohio; Bucking-
ham of Connecticut; Curtin of Pennsylvania; Fenton of New York;
Oglesby of Illinois; Parker of New Jersey; Pierpont of West Virginia;
Stone of Iowa; the Lieutenant Governor of Maryland, the governor
being ill; former Governor Farwell of Wisconsin; together with their
staffs. Two large delegations—twenty from his birthplace, Kentucky,
and forty from his residence, Illinois—were designated chief
mourners and stationed behind the family.

Twenty-five minutes after eleven Mayor Richard Wallach of
Washington and the City Council entered the room, escorting
corporate authorities from New York, Brooklyn, Boston, Philadelphia, Baltimore, and nearby communities. They were placed on
the east side of the room as were senators; congressmen; judges of
local courts; and authorized officers of army, navy, and marine
corps. Here too were the ambassadors, ministers, envoys, attaches,
and secretaries of foreign legations; each resplendent in court
costume with high collar, heavy gilded coat, vest decorated in
medals and ribbons, forming the most conspicuous segment of an
assembly garbed in black.

Adjacent to the exit, the north steps were occupied by twenty
honorary pallbearers who would be first to follow the officiating
clergy and family out of the room. Ten ladies were present. Five
were wives of Cabinet members; also the Postmaster General's

daughter, the wife of the Commissioner of Indian Affairs, the wife of Senator William Sprague of Rhode Island (the former Kate Chase), her sister Nettie, and Mrs. Elizabeth Grimsley, who was the favorite cousin of Mrs. Lincoln, having been her bridesmaid, and who had spent the first six months with her in the White House.

Almost on the stroke of noon the new President entered accompanied by the Cabinet except the invalid Secretary of State. Stopping at the catafalque for a final look at his distinguished predecessor Andrew Johnson retired to the first step to the east and in full view of the coffined remains—he himself alive only because the nerve of the assassin assigned to him had failed. To his left stood his close friend, the venerable ex-senator from New York, Preston King; and to his right, former Vice-President Hannibal Hamlin. Around him, as if grouped for a photograph, stood Cabinet members and Supreme Court justices.

Prostrated by the awful event, Mrs. Lincoln was too distraught to attend the ceremony and was under the doctor's care. So was little Taddie, who asserted that morning the beautiful day meant his father was happy in the world to which he had gone; because, said the tearful lad, "he was never happy here."

Robert was the sole member of the immediate family to be present and he had a hard time of it, weeping continually into a handkerchief. Beside him was his commanding officer, the supreme head of the Union armies, General Grant. Other relatives present were Mrs. Lincoln's two brothers-in-law from Springfield; and two cousins, one a physician from her home town of Lexington, Kentucky; the other a former general in the Union army from "Dahcotah" Territory. Seated with the family were the two private secretaries.

The room was now full. A hush hung over the assembly. The pall of black that everywhere met the eye was suggestive of grandeur and greatness rather than of gloom. These representative men from every sector of American life, standing in serried row on row, impressed the beholder with the vast power of the dead executive in his exertions to restore peace to his bleeding country. Sad though the spectacle was, it was not without elements of hope and confidence. Ready to continue the government of the people, for the people, by the people, stood a new President. Surrounded by experienced councilors, administrators, and legislators, the presence of a living successor made plain that, though treason may destroy a President, constitutional government and the liberties it assures live on.

Amid profound silence the nation collected in the East Room stood looking upon eminent death with awed hearts and respectful silence. A ticking watch denoted ten minutes after twelve. The order of service would be an invocation, prayer, eulogy, and a benediction. There would be no singing or music; the ceremony would be simple in the manner of the deceased.

The rector of the Church of the Epiphany stepped to the platform. Facing the head of the honorable departed, the Reverend Charles H. Hall read from the Episcopal burial service, "I am the resurrection and the life. I know my Redeemer liveth." Speaking in a clear, distinct voice he enunciated the scriptural teaching on immortality related in the fifteenth chapter of Paul's first epistle to the Corinthians, twentieth verse. "But now is Christ risen from the dead, and become the firstfruits of them that slept. For since by man came death, by man came also the resurrection of the dead." The reading concluded with the apostolic injunction, "Therefore, my beloved brethren, be ye stedfast, unmoveable, always abounding in the work of the Lord, forasmuch as ye know that your labour is not in vain in the Lord." A deep "Amen" welled up from the assembly.

Now Bishop Matthew Simpson stepped to the dais. In a finely

intonated voice that caused hearers to break into tears, he prayed with all the Methodist fervency that distinguished him, ending his moving plea with the Lord's Prayer in which all who could muster their voice joined—"Our Father which art in Heaven, hallowed be thy name. . . ."

The family pastor followed with a sermon that consumed more than an hour. "It was a cruel, cruel hand, the dark hand of the assassin which smote our honored, wise and noble President and filled the land with sorrow," began the Reverend Phineas D. Gurley. "But above and beyond that hand there is another that we must see and acknowledge. It is the chastening hand of a wise and faithful Father. He gives us this bitter cup. And the cup that our Father has given us, shall we not drink it? 'Whom the Lord loveth, he chasteneth.' O, how those blessed words have cheered and strengthened and sustained us through all the long and weary years of civil strife!"

Referring to what might be the divine interpretation of the event, the Presbyterian parson declared, "He will say to us as to his ancient Israel, 'In a little wrath I hid my face from thee for a moment; but with everlasting kindness will I have mercy upon thee.' " He commented on his personal relationship with the President and said he never could forget the time *in this very room* when Lincoln received a company of clergymen who had called upon him to pay their respects during the darkest days of the war and told them: "Gentlemen, my hope of success in this great and terrible struggle rests on that immutable foundation, the justice and goodness of God."

This abiding confidence in God and the final triumph of truth and righteousness was, asserted Dr. Gurley, "his noblest virtue, the secret alike of his strength, his patience, and his success." And it was this principle that seemed to him, after being near the President steadily and with him often for more than four years, "by which, more than any other, 'he, being dead yet speaketh.' "

While the eulogy was unfolding many of the audience, standing so long in one position close to one another, sought relief by sitting on the steps. "God be praised that our fallen chief lived long enough to see the day dawn and the day star of joy and peace arise upon the nation. He saw it and was glad," the parson continued, then moved forward and placed a hand on the edge of the casket, explaining that in no way could he more appropriately conclude his tribute to the departed President than by addressing to him the same language that Tacitus, in his life of Agricola, had uttered to his departed father-in-law. Sensing that this was the beginning of the peroration, a stir went through the assembly like the rustle of dry leaves in a wind and all who were seated stood up.

The concluding words of the Roman historian were now addressed to the spirit of him who was soon to be entombed: "Others who figured on the stage of life and were worthies of a former day will sink for want of a faithful historian into the common lot of oblivion; but you, our honored friend and head, delineated with truth and fairly consigned to posterity, will survive yourself and triumph over the injustice of time."

Bowing his head and pausing, he softly pronounced the concluding "Amen." The family pastor's place on the dais was taken by the chaplain of the Senate. Raising a hand in benediction, in an impressive voice the Baptist clergyman prayed, "O Lord God of Hosts, behold a nation prostrate before Thy Throne, clothed in sackcloth, who stand around all that now remains of our illustrious and beloved chief." Calling for blessings on the government, the new President, members of the Cabinet, the injured Secretary of State, and comfort for the bereaved family, the Reverend Edwin H. Gray concluded, "Oh, hear the cry and the prayer, and see the tears now arising from a nation's crushed and smitten heart, and deliver us from the power of all our enemies and send speedy peace unto all our borders, through Jesus Christ, our Lord; Amen."

The White House obsequies were ended. At once undertakers issued from the north doorway where they had been waiting together with six veteran sergeants. Closing the lid, they set aside the floral tributes, grasped the large silver handles, and carried the ebony-like container and its precious content to the portico where the hearse was waiting. Units of the procession were in line, ready, the carriages standing along the driveway.

It did not take long to empty the house of the head of the nation. Empty, except for the grieving woman who lay in a darkened room on the second floor of the west wing. Agonized and alone, her sons gone to honor their father, yesterday she was the First Lady of the land; today she was the widow of an immortal name.

5

THE procession up Pennsylvania Avenue from White House to Capitol was so extended that half of it had to double back on upcoming units. Five thousand government workers, seventy abreast, stretched from curb to curb, a solid phalanx of marching men. Delegations from nearby large cities; workers from the Navy Yard; local railroad employees and transportation people from docks and shipyards and from Alexandria and Baltimore; a fire hose company from Philadelphia of which the late President had been an honorary member; a host of fraternal lodges and societies; church bodies by the dozens; clergymen; school children and teachers; state and city officials; convalescents from military hospitals (the saddest sight in the march; some bandaged, some armless, others hobbling on crutches, all determined to pay their last respects); survivors of the War of 1812; Fenian brotherhoods and German singing societies; Italian, Swiss, French, and Polish clubs; saddle and harness makers; Seth Kinman, eccentric California hunter attired in moccasins and buckskin breeches; Chief Agonagwad of the Winnebago Indians; these, and many, many more, evidenced the public urge to venerate the honored dead.

The reverent attention accorded the beautiful hearse as it moved slowly along the avenue, especially from the Negro people, was touching. Providing a full view of the flower-covered casket the swarthy vehicle, topped by a golden eagle draped in sable, was drawn by six handsome gray horses attended by liveried grooms. Surrounding it marched the twenty-five sergeants and four officers charged with around-the-clock guardianship until final entombment. Behind the hearse the presidential mount (an athletic gray gelding from the Quartermaster Department branded "U.S.") was led by a uniformed attendant. The late rider's boots stood reversed in the stirrups in the military manner.

Enveloping hearse and escort were two military units that had formed the President's bodyguard. Family and relatives followed in closed carriages; the sons each in a separate carriage, then cousins and brothers-in-law, and the two private secretaries; six carriages in all.

Negro organizations brought up the rear of the procession, marching hand in hand to betoken brotherly love. The first group, forty abreast, was dressed in nocturnal suits, white gloves, tall black hats, and totaled thirty-eight ranks. Including brotherhoods; burial societies; benevolent, fraternal, and religious associations; four thousand Negro civilians marched and ten times their number watched.

An old proverb has it that the last shall be first and the first last. In the Great Emancipator's procession it was fitting that those whom he had set free from human bondage were both last *and* first. A regiment of Negro infantry that had proved their fighting qualities in battles around Richmond had been ordered to Washington to act as an escort regiment. They did not arrive at the Sixth Street wharf until noon. Proceeding up Seventh Street to the avenue, they found further progress blocked and halted in front of the Metropolitan Hotel which stood at that point. Reconnoitering his position the commanding officer observed the head of the procession bearing down on him. Wheeling the regiment smartly about, he ordered the band to strike up a dirge, and in this manner the Twenty-second U.S. Colored Infantry headed the Lincoln cortege to the Capitol. Perhaps it was more accident than design, but the man they were honoring would have found it an appropriate tribute.

Behind them stepped the Tenth and Ninth Regiments of the Veterans Reserve Corps, and then a Marine battalion, two artillery battalions, the Sixteenth New York Calvary, a detachment of the Eighth Illinois Cavalry, the commander of the military escort and his staff, a contingent of military and naval officers, army paymasters, surgeons, medical and hospital personnel, bureau generals and staffs, and five hundred paroled officers from Camp Parole; an impressive array of military might.

Just ahead of the hearse rode Colonel Lamon as chief marshal followed by the honorary pallbearers and the physicians who had attended the deceased. After hearse and family, President Johnson rode in a carriage escorted by mounted general officers and the First Virginia Artillery (Union) on foot. Next came Cabinet members, Supreme Court justices, diplomatic corps, and heads of

bureaus and departments according to their relative dignities. The
civil section was interspersed by military units of government
employees. Such were the Treasury Guards who carried their
regimental flag that had draped the front of the Lincoln box, the
slash made by the assassin in his leap to the stage plainly visible.

Thirty bands among the units evoked the "Dead March" from
Saul and other common-time tunes. The Marine Band offered a
dirge composed for the occasion by the general in command of
engineers. Of all aspects of the event none was more noteworthy
than the sound of it: a vibrant cacaphony that was strangely har-
monious, and that formed a framework of lament in which all things
seen could be felt. The big siege guns encircling the city roared
adieus; field artillery posted near the White House, at City Hall,
and on East Capitol Street, boomed and banged once a minute;
muffled drums thump-thumped the slow beat; and from every side
was heard the sound of bells. Church bells, firehouse bells, locomotive bells, grade-crossing bells, big bells, little bells tolled a
doleful farewell. The death march of the first American President
to be assassinated offered an immense oratorio that ranged the scale
from basso profundo to melodic treble.

Sound and sight were beyond forgetting. Particularly so from
Capitol Hill with its sweeping panorama of broad avenues and green
spaces warm under a bright April sun; the long, straight columns
of uniformed figures and polished muskets in the distance that
hardly seemed to move but kept creeping closer; the dark masses
of spectators bordering brick-paved Pennsylvania Avenue like long
bands of crape; the ornate public buildings and modest dwellings
accoutered in emblems of sorrow—a spectacle that was at once
grand and touching.

The dazzling-white Capitol structure was also attired in sable
symbols; its stately rows of pillars and windows wore the widow's
weeds. Atop the dome the figure of Armed Liberty, "The Lady of

the Capitol," was surrounded by dark decor; and the star-studded banners hung mournfully in the half position.

The slow-stepping marchers at last reached the base of Capitol Hill, turned left along the railroad tracks, climbed the north side, and moved across the east plaza. The foot soldiers enveloped the plaza in a military square. To their center the contingent of officers assembled, and behind them cavalry and artillery units took position. Back of the military formation throngs of citizenry looked on respectfully as the carriages drew to a halt at the foot of the broad central stairway and discharged their cargoes. Up the granite steps to a doorway framed in mourning honorary pallbearers and Guard of Honor formed a double line. Now the focus of all eyes drew alongside the steps and came to a stop. Abraham Lincoln was about to enter the Capitol of the United States for the last time.

The scene was similar to that of six and a half weeks before. Blue-ranked soldiers were presenting arms at his approach now as they had then. Around him, with few exceptions, were the same faces; a glittering galaxy of government officials. Overall was one awful change. Then the sun had broken through scurrying clouds as if to bless him. Now it beamed directly into his upturned face. Then he had spoken of his determination to restore the Union of States "with malice toward none and charity to all." Now he was silent.

But did he not speak more eloquently now? Did not everyone feel more keenly his great moral stature as the remains were borne up the steps and into the great rotunda? Did not his still form present a message more surely than had his lips?

"It is appointed unto men once to die," began the family pastor, standing at the head of the casket around which clustered the invited mourners, all heads bowed. "The dust returns to the earth it was, and the spirit to God who gave it. . . . Lord, so teach us to number our days that we may apply our hearts unto wisdom." The minister's words were muffled in the darkly draped chamber. "For-asmuch as it hath pleased Almighty God in his wise providence to take out of this clay tabernacle the soul that inhabited it, we commit its decaying remains to their kindred elements, earth to earth, ashes to ashes, dust to dust. . . . Wherefore, let us comfort one another with these words. Amen."

The simple ceremony was over. Guns in the outer forts stopped shaking the earth. Field artillery no longer crashed. Baying brass bands moved away. The myriad bells ceased their threnody. Slowly the people dispersed.

Under the lofty patriotic pile, that is enshrined in the heart of every American as the temple of freedom, there now reposed the mortal abode of the man at whose urging the unfinished dome had been carried upward and the work completed in spite of the troubled times. The work typified his own monumental task of reuniting a shattered Union and rebuilding the nation.

Now his head reposed on a white silk pillow. His gaunt frame, clad in the plain black suit, lay in a lead-lined walnut box. The box, six feet six inches in length, a foot and a half across the shoulders, was covered in black broadcloth adorned with rows of silver tacks, stars, and tassels; four massive silver handles were along the sides; and the interior was upholstered in plaited white satin with silk facings and edgings. Surmounting the lid a silver shield was engraved:

Abraham Lincoln
Sixteenth President of the United States
Born Feb. 12, 1809
Died April 15, 1865

The handsome casket rested on a dais ornamented in silver fringe looped with silver stars, and at each corner stood a bundle of rods bound with silver bands. The bundles were classic symbols of strength in unity, the fasces of antiquity, emblematic now of the Union. The long sides of the bier were arrayed with muskets, rifles, pistols, sabers, and cutlasses, symbolic of the military and naval services with which the President had been so intimately identified.

The rotunda was heavy with drapery. The eight large oil paintings around the circumferential wall portraying stirring scenes from early American history were completely shrouded. Statuary was also covered except for Houdon's white plaster statue of George Washington and it was hung with a black sash in the military fashion. From the frieze of the chamber extending upward into the cupola streamers of black cloth dimmed the outside light and imparted a sepulchral air. The hushed gloom made the scene a memorable one.

Abraham Lincoln lay in the ark of the Republic with his Maker.

At eight o'clock next morning the doors were opened to the public. The feminine figure atop the dome, soonest of all things in the nation's capital to kindle at dawn's earliest gleam, was but a dim shape in the haze of this rainy Thursday. Neither stormy weather nor long wait deterred Washingtonians, and three thousand an hour flowed past the venerated object until nine in the evening. Entering the draped chamber they removed headgear, spoke in whispers, and in other ways showed their respect. The eerie gloom was disturbed only by the occasional clank of arms as veteran guards moved about and by the sob of mourners affected by the sight of the familiar features so still yet so natural.

"Directly beneath me lay the casket in which the dead President lay at full length far, far below," related a newsman who had ascended the three hundred and sixty-five steps to the gallery. "Like black atoms moving over a sheet of grey paper, the slow-moving mourners crept silently in two dark lines across the pavement of the rotunda . . . and disappeared."

Throughout the night a detachment of picked veterans under a brigadier general mounted guard over their former Commander-in-Chief, not one of whom but would have gladly exchanged places. Peering into the dripping hours from her lofty perch "The Lady of the Capitol" kept vigil too, she who was as much a memento of The Tall Kentuckian who lay beneath her as he was of the Union of States he had made certain would endure. These were the last hours his attenuated frame would be part of the national capital, but his spirit would remain here as long as America lived.

To anticipate the crowds expected at the leave-taking ceremonies —the train was scheduled to depart at eight o'clock—those designated to escort the body to the train and those who would travel to the final resting place began assembling in the rotunda at six o'clock. At quarter past seven the family pastor took position at the head of the casket and raised a prayer over a circle of bent heads. At its conclusion the twelve veteran sergeants, who had taken the coffin from the hearse Wednesday afternoon and carried it up, now stepped forward and carried it down.

Following the hearse walked General Ulysses Grant, the first lieutenant general since George Washington.* His staff and a dozen other generals and admirals walked with him. In this manner did the military chieftains evidence their respect for the departed Commander-in-Chief. On the heels of the high officers rode mourners, pallbearers, and other government people, the column closed by President Johnson in a carriage escorted by a mounted guard. No members of the family were present. Four infantry companies of Veteran Reserves headed the march to the Baltimore

---

* General Winfield Scott was a lieutenant general by brevet.

and Ohio Railroad station three blocks away. No bands, no bugles, no drums sounded a single note.

At the depot the silver-trimmed coffer was carried through saluting ranks of the military, they having surrounded the building and posted extra guards at all approaches. Only authorized persons were allowed inside.

The nine-car special train stood ready, steam up, its motive power a brand-new locomotive built by the railroad, Number 238. The engineer was Thomas Beckett and C. A. Miller was the fireman. The road supervisor of engines was also in the cab. Ahead of it a sister engine stood ready to move out ten minutes sooner as pilot. Both engines were trimmed in black, brass work shrouded, Stars and Stripes bound in sable.

Six passenger cars and baggage car, all new, were also darkly festooned. Two cars at the end of the train were specials. The last one, a handsome vehicle of the Philadelphia, Wilmington and Baltimore Railroad built for its officers' travel, was reserved for family and relatives and the Guard of Honor. The President and Mrs. Lincoln had traveled in it on various occasions through the courtesy of the road's president, Samuel M. Felton. Before leaving Philadelphia it was suitably draped.

Even more magnificent was the second car from the end. Since it would carry the martyred man throughout the memorial journey it would become known as the Lincoln Funeral Car. Originally designed for his travel over military railroads, it was built in the car shops of the U.S. Military Railroad at Alexandria, Virginia, and had been completed several months before. Lincoln had not seen the car, nor is there any indication he knew about it.

Who authorized its construction is not definitely known. No official records can be located, the Smithsonian Institution having conducted diligent research into its origin. The best guess is that the Secretary of War initiated the project. Stanton was extremely solicitous of the President's well-being, continually urging him to secure better personal protection and finally insisting on detailing an infantry company and a cavalry troop to guard the White House, as well as providing personal bodyguards in civilian clothes to accompany the President. To all of this, Lincoln succumbed but heartily disliked.

Records do show the presidential conveyance was started in November of 1863. According to certain accounts the under-structure of the car employed girders instead of the conventional truss-type then in use. To the girders iron plates were riveted that reached from sill to window, thus in effect making the lower half of the car bulletproof. This gave rise to the legend of an "iron-clad" railroad coach for President Lincoln.*

Based on today's standards the vehicle would not appear un-usual but for that day it was extraordinary. Divided into dining room, stateroom, and parlor, an aisleway ran along the inside wall of the car connecting dining room and parlor, keeping the bedroom completely private. Thus located in the center, the bedroom was the most comfortable place for railroad travel.

The roof of the car was the modern raised or monitor type, allow-ing better ventilation, and was paneled inside with crimson silk gathered into rosettes. The upper deck, also paneled, was painted zinc white. Coats-of-arms of the states ornamented each panel. From seat rail to head lining sides and ends of the car were upholstered in dark green plush, set off by light green silk curtains framing the windows. Between windows the spaces were adorned with oil paintings. The woodwork was black walnut. Other appointments were equally elegant and included a beautiful silver service, wall-to-wall carpeting, cushioned chairs, carved tables, chandeliers of cut glass.

There were no beds or berths in the bedroom which doubled as

* This remains controversial. See appendix.

a sitting room, but four tufted lounges could be opened out to form comfortable sleeping accommodations. Two of the lounges were extra long to take care of the President's six-feet-four.

The exterior finish was a rich chocolate brown, hand rubbed with oil and rottenstone. In an oval panel in the center of each side an American eagle was painted on a background of national colors. Above it gold letters spelled out "United States" and gold ornamentations decorated mouldings and cornices. The car had no number or name.

Now the windows were hung with somber curtains and the furniture was encased in black. Above the windows on the outside a series of alpaca festoons was held by silver stars from which depended silver tassels. Strips of black velvet ending in silver fringe graced each window panel. Below the windows another series of alpaca festoons was caught up with silver stars. With its sixteen-wheeled running gear, the conveyance was the cynosure of all eyes and added authentic dignity to the cortege ensemble.

Inside in the front section of the car the silver-mounted casket was enfolded in the national flag and rested on a plain black-covered stand banked with a profusion of blossoms. At the other end a small coffin rested on a low stand. The remains of William Wallace Lincoln had been removed from the Oak Hill Cemetery vault where they had been kept since his passing in 1862. The twelve-year-old son would accompany his father to Springfield and there be interred with him.

At the steps of the hearse car the family pastor addressed a short prayer to the God of the living and the dead. "O Lord," the Reverend Gurley beseeched, "strengthen us under the pressure of this great national sorrow as only Thou can strengthen the weak," and voiced the final words before there would be taken away the mortal relict of him who four years ago had arrived on this same platform, unnoticed, untried, and unwanted. "Comfort us," he

pleaded on behalf of the silent, distinguished throng, "as Thou
only canst sanctify a people when they are passing through the
fiery furnaces of a great trial."

As he spoke the pilot engine slipped away.

Aboard the cars were seven who had accompanied the President-
elect from Springfield. One was the lost son. Wife Mary and young
Tad had been with him then but could not undergo the rigors of
this return. Only Robert of the immediate family could make it
and the strain had him hollow-eyed and drawn-looking. He came
just before departure and was seated in the last car alongside his
friends, the two private secretaries. Nicolay and Hay both had
made the inaugural journey but now would proceed only to
Baltimore from where they would return to Washington and, with
Robert, help clear the way for the incoming executive. Judge
David Davis also would return with them. Davis, by Lincoln's
appointment an associate justice of the Supreme Court, would act
as executor of the President's estate at Robert's request. He too
had been in the original group.

General David Hunter was another who had accompanied the
President-elect. Hunter, despite issuing an emancipation proclamation in the military district he was commanding without consulting
the President (it was a political, not a military, question), had
been stepped up from a major in the regular army. Lincoln had
continued to have faith in him. The seventh in the original group
was that hulk of man, Ward Lamon, former prosecuting attorney
of the old Eighth Judicial Circuit and Lincoln's trusted friend.
Often Lamon had slept on the floor outside the presidential bedroom before a personal bodyguard was assigned, ready to forestall
the doom he felt so keenly would surely come. He was sick over
the catastrophe, berating himself for not having remained in
Washington to protect his great friend and benefactor. Lamon

would go all the way to Springfield. On the eastward trip he had been the only one to be at Lincoln's side every mile of the way including the secret midnight detour through Baltimore.

The total number of persons authorized to ride the train leaving Washington including the military escort exceeded two hundred and fifty. The honorary Guard of Honor, made up of officers from all services, was headed by Brevet Brigadier General Edward D. Townsend representing the Secretary of War. Townsend, who was Assistant Adjutant General, was in overall command of the operation. Rear Admiral C. E. Davis represented the Secretary of the Navy. Brigadier General D. C. McCallum, Superintendent of Military Railroads, was in direct charge of the train and of the railroads over which it traveled.

Senators and congressmen from twenty-six loyal states, sergeants-at-arms from Senate and House and staff members, Illinois congressmen, and Senators Trumbull and Yates were aboard as was a special Illinois delegation that included the Springfield committee that had come to Washington to escort the remains home, the mayor of Chicago, the mayor-elect of Springfield, the state adjutant general, General John McClernand, Dr. S. H. Melvin, and "Uncle Jesse" Dubois, former state auditor and longtime friend of the deceased.*

Four governors were on the train: Brough of Ohio, Morton of Indiana, Stone of Iowa, and Oglesby of Illinois. Each governor was accompanied by a staff. Mayor Wallach of Washington and John Garrett, president of the Baltimore and Ohio Railroad, were aboard as were a number of newspaper correspondents, including the Associated Press bureau chief, and also the family pastor.

Some of the travelers went the whole distance; others came and went. As a military operation it was possible to control the riders,

* Lincoln said of Dubois: "My acquaintance first began with him in 1836. ... He was a slim, handsome young man with auburn hair and sky-blue eyes."

a control not possible on the inaugural trip when transportation
had been furnished through railroad courtesy. This time the War
Department issued a special pass to those authorized to travel.

The Lincoln car was the special charge of John McNaughton of
the mechanical department at Alexandria. With him were Tom
Pendel, White House doorkeeper, and Harry Smith, a plainclothes
White House policeman. The latter two had initimate knowledge
of the President's associates and government officials, making them
invaluable in handling visitors to the car. Two other skilled aides
were along; Frank T. Sands, undertaker, and Dr. Charles P. Brown,
embalmer. Their duties were to see that casket and corpse were in
proper condition on the train and off.

Ahead of the train schedule by two days Colonel H. L. Robinson
and Captain J. C. Wyman of General McCallum's staff finalized
transportation arrangements and confirmed ceremonial schedules
with local authorities. Riding on the train Captain Charles Penrose
of the Quartermaster Department handled subsistence and lodging
arrangements for those authorized to travel. Penrose had the distinction of having accompanied the President three weeks before
to Richmond and had walked by his side through the smoldering
streets of the fallen capital.

Forming the working guard of honor were twenty-five sergeants, a
captain, and three lieutenants, who had been selected from outstanding Veterans Reserve regiments. They were subject to the orders
of Brigadier General J. C. Caldwell of the Guard of Honor. Movement of the train throughout the trip was directed by the Baltimore
and Ohio's popular conductor, Captain J. F. Dukeheart, acting as
special aid to General McCallum.

Watch in hand, eyes glancing along the cars and at the pulsating
marker approaching the appointed hour, Dukeheart stood at the
steps of the Lincoln coach. He caught McCallum's go-ahead signal
as the general boarded the last car and uplifted his right arm. At

the stroke of eight he pulled down the arm and stepped on the
train. The muffled engine bell commenced sounding; steam roared
up the huge balloon stack; drawbars tightened; and the "consist"
of nine darkly draped coaches inched forward.

Meanwhile, in a building at the rear of the depot called "Soldiers
Rest," where incoming troops were offered a hot meal and creature
comforts before being shipped to battle fronts, a regiment of
artillery was finishing a hearty breakfast. At the sound of the
locomotive bell they jumped into formation at trackside, saluting
as the martyred Emancipator went by, not a dry eye among these
veterans who had held Paducah, Kentucky, against General Forrest
and his confederate hosts. They were the Eighth U.S. Colored
Artillery.

Regiments surrounding the station snapped to attention and stood
at present arms. The massed spectators pressing for a better look
and the distinguished guests on the platform, including the new
President, uncovered until the mortuary caravan rolled out of
sight in the direction of Baltimore.

PART III

THE LONG ROAD HOME

6

BEFORE daylight had fairly broken through the heavy mist, Baltimore's downtown streets were flooded with people. By eight o'clock they were overflowing and it was not possible to move in the neighborhood of the Camden Street station. The weather was in consonance with the event.

The local press concurred that "never has grief over the loss of a faithful public servant been so heartfelt and so universal," remarking that "almost every house was a house of mourning." Work was suspended. Schools adjourned. Horsecars stopped running. Public

97

offices closed. A solemn hush pervaded the Maryland metropolis. Baltimoreans turned aside from their daily vocations to reverence the departed Head of State.

Adjacent to the draped depot the largest uniformed assembly ever brought together in the Monument City was formed into line; they had come from camps around the city, from Fort McHenry, and from ships in Chesapeake Bay. At the entrance of the railroad station stood an impressive catafalque built for the occasion, headed by four matched, jet-black horses somberly caparisoned. The sounding of locomotive bells in a slow beat signaled that the special train had arrived. Minute guns took up the salute.

" 'Tenn-shun!" The shouted order rippled over blue ranks and the long columns snapped into tight formation. Presently the silver-trimmed repository appeared in the station entrance. "Present, Arms!" Thousands of trained hands slapped musket and rifle straight up as the cargo of departed glory was carried to an all-glass conveyance, a starry flag draped over it, and the doors shut. "Order, Arms! . . . For-warrd, March!"

Through mud and rain, arms reversed, flags edged in black, bands discoursing requiems, the procession took off from the depot and moved up Eutaw Street to Baltimore to Gay, circled Chew and Caroline, back to Baltimore and Gay to the Mercantile Exchange. The veteran reserve corpsmen closely investing the funeral carriage were, in turn, surrounded by the Second U.S. Artillery, unmounted. A squadron of cavalry headed the columns of infantry and artillery and marines and seamen, announcing approach of the line by trumpeters. Preceding the hearse a mounted platoon of officers was led by the commander of the Middle Department, General Lew Wallace.* Then followed the Washington escort in closed carriages minus family and relatives who did not take part in processions. Civil groups stretched two miles and included the

* Subsequently famous as the author of *Ben Hur*.

governor; governor-elect; state officials; mayor; municipal officers; fraternal, religious, educational, social bodies; and a closing file of police.

At Calvert Street the columns halted. The military separated their lines to each side of the street facing the center. General officers dismounted and took position along the passageway to the Exchange. Between facing lines the presidential remains were borne as the ranks presented arms, the officers saluted, and a regimental band rendered the hymn, "Peace, Troubled Soul." Placed in the center of the draped rotunda the upper lid was opened to expose the face. "The countenance still preserved the expression it bore in life, half-smiling," ran the comment, "the whole face indicating the energy and humor which had characterized the living man." Military and naval officers filed through first, then the soldiery and civil portion of the procession and finally the general public. Doors were closed at half past two, having been open to the public for an hour and a half.

The venerated object was removed to the hearse; the waiting columns were reformed; and the march was resumed to the President Street depot of the Northern Central Railroad for the run to Harrisburg. In pouring rain the famed "Baltimore Battle Monument" was passed, the sodden spectators baring their heads as the cortege moved by. Around the Mercantile Exchange the multitude was so great several persons were injured, women fainted, children got lost.

While the late President's remains were being viewed, the Washington escort was driven to the Eutaw House, and served a buffet luncheon through the courtesy of the city. Partaking of the food quickly they were whisked back in the same carriages and were in place when the march was resumed.

From the Baltimore and Ohio Railroad the Lincoln car and the officers' car were switched to the Northern Central line where

94139

EMORY AND HENRY LIBRARY

they were attached to a special "consist" of six coaches and baggage car. Willie's coffin stayed in the hearse car under guard during the switching, and would remain there throughout the journey. A passenger coach, coupled to the pilot engine, was occupied by Simon Cameron, his board of directors, and Harrisburg friends. Cameron, who had been Lincoln's first Secretary of War and was a key figure in Pennsylvania politics, had been unable to secure accommodations for his large group on the train and provided his own transportation over his own railroad.

Throngs as large as those on arrival were at the departure. For several miles out of the city the banks and margins of the right-of-way were fringed with onlookers. Coteries of bareheaded men and tearful women collected at farmhouses and crossroads as the memorial train wound its way through northern Maryland's hills toward the Mason-Dixon Line.

Back in Baltimore many disappointed citizens demanded that the Mercantile Exchange be reopened for public viewing. Their demands grew so insistent that the mayor and city council finally acceded; and next day unbroken lines of people filed through the rotunda. All was just as it had been—the decorations of sorrow, imposing catafalque, profusion of wreaths and blossoms, military guards and squads of policemen—except that the bier was vacant. Hour after hour thousands trudged by the mute symbols. So deeply had the heart of Maryland been touched that the martyr's surroundings received their equal reverence.

And this was the experience of the sixteenth President in the old Free State: four years before he had to pass through in secrecy and now he was borne through a conquering hero. One may well ask, had his wise policy of holding extremists with a firm but gentle hand so moderated controversial attitudes as to bring forth "the better angels" of their nature?

Reaching the state line at half after five, the entourage was met
by Pennsylvania's war governor, Andrew G. Curtin. With his
staff, including the commander of the state military district, he
had come down from the state capital. Just as Maryland's governor
had journeyed to meet the cortege at Annapolis Junction (first
stop out of the District of Columbia), so now the Keystone State's
chief executive was on hand to escort the remains through his
domain. The two governors joined each other in the front car, the
meeting having been carefully prearranged.

The death of a great man is always a marked event; and where
genius has fixed its shrine we, the people, watch with breathless
interest every movement of the deceased's person. The War Department was taking no chances and integrated their plans with all
parties concerned. The Adjutant General's office arranged move-
ments of the Lincoln Special with state and city officials; and to
ensure proper operation over the lengthy route the Assistant Adjutant General himself, General Townsend, was assigned to ride the
train all the way. Detailed instructions were dispatched to each
governor along the route similar to these sent to Governor Curtin:

The remains of the late President, Abraham Lincoln, will leave
Washington on Friday morning at 8 o'clock to go by way of Baltimore to Harrisburg and thence to Philadelphia and New York by
the timetable as arranged. The remains will reach Harrisburg at
8 P.M. on Friday and leave at 12 noon on Saturday for Philadelphia,
where they will remain until 4 o'clock Monday morning and then
be conveyed to New York. A copy of the timetable and program
will be forwarded to you tomorrow. You are respectfully invited
to meet the remains with your staff at such point as you may
designate to this Department and accompany them so far as you
are pleased to go. You will please signify to this Department by
telegraph where you will join the remains; whether you will take
charge of them at Harrisburg; where you will have them placed
while they remain at the capital of your State; and what honors you
desire to pay while there.

Governor Curtin had responded immediately: "I propose to take charge of the remains at the line of the State and to accompany them until they leave the State. They will be placed in the Capitol at Harrisburg. All the military honors that can be arranged will be shown. Measures are being taken for that purpose." Simultaneously he issued his proclamation to the public:

The remains of the murdered patriot, Abraham Lincoln, President of the United States, will arrive in the State on Friday evening next on their way to the place of interment in Illinois. . . . I recommend that all business be suspended during their passage through the State. Local authorities and people everywhere to join the State authorities in paying honor to the memory of the martyred statesman who has fallen a victim to the savage treason of assassins.

Commanding officers of military districts through which the train would pass were instructed to meet the remains at their state line and escort them "while they remain within your command." They were further ordered to report to the governor of the state to assist in the ceremonies and public honors as directed by the governor.

Crossing the Mason-Dixon Line at five-thirty o'clock the first stop in Pennsylvania was at York. Here occurred a touching incident. A group of ladies asked permission to lay a garland of flowers on the coffin. General Townsend granted the request with the proviso the ceremony be performed by no more than six. Accordingly half a dozen matrons, attired in all black, entered the hearse car, three to each side of the flag-draped bier, and deposited thereon a beautiful production of red, white, and blue flowers fashioned in the form of the national shield. Church bells tolled and an instrumental band rendered a requiem during the ceremony. The ladies could not restrain their tears as they offered their token of affection to the departed spirit.

A few minutes later the cortege moved northward through the
stormy night. At Harrisburg, reached at 8:30 P.M., the downpour
was so severe that before the head of the column leaving the depot
could reach Market Street, the deluge had thoroughly soaked
marchers and spectators. Nevertheless the escort was imposing
and the streets were thronged. A series of chemical lights had been
set up and these illuminated the black hearse, drawn by four milk-
white horses, and row on row of rifles and muskets. The rain was
accompanied by a severe electrical storm. It was a night of the
dead for the living.

Amid bursts of lightning, roar of thunder, and salute of artillery
guns the martyred hero was borne to the hall of the House of
Representatives and laid in front of the speaker's rostrum on a bier
banked with blossoms. From nine o'clock until midnight persevering
Pennyslvanians tramped through the soggy night to file past the
silent bier in the hushed chamber. Ten thousand, it was said,
braved the raging elements to gaze for a fleeting moment on the
familiar face.

At seven o'clock in the morning the doors were opened again,
and again the heartstruck populace poured through. At nine the
public were stopped and those taking part in the procession were
given an hour to pay their last respects to Old Abe draped in Old
Glory. At a quarter past eleven they witnessed the procession to
the railroad station and the departure for Philadelphia. From
countryside and village and town they had come, feeling the
national bereavement a personal catastrophe.

"Today the people of the State Capitol of Pennsylvania bury
their first great martyr, whose name and fame will go down in
history as the noblest in the personal annals of the world," proclaimed a morning newspaper. Avowing the spectacle would long be
recalled the *Pennsylvania Daily Telegraph* said its significance for
good would be tremendous and that although the assassination

exhibited the enormity of treason, "the mighty grief of the people illustrated the real strength of the government.

"The world was without a record in all its history connected with the government of men filled with such potent influence for good as that connected with the history of Abraham Lincoln's life and martyrdom," continued the *Telegraph*. "It may be written of him that he will continue to influence the American people in their greatness and glory."

Twenty-five years later the prophetic words were reaffirmed by Lincoln's two private secretaries in their notable ten-volume biography, when they declared that "the quick instinct by which the world recognized him, even at the moment of death, as one of its great men, has been confirmed by the sober thought of a quarter of a century." What impressed Nicolay and Hay was the extent of the emotion Lincoln's demise awakened. "It was among the common people of the civilized world," they pointed out, "that the most genuine and spontaneous manifestations of sorrow and appreciation were produced; and to this fact we attribute the sudden and solid foundation of Lincoln's fame." A reputation takes centuries to become worldwide, they said. Progress from the few to the many is slow. In the case of Lincoln, the many imposed their opinions at once. "He was canonized as he lay on his bier by the irresistible decree of countless millions."

Above all, Lincoln was canonized by the soldiery. That morning a dispatch from Washington related that 22,000 rebel prisoners being held at Point Lookout (on the Potomac) had expressed abhorrence of the assassination and extended their deep sympathy to the bereaved family, the resolutions sent through their sergeants to the War Department. From the Sixth Corps at Burkesville Junction, units of which had taken Lee's surrender, came dispatches of the obsequies there, saying that the dead Commander-in-Chief was "the one all-absorbing subject of conversation" because

he had so thoroughly endeared himself to both officers and men
that "all felt they had lost a dear personal friend."

Across far-flung battle lines, in crowded cantonments, at lonely
outposts, on ships in harbors and at sea, as the long bloody conflict
went on, they had talked about his goodness of heart. Hardly an
outfit but had a living example. How amid weighty cares he found
time to attend to wrongs of ordinary privates; how he saved
soldiers from being executed; how he commuted overly drastic
sentences. His compassion was more than a legend. He was
peculiarly beloved by the men in blue. Now that he was gone words
could not express their feelings.

The military hierarchy claimed his leniency ruined discipline,
that his pardons encouraged insubordination, and that his kindly
nature caused him to be taken advantage of by the undeserving.
Concerning a case which he handled with the Attorney General,
the President admitted both of them were "pigeonhearted." His
eyes twinkled as he confessed.

A closer look at his pardons discloses that the sixteenth President was well aware of what he was doing. He never was lost in
admiration for bumbling brigadiers and upstage major generals he
had appointed, whether they were political or professional appointees. He disliked the despotism upon which the army was based.
To compel plowboys, clerks, mechanics, and backwoodsmen to
adhere to regular army discipline overnight was unrealistic. Shoot-
ing youngsters for desertion and sleeping on post was inhuman.
Beyond everything he had to have an army and navy. He got them.

The Secretary of War reported that following McClellan's dis-
asters in the Peninsular Campaign, over eighty thousand volunteers
were enlisted, armed, trained, and sent into the field in one month's
time. On more than one occasion when an emergency arose sixty
thousand troops went into action in less than four weeks; in one
such emergency ninety thousand volunteers hurried from Ohio,

Indiana, Illinois, Iowa, and Wisconsin within twenty days. Of the
2,500,000 men who wore Union blue, *only 170,000 had to be drafted
during the entire four years.**

His sense of discrimination was keen. To bounty jumpers,
mutineers, spies, and those encouraging desertion or inciting treason
Lincoln gave short shrift. Going AWOL and sleeping on duty were
pardonable, much depending on the age of the offender and circumstances of the act. A mother or wife appearing before him was
likely to succeed. A boy under eighteen was almost certain to be
excused, a farm boy especially. Though he might be looked upon
as an easy mark, in commuting the death penalty the punishment
Lincoln imposed was no bed of roses; generally it was hard labor
for five or ten years in some far-off place like Fort Jefferson in the
Dry Tortugas. Not every appeal succeeded with him, even in cases
where great political pressure was brought to bear. Not every
woman who shed tears for his special benefit got her way. But he
was never less than just.

Of the numerous instances in which he refused to approve the
death penalty, the best known is that of the sleeping sentinel,
William Scott. It happened not long after the battle of First Bull
Run when the Union army had fallen back on Washington. Scott
was a private in Company K of the Third Vermont Volunteers
detailed to night watch at the bridge that crossed the Potomac (still
does) into Virginia near the Maryland line. His brigade had moved

---

* Speaking in the well of the House April 15, 1879, Ohio Congressman James
A. Garfield, soon to be twentieth President, said: "Do the gentlemen know
that, leaving out all the border states, there were 50 regiments and 7 companies
of white soldiers in our army from the States that went into rebellion? Do
they know that from the single border state of Kentucky more Union soldiers
fought under our flag than Napoleon took into the battle of Waterloo; and
more than Wellington took with all the allied armies against Napoleon? Do
they remember that 186,000 colored men fought under our flag . . . and of
that number, 90,000 were from the States that went into rebellion?"

Note: Of the 170,000 drafted only 46,343 were actually conscripted, the re-
mainder serving as substitutes.

into the Old Dominion, camping a mile inland in what was presumed to be enemy territory. The first night out the officer of the
guard made his customary midnight rounds and found Scott asleep
on post. The farm lad of six weeks before was court-martialed and
sentenced to be shot. Such drastic punishment aroused his comrades and they managed to get the case put before the President.
Lincoln pardoned Scott and sent him back to duty.

Those are the bare facts. They were considerably embellished in
newspaper dispatches, magazine articles, poems, and books that
spread the tale over America so that William Scott, the sleeping
sentinel who was not shot, became the best-known private soldier
of the Civil War. Regardless of embellishments, concerning which
there was scholarly bickering, the main facts are as stated. The
end of the story is heroic. To Private Scott goes the red badge of
courage.

He was among the four companies of his regiment that mounted
the first assault of the Army of the Potomac on an enemy en-
trenched line. This occurred at the beginning of McClellan's ill-
fated Peninsular Campaign. Scott took six bullets into his body
in the assault. His comrades dragged him to safety and then—

While yet his voice grew tremulous and death bedimmed his eye,
He called his comrades to attest he had not feared to die;
And, in the last expiring breath, a prayer to Heaven he sent
That God, with his unfailing grace, would bless our president.*

Political opponents charged that Lincoln catered to the soldiery
to win their votes. No reason why he should not, the same as he
sought those of all citizens. To charge that concern for their welfare
was purely selfish was doing him a grave injustice as the head of

* Last stanza of "The Sleeping Sentinel" by Francis de Haes Janvier.
Written soon after Scott's death it was first read by the celebrated elocutionist,
James E. Murdoch, to President Lincoln at a White House reception, January
19, 1863. Janvier also wrote "The Stars and Stripes" that was set to music and
played at Lincoln's first inaugural ceremonies.

the nation and an even greater misunderstanding of him as a man. The actual effect of the soldier vote on his political fortunes has been greatly exaggerated. The record shows that he won reelection handily without their help, that the civilian vote returned him to office. In one state, Maryland, the soldiers' vote did provide the margin of victory; and it helped in others. He did not need Maryland to win but he was proud of the result nevertheless. He commented to a White House secretary who was accompanying him to the War Department to get the late election returns that Maryland was "a victory worth double the number of its electoral votes because of the moral influence."

The Civil War was the first American experience with large numbers of voters absent from their legal residences. Only one state, Pennsylvania, had made provision for absentee balloting by soldiers.* All other states required citizens to vote in their district. How could military men come home when they were facing the enemy? Yet why should they lose their vote because they were in the armed forces defending their country? The identical situation held for Confederates as for the Federals.

The right to vote is wholly secured and regulated by state constitutions and laws, not by the national government. Between May 8, 1861, and October 13, 1864, voting in the field was provided by, or attempted to be provided by, nineteen of the twenty-six loyal states. "A review of the legislation impresses one that soldier voting bills were uniformly supported by the Republicans and as uniformly opposed by the Democrats," Dr. Josiah H. Benton revealed in his intensive study, *Voting in the Field, a Forgotten Aspect of*

---

* The act of March 29, 1813, authorizing soldier voting in the field was declared unconstitutional by the Supreme Court of Pennsylvania, May 22, 1862, reversing the lower Court of Quarterly Sessions. (The same Supreme Court, composed of bitter antiwar partisans, subsequently declared the U.S. Conscription Act unconstitutional—a state court declared a federal law inoperable!)

the Civil War. Soldier voting had, unfortunately, become a partisan issue, not to be resolved until later years.

The newly reconstructed states of Louisiana and Tennessee also held elections for President and congressmen. Lincoln won in both. Congress, however, by joint resolution which Lincoln signed with reluctance, declared they would not be recognized and so their votes were not included in the official total. Although not necessary to his election Lincoln earnestly desired that the reconstructed states be included just as if they had never been "out of proper relation" to the Union.

That he had been worried over renomination and reelection seems astonishing today in view of his tremendous achievements and the universal respect in which he is held. So apprehensive did he become about being renominated that he told Alexander K. McClure, a power in political Pennsylvania, "his name would go into history darkly shadowed by a fraternal war that he would be held responsible for inaugurating." McClure commented, "A more anxious candidate I have never known."

For three-and-a-half bloodstained years the war had dragged along, costing millions of dollars in treasure, thousands of lives, unending heartaches. The people were war weary. McClellan's bright and shining promises, bifurcated though they were, offered tempting relief from misery under Lincoln. Anything was better than the Republican scourge of war and destruction. The time had come to end the needless slaughter and negotiate peace. McClellan said he would do this. Such was the talk of the "peace makers."

So it came to be that Abraham Lincoln's thin sloping shoulders were bowed with the weight of the fratricide; carrying, Atlas-like, the load of a whole people in dire distress. He was all that stood between them and chaos. And he declared firmly, "This government must be preserved in spite of the acts of any one man or set of men."

7

AN unblemished sky and brilliant sun replaced the stygian darkness of the night storm and the broad acres around the state capitol were leafy and green in the bright spring morning. At the exit to the grounds the procession passed under a white arch bound in black and garlanded with fresh blossoms; the white for hope, the black for sorrow, the flowers for life eternal.

Again the silver-mounted reliquary was placed in the special railway conveyance, the United States car. Preceded by a pilot engine the shrouded cars moved sedately along the fat fields and neat towns of the Pennsylvania Railroad's main line. Through Middleton, Elizabethtown, Mount Joy, and Lancaster, each so choked with citizens the train could move with difficulty; at Strasburg Junction a large gathering of country-folk; at Parkesburg likewise; next Coatesville, beehive of the Chester Valley; then Downingtown, a stop for wood and water, the people clustering at the rear cars, uncovered and hushed; through Oakland, Walkerton, Steamboat, West Chester, artisans and countrymen joined in mourning; then Green Tree, Paoli, Hestonville, all quiet, the silence speaking. Finally West Philadelphia where a small brass howitzer of the J. Edgar Thomson Cannon Club announced the arrival and continued firing as the cars moved over the Schuylkill River to the depot at Broad and Prime Streets.

The military salute was taken up by two University Light Artillery guns posted on Broad Street south of Market. Instructed to fire at sixty-second intervals from train arrival to deposit of remains in Independence Hall, the battery ticked off the minutes with stopwatch regularity until, at eight o'clock, a sudden explosion interrupted the count. The gun barrel had overheated due to overlong firing. Two men serving the gun were injured and the life of the number one man was despaired of. Both were rushed to their homes and given medical care.

Philadelphia, then the nation's second largest city, was the first great metropolitan center north of the Mason-Dixon Line to act as host city; and although the extent of public feeling had been demonstrated by the tremendous outpourings at prior stopovers the City of Brotherly Love turned out a larger congregation than ever seen before. Half a million persons, equaling the city's population, squeezed into downtown streets. No day in the history of the birthplace of American freedom matched that of Saturday, April 22, 1865.

A select group of twenty-four army and navy officers formed a local guard of honor and received the honored dead at the depot. As the coffin was lowered from the car preparatory to being carried to the waiting hearse, it rested on stools arranged for that purpose. At this moment two comely young ladies stepped through the lines, laid a wreath on it, stepped quickly back, the tears trickling down their cheeks, and melted into the crowd. Thus Philadelphia's first token of affection was tendered by two of its lovely daughters.

All downtown was garnished in mourning. Columns of civic and social and religious associations assembled on the east side of Broad Street and displayed national flags and banners, many devised for the occasion. The most noteworthy object was the specially built hearse. Drawn by eight black horses harnessed in silver and led by grooms, the vehicle's wheels were concealed from sight by a fuliginous valance. The flag-draped casket reposed on a dais affording full view to standing spectators.

The route (from Broad Street to Walnut to Twenty-first to Arch and down Arch to Third to Walnut to Independence Square) was not traversed until darkness had fallen, but the tide of people flooding the streets did not subside. At Broad and Lombard the hearse paused while a hundred blended voices of German singing societies harmonized a lament by Mozart. All within earshot were affected.

By the time the column reached Independence Square it was well past eight o'clock. Up the graveled walk the coffin was carried between facing lines of Union League members.* Attired in all-black with white gloves these staunch supporters of the President held a tall silk hat over the heart as the remains moved by. Their band had been placed in the steeple of the State House; from it and

* Union league clubs were community organizations of responsible citizens that sprang up over the North during the war, to aid the Union cause. They were voluntary civilian groups having no connection with the government or the military but raised funds and regiments. Many continue to this day in northern cities furthering patriotic and civic causes. See appendix.

the band that accompanied the cortege identical requiems escorted
the body into the Hall. The refrains interblending from ground
and night-sky produced an otherworldly effect.

Another operation prepared by the Union League flooded the
area with light. The moment the hearse doors were opened a
brilliant flare of calcium lights illuminated the scene, the glow
coming from alternate red and white and blue lamps fitted with
colored glass. "It remained for this city to produce such effects to
such advantage," proclaimed Philadelphia's popular oversized
newspaper, the *North American and United States Gazette.* "Never
before has such a corpse been brought to Independence Hall," continued the *Gazette,* observing that the work of the Founders which
had made the Hall sacred to every American had been finished by
Abraham Lincoln; that it was fitting he should be brought into
the "Valhalla of Liberty" to commune with the spirits of the mighty
dead; and that "Philadelphia, which in life loved him with constant
affection and sustained him with unfaltering trust, will today weep
beside his bier with unaffected and heartfelt sorrow."

Philadelphia is not Philadelphia without Independence Hall. And
Independence Hall is not the cradle of liberty without the old
State House bell that pealed so loud and strong it cracked open.
The memorable angelus had announced the signing of the Declaration of Independence on the Fourth of July in 1776 and ever since
has been revered as the Liberty Bell. Now it rested in silent
significance on a pedestal wrapped in the tapestry of sorrow. Its
motto, "Proclaim liberty throughout the land and unto all the
inhabitants thereof," seemed to have issued from the lips of the
martyr lying on the dais nearby, his head toward this venerable
relic of American freedom.

Four years and two months previously, in this same room in
front of Washington's statue on the morning of Washington's birth-

day, the martyred President had addressed city officials and townspeople assembled to greet him as he stopped over on the way to take
office. Responding to the *sui generis* environment he said all the
political sentiments he ever entertained were drawn from those
given to the world "from this hall in which we stand." He avowed
he never had a feeling politically that did not spring from the
sentiments expressed in the Declaration of Independence.

"I have often inquired of myself," he said, "what great principle
or idea it was that kept this Confederacy so long together. . . . It
was that which gave promise that in due time the weights should
be lifted from the shoulders of all men, and that *all* should have an
equal chance. That is the sentiment embodied in the Declaration of
Independence," he declared and went on to state that if the country
could be saved on that basis he would be the happiest man in the
world if he could help save it. But if the country could not be
saved without giving up that principle he "would rather be assassinated on this spot than to surrender it."

Assassination was on the President-elect's mind that morning.
The night before he had been up until a late hour listening to two
reports. One was from the famous railroad detective Allan Pinkerton and the other from Senator Seward's son Frederick who had
been sent by his father to give warning of danger impending at
Baltimore. The two reports from unrelated sources formulated
unknown to each other convinced him something was afoot. Pinkerton advised he proceed to Washington at once. Lincoln declined,
saying he would carry out his commitments to raise the flag over
Independence Hall in the morning and address the Pennsylvania
Legislature at Harrisburg in the afternoon. To calm those who
seemed upset by this decision, he promised that if no Baltimore
delegation met him at Harrisburg he would reconsider.

And that was how matters stood when he had stood in the room
where he now lay. His mention of assassination had been no flight

of oratory. He was murdered for the reason he had voiced. As leader of the forces generated by the Declaration of Independence he had won the war for freedom. Through his efforts *all* Americans had been assured of life, liberty, and the opportunity to pursue happiness. He had struck off the bondsmen's shackles and for that he had been struck down.

"He may have had a glimpse into the future," the *Philadelphia Inquirer* suggested. "His eyes may have seen dimly the fate which overtook him at the moment the noble principles for which he had so long and faithfully contended were triumphantly vindicated and forever established." The *Inquirer* reporter, standing at the bier contemplating the benign countenance of the dead man, let his eyes wander over the solemn tapestried room; looked at the patriots' pictures gazing at the scene; and thought that if they could speak they would say, "We indeed won our liberty from a foreign tyrant; but we left a fetter in the land of our children to break . . . that you have now broken. Welcome, noble and worthy son, to rest and to immortality."

It was as though Lincoln had a double guard of honor around him—the living military officers with drawn sabers and the august shades of Americans whose patriotic acts had made the chamber a glorious place forever.

The hall was opened at ten o'clock only to holders of special tickets who were admitted at the county court's door on Sixth below Chestnut while the Union League band in the steeple continued to fill the night with hymns and dirges, providing a reverential setting.

Compelling the general public to wait while a privileged few were permitted to view the "champion of the people" annoyed the *Philadelphia Daily News.* "It was a desecration and makes the cup of our municipal humiliation run over," complained the tabloid-

sized newssheet which, though having local political differences,
was loyal to the administration and an admirer of the President. At
the masthead of its editorial page appeared a rippling American
flag under which were the words: "This emblem of freedom and
flag of the free/ Has been placed at half-mast on the land and the
sea/ There to remain until beneath the green sod/ Our chieftan
shall sleep in the bosom of God."

The hall was closed at midnight. Just as the hour was chiming,
three ladies entered and deposited on the casket a cross of pure
white flowers. Attached was a silken streamer inscribed: "A
Tribute to Our Great and Good President Fallen a Martyr to the
Cause of Human Freedom—'In My Hand No Price I Bring, Simply
to My Cross I Cling.'" Throughout the night the streets were alive
with people. Above the main doorway on Chestnut Street a series
of gas jets spelled out "Rest in Peace," and underneath a trans-
parency depicted the late President lying in the coffin. The display
illuminated the surrounding area and imposed a reminder of the
tragic occasion.

A determined crowd took possession of the steps at the windows
about half past three and at five the windows were opened; the
easterly one for ladies and ladies with escorts, the west for men
only. Dawn was peering over the housetops as the public poured
through the room where the Declaration had been signed, the
Constitution formulated, and was now a chamber of heroic death.
The throng increased so fast the streets were soon jammed with
those hoping to enter. Boats were landing at nearby docks, trains
were pulling into depots, wagons and buggies were rattling down
the highways, all discharging streams of anxious spectators.

By noon the police were helpless in the face of the mounting
multitude. Describing the confusion as that of a horse race or
political meeting, the critical *News* said there was no respect for
"the hour, the place, or the still corpse within." The military were

called. Excitement broke out when a rumor gained circulation that a fight was in progress. Women fainted, children were tramped on, "coats were abbreviated, bonnets demolished, shawls torn, pantaloons ripped, and hoop skirts so disfigured a coroner's jury would declare them unrecognizable."

Among those pressing to get into the hall was a former Philadelphia girl who was visiting her parents. Comely Mrs. Louise C. Olmsted, sleek brown hair parted in the middle in the prevailing fashion, wrote her husband in Brooklyn of being on the street from nine in the morning until seven that evening. She stepped into line at Third and Chestnut Streets, crept down to the wharves at less than five feet a minute and reached Fourth and Chestnut four hours later. "At last we stood where we could see the President," she wrote. "The Hall looked beautiful . . . and the poor murdered body for the sight of which all this time was made, lay there quietly sleeping. . . . Our last President certainly was a very homely man, yet there is certainly something more than ordinary in every line of his careworn face."

Another lady, the petite editor of a juvenile monthly, stood beside the martyred man. Lincoln had called her "Grace Greenwood the patriot" in recognition of her intrepid work among disabled soldiers and sailors. Obtaining a private view she was able to remain "as long as I could bear to stay beside the casket, gazing down on what seemed to me to be a dread *simulacrum* of the face of our great friend; so unlike was it, yet so like." People were saying he looked so peaceful. "But to me it was an awful peace," she wrote, "as though the soul had sunk deep beyond deep in God's rest and had left in its garment of flesh the mold of its mortal cares, its piteous yearnings, its unspeakable weariness."

So reported Grace Greenwood whose family name was Sara Jane Clarke and who married Leander K. Lippincott. While Lincoln lived she had been fortunate enough to have had the opportunity to look upon that "now historic figure and had found it heroic in its grand ungainliness." Grateful that her hand had been grasped in greeting and farewell by the hand that had performed the grandest work of the century, she was grateful too she had gazed into his eyes "whose tired lids were pressed down at last by the long-prayed-for Angel of Peace."

Two days before the President's remains reached the city, three former officers of the Union Army conducted a meeting of brother officers and formed the Military Order of the Loyal Legion. The meeting was held in Independence Hall and was a direct reaction to the traitorous praesidicide; a banding together of fighters for freedom to carry on in civilian life the aims of their former Commander-in-Chief, associating themselves in commanderies.

Military and police finally succeeded in imposing a semblance of order by excluding everyone from street crossings around Independence Square, relieving pressure on the lines of people waiting to enter the windows. All day and all night Sunday until early Monday morning the public tiptoed through the candle-lighted chamber at a hundred a minute; in twenty hours the police counted a hundred and twenty thousand persons.

More thousands were waiting in line when time ran out. As in Baltimore and Harrisburg they would not be denied. Later the entrance windows were reopened and the anxious people poured through the coffinless room. The Commissioner of Public Property promised that if demand warranted he would keep the edifice open until Saturday and that he would also retain the hearse in the Square. He did both.

The plumed vehicle had been placed at Sixth and Chestnut Streets Sunday morning and remained there throughout the day and attracted much attention. A rumor flew about in the afternoon that a keg of powder had been found underneath it. The report was false but caused a near riot. What was found was a discarded canteen mug such as that used by the soldiery and it was found under the undertaker's carriage not under the Lincoln hearse. Coffee grounds stuck in the bottom of the mug were mistaken for powder grains. The subject of assassination was on everybody's mind.

At the dark hour of 1:17 A.M. the historic assembly room was cleared of spectators to permit embalmer and undertaker to perform their tasks. Shuffling feet by the thousands had covered everything with a layer of fine powder as though "spread from a dredger box." Deftly Dr. Brown restored the familiar features to normal appearance, using a fine camel's hair brush and bit of cosmetic. At half past two the valanced conveyance waiting at the Chestnut Street entrance was loaded with the special burden and the journey resumed.

Weird flickering of five hundred flames borne by members of the National Union Club and the deep sound of requiems rendered by Beck's Philadelphia Band supplied a fitting finale to Pennsylvania's obsequies. The ghostly parade moved to the Kensington passenger station of the Camden and Amboy Railroad, people popping out of houses half-dressed, heedless of wintry blasts, augmenting the marchers. The literate *Telegraph* related that "the train which bears from us the object of our deep love and pure veneration moved away just as the first rosy tremblings of dawn flushed the verge of the eastern sky."

The observant paper offered reflections on the solemn event, editorializing on "The Sermon Yesterday in Independence Hall." There were many kinds of sermons, began the editor. Those from the pulpit were full of heavenly morality, those from the stage taught common sense on the follies of the day, and then there were those silent sermons preached by good men's lives. Of the latter the most eloquent of all "was preached all day yesterday in

Independence Hall. . . . No one could turn away without having holier aspirations."

Public schools had closed for the week. They reopened Monday morning to hold appropriate exercises, their assembly rooms tastefully attired in mourning. The exercises generally consisted of an opening prayer, group singing, passage of a resolution of sympathy, an address by school principal or invited speaker, the program closing with a benediction. Schools then adjourned for the day.

Among invited speakers was the Honorable William D. Kelley, member of Congress from the Philadelphia district. Admirer and supporter of the late President, Judge Kelley had dedicated his two-volume work on international law to Lincoln who requested the judge to make the inscription moderate, "not representing me as a man of great learning or a very extraordinary one in any respect." The husky six-foot-three Kelley first met Lincoln as President-elect in the parlor of his Springfield home and had many contacts with him in the years that followed. To the assembly of Girl's High School and Normal School the judge said the war President lived in full consciousness of his mortality and of the judgments of a just God.

"No wrecked mariner storm-tossed upon a raft in mid-ocean ever felt more thoroughly his dependence, and that of those around him, upon God, than Abraham Lincoln felt the dependence of this nation and himself," declared the former common pleas court judge who would represent his district in Congress for thirty years. He called their attention to Lincoln's farewell remarks when he left Springfield and suggested that perhaps they had read some of the speeches he had made on the way to Washington. Or perhaps they had read his state papers, "You will find in them all expressions indicative of his deep sense of dependence. . . . With Abraham Lincoln consciousness of God was ever present within himself."

A few minutes after four o'clock the Lincoln Special departed
for New York to begin the fourth day of the homeward trip.
Steaming along at twenty miles per hour, slowing down to ten or
less when passing through villages and towns, the cortege reached
Bristol shortly after five o'clock. A rising sun clearly delineated
the six bright yellow passenger cars, yellow baggage car, deep
chocolate-colored hearse carriage, and crimson official car, all
heavily trimmed in mourning.

The first stop was Morrisville on the Pennsylvania side of the
Delaware River to take on the New Jersey governor and his retinue.
To him the Pennsylvania governor now turned over responsibility
for the train since he would detrain at the next stop, New Jersey's
capital city. Other Jersey officials had come aboard as did the
Newark committee and prominent citizens.

These groups occupied the front car. The next coaches were filled
with senators, congressmen, and state delegations from the national
capital. The ex-governor of Idaho Territory and the governor of
Washington Territory were among those who had joined at Philadelphia. The enlisted guard of honor and other enlisted personnel
occupied the car just ahead of the hearse carriage. The last car in
the train, the crimson-colored special that carried the Guard of
Honor, was designated the "official" car or "officers'" car since it
served as headquarters for the officers in charge of the trip. A
recent addition to this group was handsome General John A. Dix
who commanded the New York military district which embraced
northern New Jersey and who had been one of the patriots in
President Buchanan's Cabinet. He and staff would continue on the
train to western New York.

At half after five the Delaware River was crossed and a few
minutes later the train reached Trenton. Five thousand persons
were waiting for it at this early hour. Thirty minutes the Lincoln
Special halted in the Trenton station as the travelers break-

fasted. Guns boomed, bells pealed, bands sounded, the throngs standing silent and bareheaded. There were no exercises. As the journey was resumed Princeton was passed at quarter of seven, the trackside lined with draped national emblems borne by students and townspeople. At New Brunswick an engine of the New Jersey Railroad and Transportation Company took over. The time was 8:34 A.M. as Rahway went by. At Elizabeth, eleven minutes later, groups of young men were holding aloft black-bordered banners each bearing one word: Victory, Peace, Union, Lincoln.

The Newark Market Street station was entered at fifteen minutes after nine, every vantage point overflowing with attentive Jersey-men. Convalescents of the U.S. Military Hospital stood stiffly at the salute. Other patients not so fortunate saluted from wheel-chairs or leaning on crutches. The women of Newark, seeing their menfolk remove headgear to honor the deceased, wished to express their feelings and removed their bonnets. The train lingered a few minutes and continued its eastward passage, passing anxious crowds at the Center Street and East Newark depots and at grade-crossings along the way to Jersey City.

Ever since news of the national loss had been received Jersey City's great terminal building, where six railroads ended their New York runs, had been draped in poignant symbols. The balcony encircling the vast interior was festooned with sable and filled with citizens, principally ladies and their escorts, just as had been the case four years before when he had been greeted here on the way to Washington and had spoken words of gratitude for their support. On the west wall the station clock was stopped at 7:22, the moment of his demise. Around the clock a legend read, "A Nation's Heart Is Struck."

The crash of field artillery turned all eyes to the railroad yard. The pilot engine was wheeling into sight. Backing into the station came the sad train. The late President was received—

As an honored guest;
With banners and with music,
With soldier and with priest,
With a nation weeping and breaking our rest.

The dark-garlanded cars eased to a stop as singing societies from Hoboken intoned the ancient ode "Integer Vitae"—a man of upright life. An escort column formed on the platform that included corporate officials from nearby Jersey communities, committees from New York city and state, and military officers. The column paced around the terminal building to a salvo of fifty-six guns fired by the Hudson Brigade artillery. A choral group sang "May He Rest in Peace." Outside on Hudson Street the casket was carried in a special catafalque around Exchange Place, down to the ferry-house, and aboard the "Jersey City," largest of the ferryboat fleet.

The craft got under way at once. As it left the Garden State and steamed across the broad stream, artillery ceased thundering and bells ended their cacophony. Only the steady splash of paddle wheels in motion and shrill cries of escorting seagulls broke the stillness of a "ship sailing rapidly toward an indefinite shore." Harbor activity was halted. The moored and docked ships evidenced their sentiments by wrapped masts, draped rigging, festooned sides, and half-masted ensigns. Many dipped their national flags as the elegiac vessel sailed toward the other shore.

New York was standing still to honor the memory of The Man Who Kept the Faith.

8

FROM the deck of the keening caravel it was a singular sight to see thousands of human beings tightly massed in such unlikely places as roofs, piers, docks, portholes, decks, and rigging of ships, the whole without movement and all intent on the approaching catafalque that carried the assassinated Chief Executive. Without another thought than sorrow for the terrible deed no sound escaped them; the massive scene was as silent as a photograph.

Steadily the somberly draped vessel plied the still water, its fateful symbols fluttering in the bright sun. At ten minutes to eleven the uncanny silence was broken by a chorus of deep male voices chanting an ode from the first book of Horace. The spiritual tones escorted the ferryboat into its berth at the Desbrosses Street Slip. Guns and bells let go, announcing arrival in the Empire State of the illustrious dead.

Perhaps it was the unusual scene enacted before them; perhaps it was the touching requiem being sung; or perhaps it was the sudden guns that prompted every man to bare his head as if obeying an order. Ladies burst into tears. A few boys, entranced by the otherworldly proceedings, failed to remove their caps, and received an unexpected punch in the nose for their lack of manners.

Those in the streets striving for a better look created surges the military and the police had difficulty in restraining; not that the crowds were unruly or fractious but they were so closely integrated their smallest movement was magnified to Brobdingnagian proportions. On Desbrosses Street beginning at the ferry-house every possible viewing point overflowed with avid sightseers. Awnings, sheds, fire escapes, balconies, telegraph poles, lampposts, tops of wagons were burdened with witnesses. Clusters of faces protruded at all levels; window sashes had been removed to allow more to look out. From a Tenth Street horsecar that had been halted by the impenetrable mass agile passengers took advantage of the opportunity to clamber to the roof. All went well until there came a crash, and roof and rooftoppers went down in a heap.

One side of Desbrosses was hemmed by dark gray lines of the military holding the crowd in check; the other side was occupied by metropolitan police performing the same task. The task was complicated by constantly swelling numbers so tightly packed that large amounts of clothing were lost and some even lost shoes. Women and children who fainted were borne away with difficulty. There were just too many people for the space available.

A buxom woman pushed through police lines saying she had to

leave because she was being squeezed to death. "I can stand a good deal of squeezing," she said, mopping her flushed face, "but that was too much for me"; and she strode up the street. Many ladies were accoutered in full mourning dress. Others wore black accessories of hat, gloves, purse, shoes, scarf or sash. Nearly everyone exhibited some emblem of respect and grief; either a band of black crape around the upper left sleeve or hat, or a special mourning badge such as were being sold by street vendors.

The gray-clad soldiers were New York's Seventh, the national guard regiment that had saved the nation's capital in 1861 and then had sent more officers into the Union army than any comparable unit. Presenting arms as their former Commander-in-Chief was borne from ship to shore, they formed a hollow square around veteran sergeants guarding the hearse and, preceded by regimental band and covey of general officers, began the slow-paced march to City Hall. They were followed by the Washington contingent riding in carriages three abreast, and then on foot by New York Mayor C. Godfrey Gunther and city officials, delegations from Jersey communities, army and navy officers, the press, various other dignitaries, and a closing platoon of police.

From Desbrosses Street the route went north on Hudson to Canal, east on Canal to Broadway, south on Broadway to City Hall Park. At Hudson and Canal the neighborhood was a mixture of dwellings, tenements, stores, and warehouses, populated by a charming conglomeration of Irish, German, and African. All buildings, modest and pretentious, exhibited signs of respect and sorrow; and all businesses were closed including saloons.

As the object of all eyes reached Canal Street a woman leaning from a tenement window called out, "Well, is that all that's left of Ould Abe?" Her strident voice carried afar in the solemn hush. A bystander looked up and retorted, "It's more than you'll ever be!" "O, I've nothing against him," she responded without rancor.

"I never knew him or cared for him, but *he died like a saint*," she exclaimed and crossed herself in respect. A white-haired Negress held an apron to her face and between sobs wailed, "He died for me! He was crucified for me! God bless him!" A poorly dressed woman, tears streaming down her cheeks, cried, "Ach, my poor boy. Killed at Antietam for him! Now both are in heaven. God be with them!" Bystanders were visibly touched by these exclamations telling of broken hopes and enduring faith. The atmosphere of respect and affection moistened the eyes of many to whom tears were strange.

A brawny backwoodsman, who looked as though he could cut six cords of wood a day and still have plenty of time left over, pressed forward in the spectators as the cortege drew near. "Don't walk on my feet!" cried an irate individual. "Excuse me, sir," apologized the weather-beaten woodsman, "but I *must* see the coffin." "Why *must* you?" "Two of my brothers died in the same cause he did," replied the big fellow sadly. "Besides, he's one of my craft. I could never go back to the woods again until I see and bless his coffin." The attentive crowd parted as best they could to let him through.

Wheeling into Broadway, the column made one of those inexplicable halts that seem inevitable in public processions. An elderly lady holding the hand of a little girl stepped from the curb and addressed a bronzed veteran standing there. "Please, sir," she said as the little girl looked up at him in awe, "please shake the hand of my granddaughter. She wants to remember this day all of her life." The husky enlisted man folded the tiny hand in his broad palm for a moment and replied, "I too shall remember this day for the rest of my life. I've got on the all-firedest tightest pair of boots that ever cursed a soldier's feet."

Broadway, Manhattan's spinal column, presented a sepulchral appearance. From the Battery to Union Square there was not a building but had assumed a garb of grief. The street was one long cortege. Elaborate and ingenious and costly as the decorations were, it was the expressions of sentiment that accompanied the decorations that were so impressive. Though many might be characterized today as naïve and sophomoric, one may well ponder whether today's sophistication exhibits anything gained or something lost.

New York was then as now a city of imposing processions. Not too many years had gone by since the Erie Canal celebration, the Harrison funeral, the Taylor procession, the Atlantic cable celebration, the Japanese reception, the Prince of Wales parade, and the war demonstration of 1861. Just a few weeks previous had been the great peace celebrations. All had been memorable events, unsurpassed by any city on the continent. "But the great procession of yesterday was different from all others," the *New York Herald* avowed. It was different because it came from the heart.

This was no contrived display. No politician or military chieftain could order so many people to turn out in such tremendous numbers and decorate their homes and buildings, thereby telling the world of their affection. The quotations on store windows, the biblical verses on banners, the patriotic references, all demonstrated how deeply Manhattanites felt about the martyred man in their midst. It was spontaneous testimony.

Resuming the march the column reached the west gate of City Hall Park at fifteen minutes to noon and passed in front of the Astor House at Barclay and Vesey Streets where Lincoln and his family had stayed on the inaugural trip and which now displayed banners reading, "If misfortune comes, she brings along the bravest virtues"; "Heaven but tries our virtues by affliction and oft the cloud that wraps the present serves but to brighten all our future days"; and "Only the actions of the just, Smell sweet and blossom in the dust."

Turning around the south end of City Hall Park the column

moved by St. Paul's Church and then past Barnum's American
Museum at Broadway and Ann Streets. Over the main entrance
Barnum had placed an urn, on the urn the well-known motto,
"Dulce Est Pro Patria Mori," and over the urn the single word
"Lincoln."

The cortege marched up Park Row to Printing House Square
and its numerous newspaper plants. Across the square City Hall,
garbed in tokens of sorrow from dome to basement, tendered
municipal tribute. The cupola pillars were swathed in sable; the
roof cornices held festooned valances; the windows were hung with
strips of mourning; and the portico pillars were spiraled in swarthy
ribbons. Spread along the balcony balustrade, the community's
memorial message proclaimed in white letters on a black background: "The Nation Mourns."

From the balcony the scene was one never to be forgotten. A
noonday sun sent summertime heat on a concourse of bared heads
that completely pervaded the park and all adjacent streets. Distant
artillery thundered. Steeples wailed. The spire of nearby Trinity
Church chimed "Old Hundred." Near and far as one could see
scores of thousands of red-white-and-blue symbols of liberty hung
at the half position and many were rimmed in sable. Windows and
rooftops were overburdened with citizenry straining for the sight.
Trees in the park, budding spring green, were bent with the weight
of determined sightseers. Holding open the esplanade in front of
the Hall blue-uniformed police stretched from east to west gates.
On the esplanade stood the Guard of Honor, the Seventh Regiment.
At the iron railing marking the plaza's south limits the shining pates
and whited temples of War of 1812 veterans revealed the thin
ranks. On both sides of the broad steps to the Hall ranged a thousand members of the Saengerbund, Liederkranz, and Orion musical
societies attired in all-black with tall black hats and white gloves.
Overall arched an azure sky.

The flag-draped cargo was carried across the esplanade as male voices evoked the "Pilgerchor" from *Tannhäuser:*

> *Der Gnade Heil ist dem Büsser beschieden,*
> *Er geht einst ein in der Seligen Frieden!*
> *Vor Höll' und Tod ist ihm nicht bang',*
> *Drum preis' ich Gott mein Lebenlang.*
> *Halleluja Ewigkeit.*
> *Halleluja Ewigkeit.**

To the familiar chorus of the returned pilgrim the cynosure of all eyes was conveyed up the steps into the rotunda and up the winding stairs to the landing opposite the Governor's Room where an elaborate setting was ready to receive it. All present retired to permit embalmer and undertaker to perfect their arrangements.

Now the photographer, who had been granted the exclusive right, came forward and took pictures. The heavy drapery so dimmed the daylight that the slow wet-plate process then in use required half an hour for the photographing operation. Artists from illustrated media sketched the historic scene at the same time; members of the press were also admitted.

Next day the press, commenting on the appearance of the deceased, said the face was shrunken, mouth compressed, and face around the eyes discolored. "But upon the whole," the *Tribune* dissented, "the ravages of death have not been severe." The *News,* an afternoon paper, rewrote the *Tribune's* piece and restated the same theme. The *Herald* saw traces of the life-and-death struggle in the countenance and maintained primary signals of decay were apparent. The *World,* an antiadministration organ, declared the face was pale, shrunken, and haggard; and that "death had set its seal there unmistakeably and the embalmers had been powerless to conceal it."

The man lying in the coffin, averred William Cullen Bryant's

* From the Elder Pilgrims' Chorus, Act 3, of Richard Wagner's opera.

Evening Post, was "but a sad reflection of the real person" and not the "genial, kindly face of Abraham Lincoln but a ghastly shadow." Perhaps these were the words of Mr. Thanatopsis himself since the *Post's* publication office was just down the street at Nassau and Liberty; and perhaps it was he who wrote that "the thousands seeing our martyred President for the first time can gain but a poor idea of his homely, kind, intelligent countenance as it was illumined by the vitality that reflected the good and generous soul of the living man." Henry J. Raymond's *Times* concurred. "To those who had not seen Mr. Lincoln in life the view may be satisfactory," said the *Times,* "but to those familiar with his features it is far otherwise; the color is leaden, almost brown, the eyes deep sunk, cheek bones unusually prominent, cheeks hollow, lips tightly compressed, receding forehead—this is all that remains of *the man whom goodness made great.*" *

How did the sixteenth President look when alive?

By his own admission he was homely. One recalls numerous anecdotes in which he called himself ugly (he recognized his shortcomings) and one in particular reveals his identification with the great family of mankind. He told his secretaries of a dream he had the night before about being in a great assembly of people through which he was making his way. As he passed along someone spoke up, "He is a common-looking fellow." Lincoln in his dream turned to the speaker and replied, "Well, friend, the Lord prefers common looking people; that is why he made so many of them."

* Several New York papers announced the deceased would not be exposed to the public thereafter and the viewing in New York was for the last time. Though not specifically stated in the accounts there were rumors the face had turned black. It was said the "cosmetic" used in Philadelphia had been chalk and that it covered the entire face. Others disputed this and maintained that only around the eyes was the skin discolored (due to shock of the explosion) and that his natural hue was saffron. Those in position to know, embalmer and undertaker, were silent. General Townsend, in his daily report to the Secretary of War, wired: "I have examined the remains and they are in perfect preservation. We start for Albany at 4:15 P.M." The general can be accepted as a reliable witness.

Matched against predecessors and successors Abraham Lincoln was the homeliest of American Presidents. In his lifetime he sat for a known thirty-one different photographers on sixty-one occasions and for an estimated sixty-seven painters and sculptors. To date 119 separate photographic views have been located, making him one of the most depicted Presidents until the advent of motion pictures and television. His likeness has been reproduced untold millions of times on postage stamps, bonds, bills, and on the copper penny (which he would have appreciated the most). His portrait is seen worldwide; and he can be characterized as his country's greatest and finest export. In the United States more businesses, financial institutions, and noncommercial enterprises are named for him than any other American except Washington. Everybody knows Abraham Lincoln. He is Mr. America.

Why should there be any question about his appearance?

His law partner, Billy Herndon, an acute observer, had studied Lincoln closely for twenty-five years and described him, "His cheek-bones were high, sharp and prominent; his jaws were long and upcurved; his eyebrows cropped out like a huge rock on the brow of a hill; his long sallow face was wrinkled and dry and leathery," thus nearly duplicating the death-describing newspaper accounts. Herndon added a comment that has become a classic: "Melancholy dripped from him as he walked." If that is how Lincoln looked in life then how could he have looked otherwise in death?

That in death his appearance was not the same as in life goes without saying; no one's is. Friends saw that something was greatly missing. They had known at firsthand the man the rest of us see only in likenesses. The difference was his personality. Said Ohio newpaperman Donn Piatt, "His face brightened like a lit lantern when animated. His dull eyes would fairly sparkle in fun or express as kind a look as I ever saw when moved by some matter of human interest."

Ward Lamon declared that Lincoln was a "plain, homely, sad, weary-looking man to whom one's heart warmed involuntarily because he seemed at once miserable and kind" and wrote of the "hollow-set eyes with dark rings underneath the long, sallow, cadaverous face."

What especially struck General Sherman was that Lincoln's arms and legs seemed to hang almost lifeless and his face appeared careworn and haggard when at rest or listening; "but the moment he began to talk, his face lightened up; his tall form unfolded and he was the very impersonation of good-humor and fellowship." Marquis de Chambrun, who accompanied the Lincolns at City Point, was particulary moved by the President's good nature and noted that he laughed easily, either at what was being said or what he said himself. "But all of a sudden he would retire within himself," Chambrun related, "and then he would close his eyes and all his features would bespeak a king of sadness as indescribable as it was deep."

There lies the problem. Artist and sculptor and photographer have been unable to capture the vital force, the spiritual power, the tide of genius, animating the physical configuration. Those artists who tried turned out "prettified" portraits, doing no justice either to man or charisma. The difficulty continues. Can external image depict internal characteristics? Can *Honest* Abe be portrayed? His friendliness? His wisdom or compassion? Attempts to do so should never cease for art speaks in ways words never can.

A staunch friend and political associate, Isaac N. Arnold, put a knowing finger on the difficulty when he said Lincoln was "easily caricatured but difficult to represent as he was in marble or on canvas." Arnold, member of Congress from the Chicago district who penned two Lincoln biographies and knew him intimately, made the sagacious observation that "the tenderness of his heart was apparent in all the actions of his life."

Thus it will ever be that the Abraham Lincoln we see is the place where the spirit dwelt. But whatever manner in which he is depicted, caricatured, or prettified, The Homely Man from Illinois will ever appear to plain people as the charismatic image of freedom. They will see *into* his likeness what the outside of the building not made with hands does not reveal.

From the moment the doors were opened at one o'clock a continuous stream of New Yorkers flowed by the bier. Throughout the warm afternoon, cool evening, chilly night, bright dawn, and sunny morning hours until the flow was shut off at noon, the course of the stream was never broken. At midnight the number of persons straining to get in was greater than in the daytime.

This was because the extent of the multitude was visible in the daylight and prompted people to return at a late hour in order to avoid the crush. So many thought alike, the crush was worse during the night when it was difficult to judge the impossible task in the dimly lighted streets. Where thousands assembled in the daytime tens of thousands gathered in the night, determined to gratify their earnest desire.

Admittance to City Hall was through the basement door on the east side, thence along the passageway to the rotunda, up the west stairway, passing the bier at the top, down the east staircase and out the Hall's rear exit. Those with tickets of admission—thousands of tickets were distributed through political, social, and commercial channels—entered from Broadway, ascended to the Governor's Room, and viewed the remains from the other side of the catafalque.

Ticket holders lined up twenty abreast along Broadway and twenty deep down Murray Street. The general public inundated Printing House Square, halting all traffic and extending on Chatham Street to East Broadway, up the Bowery for three quarters of a mile, fed by the tributary streets, Centre, Baxter, Mulberry, Mott,

and Elizabeth. No man could count the turnout. Yet the patience of
the public in the face of the improbable task, noted an observer,
"was as of a host of apocryphal Jobs"; for the odds in reaching
the deceased were no better "than accession to the pearly gates."

Broadway never presented a more startling aspect. Above Fourteenth Street it was deserted while below Spring Street it was
impossible to negotiate, so massive was the throng of people. From
twilight to dawn City Hall Park and adjacent streets were more
crowded than on a midsummer afternoon.

The thoughts of millions were voiced by the copublisher of the
Post who told the Athaeneum Club that not in human history had
there been so universal, so spontaneous, so profound an expression
of respect and reverence. "In all churches without distinction of
sect, in all journals without distinction of party, in all workshops
and counting houses, from the stateliest mansion to the lowliest
hovel, you hear but one utterance and you see but one emblem
of sorrow."

Hour upon hour metropolitan New York paid their personal
respects—the high and low and the plain and fancy—only a moiety
of whom had supported the late chieftain with ballots. Yet there
were many who felt as if they were treading on holy ground. Some
ladies attempted to touch his brow or kiss the pale face. When
prevented from doing so they cried out in protest and would not
pass on. Compelled by strong gentle hands to give way they resisted
and wept. One lady managed to return three times and was barely
stopped each time by an alert guard from carrying out her purpose.
Many touched the bier in passing as if something of the goodness
within might flow out to them.

For here lay the man who had commanded an army greater than
that of any monarch who ever trod the earth, who had wielded
authority less restricted than that conferred by any constitutional
government, who had disbursed sums of money equal to the

exchequer of any nation in the world, who had brought to successful conclusion the greatest civil conflict ever witnessed in human
history, and who had moved through the storm and stress with a
forgiving heart.

Party factions had not marked him in spite of bitter invective
leveled against every move he made. The sharp weapons of partisanship from party members had recoiled harmlessly (though none-
theless painfully when they had sought to replace him) from the
shield of his sturdy character. Treason and turmoil had not sullied
his integrity nor poisoned his compassion. Here was the man who
had won new life for the nation and yielded his own in return.

Enormous power had been willingly granted him, explained
those in position to know, because it was felt he would not abuse
it. If proof were needed, it appeared the day before he was shot.
He had issued instructions to cease all drafting. Every man passing
the still form knew he had done this, knew he intended that all
Americans should return to peaceful pursuits.

And now he was among these people who had given him a dubi-
ous welcome when he had traveled through their metropolis on his
way to be invested the head of their government. These were the
citizens who had voted against him—*twice*. Who had entertained
grandiose notions of seceding from the Union so they could get rich
quick by trading with both sides at once, who had repeatedly
elected to office demagogues encouraging that separation, and who
had indulged in anti-American bigotry that had culminated in disgraceful draft riots.

These were also the same people who, when the emergency burst
upon them, mobilized their militia in response to his call and within
a few hours forwarded a regiment, quickly followed by others, to
guard the nation's capital against invasion. These were the same
people who organized a Union Defense Committee that raised and
equipped regiments and naval units, who handled millions of dollars

through their banks and counting houses for carrying on the war,
who contributed more than twenty million dollars in war taxes
and two millions in voluntary contributions for soldiers' and sailors'
welfare. These were the same people who sent ninety thousand
volunteers into Union service.

Now, in the presence of the Grim Reaper, partisanship was
stilled. Now he needed their help no more; now he was beyond their
cavil and waywardness. And now he was savior of the nation,
harbinger of peace, father of the people, martyr of the Republic.
This was his triumphal march—dead.

City Hall entrances were closed at ten minutes to noon, shutting
off thousands waiting along tangential streets. A private viewing
was accorded the governor, ex-governor, members of foreign con-
sulates, and prominent citizens. Just before one o'clock the coffin
was closed. The ever-present Washington sergeants, attired in
light-blue uniforms of the Veterans Reserve, stepped forward and
bore the narrow black reliquary down the curved stairway, out
to the esplanade, and placed it gently in the magnificent hearse.
Again the gray-clad Seventh Regiment acted as local escort. They,
and the serried ranks of Union-blue troops, wore a band of crape
around the upper left sleeve. The officer's Guard of Honor, in addition, wore a commemorative medallion on the dress coat. (Struck
off by the Philadelphia mint the medallion portrayed Washington
on one side, Lincoln on the other.) The metropolitan police, every
shift on duty, had pinned on their left breast a white satin badge
inscribed, "We Mourn Our Country's Loss, Abraham Lincoln,
April 15, 1865."

Scheduled to leave at 1:00 P.M., the movement did not begin until the hour hand was pointing toward two, the delay occasioned by bringing improperly placed military units to the head of the column. Amid spine-tingling roll of drums and sob of dirges, the plumed vehicle moved into Broadway. Up America's Main Street to Union Square the funebrial cavalcade proceeded, turned on Fourteenth to Fifth Avenue, up the Avenue to Thirty-fourth Street, over to Ninth Avenue and down to Thirtieth, thence to the Hudson River Railroad depot.

Not far from the railroad station the coupé of General Scott was descried drawn up alongside the sidewalk. "I immediately alighted and after greeting my old commander, conducted his vehicle to a place in the procession," related General Townsend in his report. "Though pale and feeble, the old General insisted on walking into the depot and paying his parting respects to the late President."

It was a day of oriental sunshine and balmy air and gentle breezes, one of the most perfect days of spring. Street vendors did a thriving business selling mourning badges and buttons bearing the likeness of the Emancipator. Of more than passing interest was that copies of the Farewell to Springfield and the Second Inaugural Address were selling on the streets as fast as the day's newspapers. The Second Inaugural also appeared in many show windows, shrouded in sable or garlanded in blossoms. The newspapers ran pages of description between rivers of black, having stationed reporters along the route to picture the overall scene. Every detail of the day was chronicled.

Marchers in the concluding portion of the procession had to go bareheaded most of the way in acknowledgment of the plaudits of the spectators. Lincoln's funeral applauded? In New York? Why was this?

The Joint Municipal Committee in Charge of Obsequies, as it was called, composed of appointees from the Board of Aldermen and the Board of Councilmen, declined to allow Negroes to march either as individuals or as societies. The untoward development caused the *Evening Post* to expostulate that the edict was mortifying and humiliating. "Our late President was venerated by the whole colored population with a peculiar degree of feeling," the *Post* exploded, "and [they] looked upon him as the liberator of their race. We have accepted the services of colored citizens in the war and it is disgraceful ingratitude to shut them out of our civic demonstration."

Caught between the prejudices of constituents and moral justice (to say nothing of American patriotism) the committee excused their stand on the ground that Negroes in the procession would cause trouble and recalled the lynching of innocent colored citizens in the draft riots. Police Commissioner Thomas Acton and Mayor George Opdyke retorted they would provide the necessary police protection to prevent trouble. The committee refused to yield.

This understandably aroused unpleasantness when the regulation was announced in Negro churches. At Shiloh Church a number of white citizens were present to discuss the matter and determine a course of action. Some Negroes wanted to march regardless but this was not encouraged although they had every reason to feel as they did. Wiser heads prevailed.

Final control of the obsequies was not in the hands of city authorities but with the War Department. On Monday morning General Dix received a telegram from the Assistant Secretary of War reading: "It is the desire of the Secretary of War that no discrimination respecting color should be exercised in admitting persons to the general procession tomorrow. In this city a black regiment formed part of the funeral escort."

Tuesday's newspapers announced that all colored people and their societies who wished to join in the procession could do so by forming on West Reade Street at twelve o'clock, their right resting on Broadway. Two hundred strong they marched as the last division in line, their ranks closed by a contingent of police. At the head they bore a banner that proclaimed: "Abraham Lincoln, Our Emancipator"; and the reverse side read: "To Millions of Bondsmen He Liberty Gave."

"The part of the line which contained the colored citizens was almost everywhere greeted with irrepressible cheering and waving of handkerchiefs," the *Post* reported. "The populace spontaneously recognized the meanness and cruelty of the prejudice that would have shut them away from the equalizing sorrows of the bier. . . . Fifth Avenue awarded them a continuous ovation."

And that was how the Lincoln cortege came to be applauded on the march through New York City. And thousands of immigrants standing along the way who had brought with them their Old World prejudices learned that America meant getting along as well as getting ahead, that American freedom required discipline to accept those different from themselves just as they in turn expected to be untrammeled in their differences, that although this bond of fraternity was not easily acquired—not even by the original settlers—it was a goal toward which all Americans raised their hopes for a happier future. America meant plurality merged into acceptability.*

At about four o'clock the hearse, in the forefront of the lengthy procession, reached the railroad depot. At quarter past the hour the station bell clanged a warning and the conductor called the final "All a-bo-oard!" The Lincoln Special of the Hudson River Railroad moved out of the old Dutch *staadt* of Nieuw Amsterdam bound for Albany. But Father Knickerbocker was not yet done with his heroic guest. Community leaders desired to tender formal expres-

---

* "He is an American," said de Crèvecoeur in *Letters from an American Farmer*, "who, leaving behind him all his ancient prejudices and manners, receives new ones from the new mode of life he has embraced, the new government he obeys, and the new rank he holds."

sion of respect and to say some things that were in the heart.
Accordingly arrangements had been made to conduct an outdoor
program in Union Square immediately following the departure.

In the square a speakers' stand suitably decorated in national
colors and festooned in mourning was filled with members of the
clergy, prominent citizens, and public officials. Ex-Governor John
A. King presided and introduced the speakers to a sea of faces
around him. First the Rev. Stephen H. Tyng delivered a prayer.
The multitude, as if a single person, stood with bowed heads. At
its end the augmented band rendered the now-familiar "Dead
March" from *Saul*.

George Bancroft stepped to the front of the platform. A former
Secretary of the Navy under President Polk and founder of the
Naval Academy at Annapolis, Bancroft was also an historian, widely
known for his ten-volume *History of the United States*. "Our grief
and horror at the crime, which has clothed the continent in mourning, find no adequate expression in words, and no relief in tears,"
he began and continued for an hour. He prophesied that echoes of
Lincoln's funeral knell would vibrate throughout the world and
that the friends of freedom of every tongue and in every land were
mourners. Concluding the scholarly address with a stirring peroration, the able speaker asserted that the blow aimed at Lincoln
was aimed "not at the native of Kentucky, not at the citizen of
Illinois, but at the man who, as President in the executive branch
of government, stood as the representative of every man in the
United States." The country may have needed imperishable grief
to touch its inmost feelings, he said. "The grave that receives the
remains of Lincoln receives the martyr to the Union . . . the manner
of his end will plead forever for the union of the states and the
freedom of man."

Bancroft was followed by the Rev. Joseph P. Thompson who read
the Second Inaugural Address, bringing home to every listener the

force of the dead man's compassion in the immortal lines, "With malice toward none; with charity for all; with firmness in the right as God gives us to see the right, let us strive on to finish the work we are in . . ." The hushed throng then heard the Reverend William H. Boole read the ninety-fourth psalm.

The Reverend E. P. Rogers invoked a prayer followed by appropriate musical selections by the band. Rabbi Samuel M. Isaacs read passages from the Talmud (Old Testament) and concluded with a short prayer. Next the Reverend Samuel Osgood read a hymn, and then an ode, both composed by William Cullen Bryant for the occasion. The aged prelate, Archbishop John McCloskey, scheduled to pronounce the benediction, sent word he was unable to attend because of fatigue incurred by participation in the long procession. The Reverend Roswell D. Hitchcock of Union Theological Seminary substituted and closed the exercises.

This was Bryant's ode:

> Oh, slow to smite and swift to spare,
>   Gentle and merciful and just,
> Who, in the fear of God, didst bear
>   The sword of power, a nation's trust.
>
> In sorrow by thy bier we stand
>   Amid the awe that hushes all,
> And speak the anguish of a land
>   That shook with horror at thy fall.
>
> Thy task is done; the bond are free.
>   We bear thee to an honored grave,
> Whose proudest monument shall be
>   The broken fetters of the slave.
>
> Pure was thy life; its bloody close
>   Hath placed thee with the sons of light,
> And the noble host of those
>   Who perished in the cause of Right.

PART IV

JOURNEY THROUGH THE PAST

9

THE impact on Manhattan of Lincoln's death was far greater than related in the foregoing chapter; for in addition to the emotional effects were the consequences upon financial and mercantile markets. Lincoln was shot on Good Friday and most brokers, commission houses, and exchanges had closed for the holy day. Early Saturday morning the news hit the business community with hurricane force, the press issuing special editions.

"A stroke from Heaven laying the whole city to instant ruin could not have startled us as did the word that broke from Ford's

145

Theater," the *Times* began its account. The *World* said, "Never before in history has there been an occasion so fraught with public consequence that was at the same time so like an overwhelming domestic affliction." The *Post* noted that the catastrophe "paralyzed business."

The Stock Exchange Board adjourned without consummating a single transaction and agreed to withhold all deliveries until Monday. No trading took place in the Gold Room, Public Stock Board, Petroleum Board, or at any mercantile exchange. Wall and William and Pine Streets shut down early. A few brokers who had the bad taste to try and "make a price" on gold in the midst of the demonstrations of grief and sympathy could find no takers. The Custom House closed at eleven. Banks stopped at noon. The Sub-Treasury had little to do since business activity was suspended. The mayor issued a proclamation recommending that commercial activities cease, but his advice was not needed since business shut down voluntarily out of respect for the honored dead.*

How financial and commodity markets would react to the catastrophe when they reopened Monday was a question fraught with not a little apprehension. Would the price of gold rise? Or would it fall? The usual reaction of free markets in securities and commodities—which are indexes of public confidence as well as of supply and demand—is to sell off on unfavorable news and to panic on really bad news. Confidence is the lifeblood of the business world as it is of the political. When confidence is shaken or lost the safest policy is to take a cash (specie) position. Thus the price of gold rises when many buyers enter the market for it, due to their urgent desire to hold it instead of securities or commodities. Uncertainty always being present in human operations, the government was especially apprehensive of what would happen when markets reopened.

* Saturday was a full work day.

Secretary of the Treasury Hugh McCulloch wrote the assistant secretary in charge of the New York Sub-Treasury calling attention to the prompt inauguration of a new President and emphasizing that the same administrative officers would continue in office, that the wheels of government had not stopped a single moment. "My belief is," McCulloch wrote, "that this great national calamity will teach the world a lesson which will be of the most beneficial character to our republican form of government . . . an event which would have shaken any other country to its center does not even stagger for a moment a government like ours."

The Treasury secretary was expressing a hope; he might even be "whistling in the dark" since there was no precedent for what the present catastrophe might bring forth. He was, however, declaring unwavering faith in the Republic. And his faith would be fully justified by subsequent events. Early Monday New York wired him: "Everything today quite as satisfactory as could be expected," and followed with a letter that represents one of the most heartwarming epistles ever sent by a federal official:

U. S. Treasury

New York, April 17, 1865.

Hon. Hugh McCulloch,
Secretary of the Treasury,
Washington, D. C.

My dear Sir:

Yours of yesterday received this morning.

I am happy to inform you that it has not been necessary to do anything whatever to protect the Government credit, the people having protected it without any action on our part.

The dire calamity which has befallen us has cemented the nation; and the Government is unquestionably stronger today than ever since its formation.

Very truly yours,

John A. Stewart,
Ass't Treasurer U.S. at New York

What occasioned this remarkable message was that when trading was resumed: (1) The price of gold, which had been falling on the good news of the capture of Mobile and surrender of Johnston, rose only to where it had been prior to those events. Trading in the Gold Room was dull, and that was also the case on other exchanges. "The revival of confidence following the news of Saturday had a potent influence in putting the gold premium back to where it was prior to Friday's sad event," noted the *Herald's* financial editor Tuesday morning. "Monarchical Europe may take a lesson from this; for in no other country could a similar event have occurred without violent depression of public funds." (2) Government securities advanced. (3) Public shares showed gains, especially railroads. (4) Bonds held firm.* (5) Commodity prices were steady.

Markets stayed open only Monday and Tuesday, did very little business, and shut down on Wednesday in consonance with the obsequies in the White House. The hearts and minds of the American people were not on gold or business.

For twelve consecutive days the community had, in company with the entire Union, abstained from secular occupation and voluntarily devoted themselves to expressions of respect and sorrow. Measured by the value of the vast industrial and com-

---

* Two decades later Secretary McCulloch disclosed that "a few bonds were offered at some points below the market rates of the day before. Through a trusted agent they were purchased . . . and the market resumed a healthy tone. In one or two other cases the market was steadied in the same way."

mercial and financial community's standing still, this was an amazing self-sacrifice. "It forms," avowed the *Times,* "not only the grandest oblation ever made on the altar of departed worth, but raises the character of the whole nation far above the imputations of sordidness and concern with Mammon so falsely ascribed by outside commentators." Even more to the point, it was a direct refutation of the hoary theory that republics are ungrateful to their public servants.

Further encouraging demonstrations of public confidence appeared when the financial markets reopened Thursday. Gold continued to slide back to preassassination levels, and subscriptions to the popular government 7-30 bonds increased to a higher rate than for many weeks previously. From the day Lincoln was shot to the day his body left New York, the American people evidenced their faith and loyalty by subscribing thusly:

April 14—$3,642,300	April 20—$3,062,300
15— 3,710,250	21— 2,743,500
16— Sunday	22— 4,110,900
17— 2,651,700	23— Sunday
18— 2,701,300	24— 4,271,650
19— Obsequies	25— 4,023,550

"We are the greatest people on the globe," unblushingly admitted Horace Greeley, referring to the above record. "The assassination of the head of an European government would have convulsed their society," he explained, "collapsed their credit, struck down capital seeking investment, and precipitated a drastic fall in values. But look what happened when this nation, now in the fifth year of a civil conflict unparalleled for costliness and bloodiness, had its beloved head brutally murdered. The people have rallied as one man to support the administration; increasing their faith in the power to govern; and intensifying their purpose to purify the

Republic and establish it forever, cost what it may. We are seeing the footprints of history in the incidents that mark the progress of this crisis."

Amazing also was Police Superintendent John A. Kennedy's report. This was the same Kennedy who, four years before, when introduced at the Astor House, had responded to Lincoln's compliment on the fine police arrangements by saying he had but done his duty. To which Lincoln had replied, "Well, a man ought to be thanked when he does his duty right well." This was the Kennedy who, after his detectives had uncovered the Baltimore assassination plot, was so apprehensive for the President-elect's safety in crossing Maryland that he went personally to accompany him but missed the meeting. This was the same Kennedy who almost forfeited his life when draft rioters beat him to a bloody pulp from which he never fully recovered. Now the intrepid head of "New York's finest" had remarkable news. His report stated that from the day the President died there had been fewer arrests for drunkenness, disorderly conduct, and all other crimes than at any time since New York contained more than a hundred thousand people. Moreover, during the processional when more persons than inhabited the city choked the streets and a hundred thousand were marching, not a single accident occurred and not a single arrest was made. So deeply had the passing of the man they had voted against touched the inner reaches of their hearts.

Literary, social, and educational groups scheduled meetings Thursday evening to commemorate the historic event. Among the speakers at the New York Historical Society proceedings was the Reverend Roswell Hitchcock, distinguished professor of church history, who delivered an erudite address, assigning the martyred Chief Executive a place next to The First President and declaring "the latter gave us Union and Liberty; while Lincoln has conserved the Union and made Liberty universal."

In describing various aspects of the event the press included personal recollections. Henry Raymond related what he said was "a characteristic act of Mr. Lincoln." When the Union Army occupied Charleston, wrote Raymond, the President asked the commanding general to inquire for the family of the late James L. Petigru. Petigru, an eminent lawyer, had been considered by the President for justice of the U.S. Supreme Court. In devotion to the Union Petigru had stood firm and immovable, almost alone in his city when the Palmetto State had announced itself a republic. "I tell you it *is* a fire!" the white-haired jurist had cried when Charleston's bells rang out the secession news. "They have this day set a blazing torch to the temple of constitutional liberty!" And when he went out to Fort Sumter to say good-bye to the Union before the Stars and Stripes was hauled down "the tears rolled down his cheeks as he deplored the madness and folly of the time." Like other Union men trapped in the South he was reduced to poverty by his partiotic course. Lincoln asked the Union general to provide the Petigru family with whatever they might need and enclosed fifty dollars cash in the letter as a personal contribution toward their wants. "We are glad to learn," said the *Times,* in reporting an act which has also become an American characteristic—helping people in distress —"that help was being sent to Charleston from Boston and New York to relieve the suffering of the city."

Bryant's *Post* published several letters from Francis B. Carpenter, painter of the renowned canvas, "Lincoln Reading the Emancipation Proclamation to His Cabinet," that now hangs in the Capitol.* Carpenter had lived six months in the White house drawing the figures from life and became well acquainted with the Presi-

* Located in Senate wing, west stairway.

dent. He wrote about Lincoln's favorite poem, "O, Why Should the
Spirit of Mortal Be Proud?" which he had heard Lincoln recite
on several occasions. The President said he did not know the
name of the author and declared he would have liked to have been
he.* Carpenter followed with another letter saying that a favorite
was O. W. Holmes's "The Last Leaf" and that Lincoln was particularly fond of the stanza: "The mossy marbles rest/ On the lips that
he has pressed/ In their bloom./ And the names he loved to hear/
Have been carved for many a year/ On the tomb." "For pure
pathos, in my judgment," Lincoln had asserted, "there is nothing
finer than those six lines in the English language."

"While I am writing," continued Carpenter in his April twenty-
second letter from 90 West Forty-fifth Street, "I am reminded of a
conversation that took place between us about that time which
may be of interest to your readers." Carpenter was referring to
dispatches describing an elaborate conspiracy matured in Richmond to assassinate or abduct the President. The account related
that five hundred to a thousand picked men were to be sworn in
to accomplish the daring deed. Carpenter asked Lincoln several
days after the account appeared whether he had seen it, and the
President replied he had not nor had he even heard of it. The artist
went into detail, at the conclusion of which Lincoln smiled and
remarked, "Even if true, I do not see what the rebels would gain
by killing me or getting possession of me."

He said he was but a single individual and that it would not
help their cause or make the least difference in the progress of
the war. "Everything would go on just the same," Lincoln maintained and told Carpenter he began receiving that kind of letter

* The *Post* noted the author was William Knox, a Scotch poet of considerable talent. The poem could be found in *Scotia's Bards*, a volume of selections
from Scottish poets published in 1853.

soon after he was nominated at Chicago. The first one or two, he admitted, had made him a "little uncomfortable" but after that he came to look for a regular installment of them in each week's mail. It was no uncommon thing to receive them now; but, said Lincoln, they had ceased to bother him. Eighty such letters were found tucked in a pigeonhole of his desk.

"Greater love hath no man that this," quoted *Harper's Weekly* in the first issue to catch the news, "that a man lay down his life for his friends." The citizenry of Manhattan agreed, and for two more days those unable to get in to see him lying in state moved through City Hall with its mourning symbols intact. They wanted a part of him and snatched mementoes to remember him by, cut silver stars from the enveloping curtains, and severed trimming from the dais, until police arrived to protect the symbolic materials. Such souvenirs may be seen today preserved in museums and historical exhibits. Families inheriting the tokens regard them as cherished heirlooms and say proudly, "This silver lace is from the bier on which President Lincoln lay in state in City Hall."

Though prior cities had continued the lying-in-state decorations for a few days or as long as a month—Baltimore at the Mercantile Exchange, Harrisburg at the state capitol, Philadelphia at Independence Hall—and succeeding cities would continue the practice, that had not been possible in the nation's capital. The East Room of the White House and the rotunda of the Capitol had had to be cleared promptly. But the resourceful commissioner of public buildings found a way to accommodate all who wished to honor the departed Emancipator. He placed the bier upon which the casket had reposed underneath the rotunda in a vault. Here it has remained ever since and may be seen today, a hundred years later.*

*Open to the public free. The vault is the *second* level below rotunda floor. Is not a part of the regular sightseeing tour. Ask. The caskets of Presidents John F. Kennedy and Herbert Hoover also rested on this bier as have those of General Douglas MacArthur and the Unknown Soldiers.

The crimson-colored officers' coach and the sepia-toned hearse conveyance that would make the total trip were lightered across the river from Jersey and placed on the Hudson River Railroad tracks at the main passenger station on Chambers Street. Here the nine-car "consist" was made up, decorated, and hauled uptown to the Thirtieth Street depot. Thoughtfully the management assigned the same two coal-burning locomotives that had drawn the inaugural special. The *Union* would pull the cars (states) while, symbolically, the *Constitution* would act as pilot.

Instructions and Timetable for Lincoln Special

Tuesday, April 25, 1865

Lve. New York		Lve. Hyde Park ...... 7:56 P.M.
29th St. ....4:00 P.M.		Staatsburg 8:08
Manhattanville 4:20		Rhinebeck 8:24
Yonkers 4:45		Barrytown 8:40
Dobbs Ferry 5:00		Tivoli 8:52
Irvington 5:07		Germantown 9:10
Tarrytown 5:15		Catskill 9:27
Sing Sing 5:30		Hudson 9:38
Arr. Peekskill 5:57		Hudson 9:41
Lve. Peekskill 6:00		Stockport 9:52
Garrisons 6:26		Coxsackie 10:00
Cold Spring 6:33		Stuyvesant 10:07
Fishkill 6:50		Schodack 10:26
North Hamburg ...7:06		Castleton 10:37
Arr. Poughkeepsie 7:25		Arr. East Albany ....10:55 P.M.
Lve. Poughkeepsie .....7:40 P.M.		

Train has right of track over all other trains bound in either direction; and trains must reach stations at which they are to meet, or let special pass, at least 10 minutes before special is due.

A "pilot" engine will leave New York 10 minutes in advance of special, running 10 minutes ahead of published schedule to East Albany. Pilot engine has same rights as special, and at stations where trains meet or pass it, they must wait for special. The special will run at a slow rate of speed through all towns and villages.

Train No. 10 will, on this day, leave Thirtieth St. at 4:15 P.M. All station masters, trackmen, drawbridge tenders, switchmen, and flagmen, will be governed by the general rules of the company.

Considering the record crowds and the pageantry of the nation's largest cities it would seem that the peak of public response had been reached and that little new or impressive could be expected. Yet noteworthy features were manifested on the 142-mile run to Albany. This being the fifth day after leaving Washington the additional time permitted greater attendance of uniformed organizations and more elaborate pageantry. Communities along the route had perused the dispatches describing cortege and ceremonies from city to city, and there arose the human motive to improve what had gone before. Competition is a normal American trait. Pride is another. The prideful efforts of each community along the way made their efforts more meaningful to themselves; and, alarmists to the contrary notwithstanding, that was eminently desirable.

Hastings-on-the-Hudson, residence of naval hero Admiral David G. Farragut ("Damn the torpedoes! Full speed ahead!") constructed an elaborate arch by popular subscription. The four-columned triple archways were adorned with mottoes and inscriptions; a principal one saying, "We will cherish the memory of Abraham Lincoln by supporting the principles of free government for which he suffered martyrdom." Tarrytown painted the side of a building to represent the American flag and surmounted it with the admonition, "Bear him gently to rest." Young ladies dressed in white stood on a platform in front of the flag with bowed heads clasping one another's hands. Ossining put a twenty-five-foot arch over the tracks; the columns striped black and white, the velvet verges entwined with evergreen, a kneeling Liberty at the keystone. Cold Spring, where the famed Parrott artillery was forged, built a graceful arch alongside the track. Under it a young lady represent-

ing Liberty-in-Mourning was attended by a kneeling soldier and
sailor; around the tableau stood members of the local Union
League under whose auspices the memorial was constructed.

The west bank of the river, from Palisades to the state capital,
was margined with people on the hills, along the woods, in the
havens and harbors, and at villages and towns. Structures on both
sides of the Hudson were garnished with emblems and mottoes;
flags on riverboats were at half-mast; minute guns crashed as the
somber special steamed onward. Assemblies of militia, cadets of
military schools, firemen, policemen, and other uniformed units
saluted at Yonkers, Dobbs Ferry, Irvington, and Peekskill. Opposite
West Point, at Garrison's Landing, a thousand gray-clad cadets of
the Military Academy and a company of blue-uniformed regulars
presented arms in impeccable formation, the officers uncovering, the
band evoking a requiem, while high upon the parade ground
Academy guns puffed blue smoke, the reports booming and
echoing along the river valley.

The sun was sinking as the train pulled into Poughkeepsie, cast-
ing a mellow glow over the historic event. The steep hillsides were
carpeted with twenty thousand persons, perhaps more. Guns roared,
bands sounded, the throng stood still for fifteen minutes as the
travelers detrained and partook of a hasty buffet supper. Ten
minutes after eight, when movement was resumed, stars twinkled
and night lights dappled the smooth-running river.

More illuminations appeared. The way of the martyr was being
lighted. This was another unique characteristic of the Albany run.
"As we sped over the rails at night," related Chauncey Depew, a
member of the New York State committee, "the scene was the most
pathetic ever witnessed. At every crossroads the glare of in-
numerable torches illumined the whole population from age to
infancy, kneeling on the ground, their clergymen leading them in
prayers and hymns."

Rhinebeck was reached at about half past eight and displayed the first marching torches. Barrytown, Germantown, and Catskill posted torches around their depots and the houses blazed with candles and lamps. Torch-bearing townspeople at Hudson, a three-minute halt, moved alongside the train to the beat of a dirge. Coxsackie, Stuyvesant, Castleton, all revealed themselves in an abundance of glowing fires. The end of the run, East Albany, reached on schedule at eleven o'clock, was a mass of flame; night was turned into day.

Removed to a glassed sarcophagus, the hero's receptacle was ferried over the river to be greeted by military honor guards and the Albany fire department equipped with flaming torches. The scene was worthy of a Rembrandt. "And so, once more, Mr. Lincoln goes up State Street. The last time I saw him he was moving up the same street; and in only four years," lamented the observer, "I have turned from the sight of the living to the dead." The remains were borne into the assembly chamber of the capitol where, on the occasion of his prior visit, he had voiced heartfelt thanks to a joint session of legislators. Now he was placed in front of the speaker's stand on a simple bier of silver-trimmed black velvet and an American flag was draped around the casket by the daughter of Thurlow Weed, the Empire State's party leader.

10

LIKE Lincoln, Thurlow Weed had come up the hard way. Both were tall men, awkward in appearance, soft-spoken, easygoing. Both had the ability to get along with people. Weed's schooling, like Lincoln's, had been "by littles." At the age of eight he was pumping the bellows in a blacksmith shop for six cents an hour. He served apprenticeships in print shops at Catskill, Manlius, and Norwich; and at Rochester edited the weekly *Telegraph*. Moving to Albany in his one term as assemblyman, he founded the *Evening Journal* which he edited for the next twenty-five years and sold for a handsome sum.

Though he continued in the newspaper field to the end of his days, Weed's talent and passion was politics. He made Seward governor in 1838, William Henry Harrison President in 1840, General Zachary Taylor President in 1848, Seward senator in 1849, and tried to make him President in 1860. His success as leader of the New York State Republican Party derived from a pleasing personality, shrewd political judgment, and a way with men. He was also a man of his word. His protégé, Seward, said he had no idea dictators could be such amiable creatures. Weed died a millionaire at the ripe age of eighty-five.

A contemporary politician, whose name and fame are so interwoven with the Albany Republican that confusion continues to this day, was William Marcy Tweed, Manhattan Democrat, and Grand Sachem of Tammany Hall. Like Weed, Tweed was tall, softspoken, friendly. He got his start as foreman of a volunteer fire-engine company and was elected alderman. So venal did the Board of Aldermen become they were dubbed "The Forty Thieves."

The Tweed "ring" decreed that invoices must be half fraudulent, the fraudulent half going into the ring's pockets. He raised the "take" to 85 percent. The New York County Courthouse cost taxpayers twelve million dollars, at least two thirds of it fraudulent. Justice finally overtook the boodlers and the grafting ex-volunteer fireman was clapped into jail. Slipping out of jail disguised as a woman, Tweed skipped to Spain where he was identified by a Nast cartoon. (Thomas Nast waged an unremitting campaign against Tammany miscreants in the course of which he originated the Tammany Tiger, based on Tweed's fire-engine emblem.) Brought back, tried, sentenced, and incarcerated in the old Ludlow Street jail, Tweed died a broken man in his fifty-fifth year. From New York City alone it is estimated he and his ring filched a hundred million dollars.

Thurlow Weed, in contrast, had a code of honor; he was personally incorruptible. He never urged appointment of a relative to public office, never supported a bill he believed injurious to public welfare, never opposed one that benefited the people. He rejected proffered bribes. (Greeley said he witnessed such an attempt.) Yet Weed did resort to political bribery, tendered legislative favors to achieve party ends, distributed patronage to extend party voting power, and otherwise operated as party "boss."

Weed, Tweed, and Lincoln were three contemporary personalities who rose from humble beginnings to fame in the classical American manner. They typified the political best, worst, and inbetween. One was the greatest statesman the United States ever produced, the other a scoundrel, and the third moved in a twilight zone. The contrast is the more striking because Lincoln had as many temptations to deviate from rectitude as any politician. The lesson to be learned from his career is that success in politics can be achieved through virtue the same as in every other human endeavor. To state the proposition conversely, wrongdoing is not a necessary concomitant of political practice.

In politics more is heard about the frailties and failures of human nature, but every form of human endeavor has its ethics. Should a medical doctor treat a patient for a disease he knows is incurable but the patient does not? Should he so inform the patient or should he remain mute and send his son to college on the proceeds? Should an attorney representing a guilty client plead not guilty and try to free him by every trick and subterfuge? Or should he merely see that the client is accorded full legal rights? Should a businessman make and sell a product he knows is inferior and fob it off on the public? Or should he acknowledge the inferiority? Examples can be continued *ad infinitum*.

To be sure, it is easier to be crooked in politics than in any other legitimate field of human activity; its techniques invite duplicity and chicanery. There is continual ambivalence between the good of the people and the private advantage of the politician. Besides, the differences between the moral code of the individual and that of the aggregate present fine distinctions little appreciated by the masses. So the temptation is strong to take the most profitable way.

Tweed did. But he committed acts against which the body politic had erected protective barriers; his acts were criminal. What about Weed? By benefiting the party and not himself did that make his transactions moral and ethical? A determination rests upon the point of view or the reference taken. Politically the acts in question would be adjudged *amoral;* that is, not subject to ordinary judgments and distinctions. He operated in a hazy area where moral confusion arises. Nor can the issues be pinpointed. Except to note that Weed did not transgress the law. The public rightfully viewed him with suspicion as they rightfully do every political "boss." Do ends justify means? That is the dilemma projected into public politics. If they do, then how far? If not, why not?

The seesaw extends to many political maneuvers. Money and how to get it for political purposes is a prime source of ambivalence. Voters are not in the habit of paying for a candidate's expenses; so support is sought from those who need legislative and governmental favors, notably the underworld. Alliance of crime and politics corrupts government and suborns justice; yet the alliance is melded by unrelenting needs on both sides. Hypocrisy, deceit, nepotism, chicanery, brutality are so indelibly identified with the exercise of political power as to bring the governing process into disrepute regardless of whether its form be democratic, autocratic, despotic, or parliamentary.

Historians and biographers overwhelmingly treat Lincoln's political life with diffidence, dismissing it arbitrarily with some hasty label like pragmatist (a favorite), practical politician, realist, and then forego further elaboration. There are good reasons for the avoidance. Politics cannot be embodied in a snappy quote or clever phrase; it is too complex a subject. The generality of persons do not comprehend its elementary principles and probably never will. Nevertheless they demand their hero be pure as driven snow and prefer not to consider his clay feet. The essential thing is that the hero slay the dragon.

This poses a problem with Lincoln. He did not slay the political ogre. Quite the contrary. He was Mr. Politician himself, adept at the very thing the people distrusted, and rose up the heights for no other reason. Some like to paint the lily by arguing Lincoln rose beyond politics into the realm of statesmanship. He surely did, but statecraft is politics by whatever name.

"Politician" has come to mean a person skilled in human relations—always with a sinister connotation—and refers to group manipulations but not necessarily so. *Politikos* derived from the Greek *polis,* the city, in connection with their wonderful form of self-government, then a new thing in the world. Self-government required the citizenry to discuss and vote on all matters affecting relations with one another as a society, and also with the other groups inhabiting the globe. To properly exercise this right of suffrage the Greek citizen had to understand politics for his own well-being. That was the key fact of Hellenic democracy as it is of American republicanism.

The American system of government was also a new thing when it came into the world, and it continues to be unique. That "all men are created equal" is a goal that has run through the bloody annals of mankind like a golden thread; but common responsibility for common direction of the community did not find full political expression until the New World produced it in these United States. The American citizen, to service his personal interest, like his Hellenic counterpart, should understand politics. That noted philosopher of Harvard and Spain, George Santayana, made an ob-

servation to the effect that an American has a difficult task to perform in having to be saint, scholar, entrepreneur, soldier, and
politician, all in one person.

Public politics in its broadest sense deals with social behavior.
When thus comprehended, to derogate politics and disparage its
practitioners amounts to flagellating one's self, family, and neighbors. Among the various social aspects of man's behavior—political,
economic, religious—the differences are defined by points of view,
by the references taken, or by arbitrary limits of analysis and
interpretation. No sharp boundary lines delineate the components
of social behavior as on a surveyor's plat; human conduct is inter-
related and interdependent, for man is a whole being.

What is important is to know the *purpose* of a political act. Does
it or does it not contribute to the commonweal? Here again are
many answers, each relative. "Commonweal" embraces the complete spectrum of man as a society. Involved in the problem also is
whether politics deals only with skills and techniques or includes
values and ideals. The primary task of political action should be to
insure the existence in the state of the good, the true, and the
beautiful. Unless it strives for these goals, it fails its first duty
toward the citizenry. Philosopher Santayana held that the criterion
in politics is moral. He maintained the *modus vivendi* was not man
as he appears to the senses, but rather "an inner proclivity to action
and passion that animates him."

Lincoln's "political education" commenced when he was twenty-
three. In his very first electioneering handbill he explained his
motivation, displaying at this early age remarkable human insight.
"Every man is said to have his peculiar ambition," he said in the
final paragraph. "Whether it be true or not, I can say for one
that I have no other so great as that of being truly esteemed of my
fellowmen by rendering myself worthy of their esteem."

In this, his first try, he was defeated; the only time in his public
career he lost a *popular* election. The next year he was appointed
postmaster at the tiny village he called home, New Salem.* Then
he ran again for the legislature and won; being second by fourteen
votes to top man. For the succeeding quarter of a century Lincoln
engaged in political activities, which have been frequently denoted
as his years of "greasy politics"—a term that implies a measure of
underhanded dealing or that this part of his career was sinister and
need not be told. Nothing could be more distant from the fact.
There are good and bad sides to politics.

Lincoln knew both sides. Speaking on the State Bank Bill he
declared, "It is the politician who is first to sound the alarm. . . .
It is he, who, by these unholy means is endeavoring to blow up a
storm that he can ride upon and direct." Then he let loose both
barrels. "Mr. Chairman," he said, "this movement is exclusively
the work of politicians; a set of men who have interests aside from
the interests of the people; and who, to say the most of them, are,
taken as a whole, at least one long step removed from honest men.
I say this with the greater freedom because, being a politician
myself, none can regard it as personal." **

Lincoln's description "to blow up a storm that he may ride upon
and direct" is another way of saying to so agitate an issue that it
will result in political benefit to the agitator. From the four corners
of a room (issue) the politico sweeps dust and when the turmoil
has served his purpose (dust is everywhere) sweeps it back again,

* Now reconstructed and free to the public.
** Thus spoke Lincoln before the Tenth General Assembly of Illinois,
January 11, 1837. Among the members were a future presidential candidate
(Douglas); six future U.S. senators (Ewing, Edwards, Shields, Breese, Brown-
ing, and Douglas); eight congressmen; three state supreme court judges; a
Cabinet member (Browning in President Johnson's); seven state officers; and
two generals of the Union Army. These were the "greasy" politicians to whom
Lincoln addressed his words of political reality.

making himself a great personage by the vigorous sweeping and a hero if he can manage it. Substance of the issue matters little.

A similar maneuver is setting up a bogey to be knocked down, called the strawman tactic. This is the contrived crisis, the artificial issue, the sort of maneuver Lincoln likely had in mind when, asked what he deemed to be the most valuable ability for a winning politician, replied, "To be able to raise a cause which shall produce an effect and then fight the effect."

The tactic is not confined to public politics; it occurs in every area of human endeavor, wherever men gather in groups. Man is a political animal and must be dealt with as he is, not as one thinks he ought to be. He is encountered in the arena of public politics both as an individual and as a group.

The differences between individuals acting alone and as a group are as noon and night. Cognizant of the distinctions, skilled politicians act accordingly. That is their business. Because the business is so little understood by the body politic, it is viewed as a "black art" and stigmatized as the Machiavellism of the governing process.

Lincoln told a temperance society that human nature is God's decree and "can never be reversed." He noted the Bible teaches us that all men are sinners and said he reckoned we would have found that out by just looking around us. Despite the negative components present in mankind he believed that "the human instrumentalities, working just as they do, are of the best adaptation to effect His purpose." Well aware of the realities of human existence from a quarter century of practicing law at the circuit level, he encountered men of all characters; and into his presidential office came frauds, hypocrites, liars, bootlickers, and double crossers looking for favors. At times he grew so discouraged that he gave vent to his otherwise well-controlled feelings, denouncing "every foul bird and every dirty reptile gorging on the filth of war's corruption and hatred." Lincoln saw man as he is, but looked for the best and acted in the interest of the greatest number. "Where there is no vision, the people perish." *

On moral and ethical questions Lincoln was preeminent. "He had a wider and deeper comprehension of his environment and of political conditions especially than men who were more learned," observed Herndon in the biography that has become American folk literature. "Although he cared little for simple facts, rules and methods," Herndon pointed out, "it was on the underlying principle of truth and justice that Lincoln's will was firm as steel and tenacious as iron. . . . He scorned to support or adopt an untrue position as his conscience prevented him from doing an unjust thing."

Lincoln's apparent paradox of appearing pliable on some things, Herndon explained, was due to his flexibility on non-essential matters; but on moral and ethical principles he was "immovable as a rock. . . . When justice, right, liberty, the government, the Constitution, the Union, humanity were involved," said Billy, "then you may all stand aside. No man can move him. No set of men can. There is no failing here. This is Lincoln."

That beneficent ends can accrue from political manipulation pains the high-minded. However unworthy may be the hands, politics does deal with ideals as with techniques. The history of the United States illuminates this basic principle; the principle voiced in the age of Pericles and Plato that the political process in democratic governance can be one of sublimation. That is the way Lincoln operated. He followed in the footsteps of the Founding Fathers, carrying forward their hoped-for ideals of American freedom.

* "Honest statesmanship is the employment of individual meanness for public good," Lincoln once remarked to his secretaries, revealing his realistic understanding of human nature.

Had he not been nurtured in the American tradition, Lincoln likely would not have so ably resolved the political upheaval that marked his administration. The nation exists today and the Constitution stands inviolate because the sixteenth President was schooled in the grassroots of American politics that embraced all manner of political activity. Hours and days he devoted to party work, caucuses, and conventions; writing party circulars, making speeches, devising strategy, formulating policies (he worked his way up to party leader). And he put in long hours and many days as a legislator, attending legislative sessions, doing committee work, passing on appeals and appointments, evaluating bills, sponsoring legislation, answering correspondence, and speaking in the legislative chamber. He developed into a skillful politician.

Denigrating Lincoln for political activities because the art of political practice is not comprehended by the denigrator or because it is viewed as being on a low moral level, does not detract from his character. This note of caution is sounded since more has been published on Lincoln than on any American public figure and his daily life has been chronicled from birth to death.* Yet his political career has received less intelligent treatment than any phase of his life; even notable biographers parrot the cliché of "greasy" politics.

His early career is seldom narrated, for example, without referring to the logrolling tactics used in getting the capital of Illinois moved from Vandalia, located in the southern part of the state, to Springfield, a central location. The implication is that Lincoln's tactic was reprehensible. The practice of you-vote-for-my-bill-and-I-will-vote-for-yours, *quid pro quo,* is as old as politics and has been standard procedure around the globe long before "Absalom stole the hearts of the men of Israel." Logrolling can be used

* *Lincoln Day by Day.* Lincoln Sesquicentennial Commission. Washington, D.C. 3 vols.

dishonorably of course; just as Absalom so used it in attempting to unseat his father, King David. Lincoln utilized the tactic honorably in Vandalia, in Springfield, and in Washington.

Consider the Thirteenth Amendment. Today one would assume that such a great moral resolution as abolishing human slavery would have no difficulty in being placed on the statute book and especially in 1864. The Senate readily passed the amendment but it failed to get the needed two-thirds majority of the House. Lincoln suggested in his annual message that the House reconsider and vote again before the newly elected Thirty-eighth Congress took office. The fall election had indicated the incoming Congress would vote in its favor, he told them, and it would stand forever to the credit of the Thirty-seventh Congress if its members would honor themselves by abolishing slavery in the United States.

Even this direct patriotic and moral appeal did not insure the outcome in the House. Foresightedly Lincoln had prepared for ratification by the states. That would be close, too, and it had taken the power of his office exerted through Assistant Secretary of War Charles A. Dana to bring Nevada into the Union in order to get the needed three quarters. He told Dana, "It is easier to admit Nevada than to raise another million soldiers"; and pointed out that the amendment abolishing slavery was the equivalent of new armies in its effect on the people of the nation and on the outcome of the conflict. Three congressmen in particular needed attention, and "whatever promise you make to them I will perform." Two wanted internal revenue jobs and the other a lucrative custom-house appointment. They got them.*

When the amendment itself stuck in the House, again the President used the powers with which he was clothed to secure needed votes. One congressman wanted a federal job for his brother in New York; another whose congressional seat was being contested

* As "lame duck" congressmen they would soon be out of a job.

was given assurance of the Administration's support; and a third
was promised friendly votes in adverse legislation that affected a
client for whom he was attorney. The scene in Congress on
January 31, 1865, was a memorable one. The Thirteenth Amendment was given the necessary two-thirds majority by a margin of
three votes. That was how close the President had calculated. An
artillery battery posted outside the Capitol let go a hundred-gun
salute when the measure was passed that legalized his proclamation
declaring all persons held as slaves are and henceforward shall be
"forever free."

Thus, in brief, did the President bring Nevada into the Union
and assure passage in the House of the constitutional means to free
the bondsmen—by patronage. Can there be greater sublimation of
political technique than gaining legal liberty for four million slaves?
Who will denounce the political actions as "greasy" politics? Cannot
lowly means achieve the highest ends? Of course they can. "The
passage of this amendment will clinch the whole subject," Lincoln
told Congressman James S. Rollins, a large Missouri slaveholder,
asking for his affirmative vote. "It will bring the war, I have no
doubt, rapidly to a close," Lincoln predicted. Rollins agreed and
voted aye.

Discerning Dana declared that Lincoln was a supreme politician.
"He understood politics because he understood human nature," said
the future editor of the *New York Sun,* and asserted: "There was
no flabby philanthropy about Abraham Lincoln. He was all solid,
hard, keen, intelligence combined with goodness."

Patronage is one of the coins of the political realm on which
Lincoln has been given rough treatment. No biography overlooks
mentioning the horde of officeseekers that overran the White
House. They were a great tribulation to the President and he so
attested on several occasions. To an old friend he remarked that
although in the midst of war his great problem at the moment was

to decide among several applicants for a small-town postmaster-ship. To critics of his course he would say that he had to run the machine as he found it.

The machine he found was composed entirely of political appointees. Every federal job from mailman to Cabinet officer was political. There was no civil service then. National government meant party government. For thirty prior years the opposition party had controlled the federal machine (except for eight Whig years) and all places were filled with their men. Many officeholders were southern sympathizers or outright secessionists who had to be replaced in any case. Despite these imperatives Lincoln retained some whose skill and experience and loyalty made their services valuable, the number varying from department to department.

Studies made of Lincoln's patronage operations corroborate the fact that no President was ever confronted by a more difficult situation and that he distributed the offices as wisely as could be done under the unusual circumstances. Left unsaid is that the purpose of the political system was to retain the governing process in the hands of the people; to prevent seizure by a "man on horse-back," a king, an emperor, or similar autocrat. The American method was devised to defeat such would-be despots; it was democratic all the way. Every four years the people decided who would act as their representatives in running the federal machine.*

Just as there are different media of exchange in the economic world such as coins, bills, checks, bonds, and debentures, all of which are money, so in the political world patronage, logrolling, vote-getting, favors, and so on, represent political "money." And

* The number of federal jobs Lincoln had to distribute amounted to 1,520. The total bureaucracy amounted to 37,000. Today federal bureaucracy reaches 2,500,000, a bigness that increases the Chief Executive's difficulty in getting his policies implemented. Officeholders under civil service do not readily respond to political direction. The bureaucracy, with unions, and with lobbies in Congress, is primarily concerned with its own self-preservation, not the people's.

just as regular money can secure good ends or bad, political "money" can be utilized likewise. Lincoln employed his political capital to such advantage he made himself a political millionaire— a statesman. Indeed he employed it so well in behalf of his country- men as to make himself a political multimillionaire—a great statesman.

Or to state the proposition in terms of the people, he sublimated the manipulations of "greasy" politics to procure for the body politic the greatest benefit for the greatest number; bringing the power of the state to achieve its primary objectives of the good, the true, the beautiful.

11

A FEW feet from where he now lay Lincoln had stood and addressed a joint session of the legislature. "Most gratefully do I thank you," he had told New York's solons, "in behalf of the nation and in behalf of civil and religious liberty for all time to come." He did not propose, he went on, to speak of the policy of the government at this time, but when the time came (at inauguration), "I shall speak as well as I am able for the good of the present and future of this country—for the good both of the North and South of this country . . . and of all sections of the country."

172

On this same day that the seceded states were organizing a national government he had pleaded, "If we have patience, if we restrain overselves, if we allow ourselves not to run off in a passion, I still have confidence that the Almighty, the Maker of the Universe, will, through the instrumentality of this great and intellectual people, bring us through this as He has through all other difficulties of our country." The legislators cheered as he concluded, "Relying on this, I again thank you for this generous reception."

Albany was the third state capital through which he had passed on the inaugural journey. He would pass through five altogether: Indianapolis, Columbus, Albany, Trenton, and Harrisburg. From each he had received a formal invitation to be their guest and to deliver an address. He appeared before four legislatures in joint session and at one, Trenton, spoke separately to Senate and Assembly.

He did not address the Indiana Legislature as a body; why not is not clear. The speech he had marked "For Indianapolis," he delivered from the balcony of the Bates House (now Claypool Hotel). The context was equally suitable for a legislative body and he may have intended it so. There was no political reason for not addressing the Hoosier legislators; the next morning he met them at the State House, individually, informally, cordially. After the hand-shaking he returned to the hotel and prepared for the run to Cincinnati. The legislators meanwhile voted to adjourn long enough to see him off, and they joined the farewell throng at union station.

When he left Springfield, Lincoln could not, of course, foresee what he would encounter along the way. All doubt was dispelled by the first major city, Indianapolis, which had overwhelmed him. The largest wintertime crowd ever gathered in Indiana's new capital city accorded him a rousing reception, and their enthusiasm moved him to address them at once. From the standpoint of numbers reached the entire tour was an unqualified success. Albany was no exception, engulfing him in an ocean of well-wishers.

Lincoln's trip to the nation's capital to take office was in the tradition of the first President. George Washington had made a triumphal tour from Mt. Vernon, Virginia, to New York City in a horse-drawn coach; but Lincoln's journey somehow achieved special status in the public mind as being uniquely Lincolnian. The return trip was a logical sequel; one almost might say a compelling sequel. Whether the extended itinerary of the inaugural tour was Lincoln's original idea or whether it was suggested by others will never be known with certainty. Those with whom he might have discussed the subject left no documentary evidence nor did he mention the subject in the presence of those who did. Private Secretary Nicolay, who occupied an office with him from a few days after the nomination until the departure for Washington, did not learn of the exact route until late in January; and on the twenty-seventh wrote his sweetheart in Pittsfield that "Mr. Lincoln yesterday determined definitely to start from here on his way to Washington on the 11th of February." The press had speculated on the route. *New York Herald* correspondent Henry Villard, whose dispatches appeared in Associated Press papers, reported January 19, "It was but yesterday I had occasion to converse with Mr. Lincoln on the subject of his impending trip to Washington City. He stated he had not as yet fixed the date of his departure nor selected the route."

The newspaper reports created a flow of invitations. A delegation from the Indiana Legislature came to Springfield on January 22 bearing official greetings, another group arrived four days later, and a committee of Indianapolis citizens appeared on the twenty-eighth. A Cincinnati citizens' committee wrote an invitation on February 1. New York's Governor Morgan invited him in a letter dated the fourth. A personally written invitation arrived from New Jersey's governor, and another came from Ohio's. The Massachusetts Legislature dispatched a personal representative bearing a handsomely engrossed parchment signed by the governor inviting him to Boston. To this Lincoln responded at once excusing himself, "I am constrained to say want of time denies me the pleasure of accepting." Dayton, Cleveland, Harrisburg, Pittsburgh were among cities sending delegations and letters of invitation. The President-elect received more invitations than he could fulfill.

Doubtless he felt, as his secretaries said, that it would not only be a gracious act to accept as many as he could of these invitations in which all parties freely joined; but "both the people and their Chief Executive would be strengthened in their faith and patriotism by closer acquaintance." Law-partner Herndon said Lincoln told him "a man named Wood" recommended by Seward (others say by Weed) would be in charge of the trip as a sort of general manager. Herndon also noted that his law partner was the most "shut-mouthed" man he ever knew and that Lincoln habitually kept political plans and purposes to himself.

However, everyone knew, and it was reported in the press, that Lincoln was working on the inaugural address. What no one seems to have known (at least it went unreported) was that he was, at the same time, composing his journey speeches. He composed them as he sat for an hour or so each morning in a room at the St. Nicholas Hotel. The room was the "studio" of sculptor Thomas D. Jones of Ohio, who was doing the bust from life. How many speeches Lincoln completed is not known; a few have been preserved, and are on deposit at the Library of Congress.

During the 1,904-mile, twelve-day expedition to the nation's capital Lincoln delivered twenty major addresses, half that many semimajor speeches, and countless talks and greetings. Never before had he uttered so many public words in so short a time (his senatorial canvass with Douglas in 1858 came close); never would he again. Presidential candidates in that era did not make speeches toward getting themselves elected. They did no whistle-stopping, baby-kissing, or similar ballyhooing, as practiced in these raucous times. In those days of chivalry it was not considered proper for an aspirant to so high an office to take to the hustings and tell of his own virtues. Others did that for him. The candidate had to take the stance the office was seeking him, not he it. So Lincoln stayed close to home and said nothing during the frenetic 1860 campaign. The only talking he did was to deny erroneous statements attributed to him.

But the travel to Washington was unfettered by restrictions.* The journey offered an opportunity to reach hundreds of thousands of fellow citizens to whom he could explain the boil-and-bubble political trouble upending the nation. He could try to quiet the rising storm. Seven states declared themselves severed from the Union. He *had* to say something; many citizens were hoping that in some way, somehow, he could bring about a quick and decisive solution.

Imagine the reaction, especially of political opponents, had he said nothing en route. He would have been denounced as shirking his responsibilities and sneaking into office; he would have been castigated as a coward, particularly in view of the nasty things said of him when his life was endangered in Baltimore. Courageously he took the long road to the national capital in order that he might see and be seen, talk and be talked to, make clear that a new leader was on the way to take over. "The power of Mr. Lincoln is not in his presence or in his speech but in the honesty and gloriously refreshing sincerity of the MAN," wired Horace Greeley to his newspaper on boarding the inaugural special in Buffalo. "His passage through the country has been like the return of grateful sunshine after a stormy winter day. The people breathe more freely and hope revives in all hearts."

* A President did not make political speeches while in office either. His public utterances were confined to official business, proclamations, state messages. Even his communications to Congress were not voiced in person as now but were read by the Speaker's clerk.

Did Lincoln err in making the journey to Washington an extended speaking tour—as both political opponents and cloistered historiographers have complained? Was his lengthy itinerary a mistake—as Lamon maintained in the biography bearing his name but which was composed by Democrat Chauncey S. Black? Did critics and detractors possess greater knowledge than that vouchsafed America's ablest Chief Executive? Or were they politically motivated? For a hundred years Lincoln has been disparaged for his performance on this trip.

"When a first-class mind is filtered through an inferior one it becomes unrecognizable," observed an attorney whose father had been associated with Lincoln. That is why there are so many different Lincolns. We see him through lesser minds. The burden of proof, therefore, rests with those who set themselves up as more wise than he, who pontificate he went dumb on the journey (yes, they said these things in cold type), that he did not know what he was talking about, that he tried to say nothing, and that he should have kept still. They yank him out of character the moment he steps on the train at Springfield and give his character back to him when he reaches Washington, creating a hiatus the veriest novice in fiction would know better than to perpetrate. Make no mistake about it; Lincoln retained his faculties throughout the inaugural travel. He stayed in character.

All caliber of minds agree that Lincoln's wisdom involved simple processes of logic that reached inevitable conclusions. That being so, would not his prime purpose for extending the route have been to make the travel yield the greatest return? And would not that return have been primarily political? That he prepared the speeches in advance showed how important he deemed the contact with the people. Some history interpreters aver that he did not *want* to say anything that would reveal forthcoming policies and plans. The contrary was true. He deliberately composed his remarks to disclose his thinking; something on the order of what today is called a "trial balloon." Though not labeling what he said as official, he did expose, bit by bit, his plans as he moved eastward. Some astute newspapermen caught this.

The Columbus (Ohio) correspondent of the *Cincinnati Commercial* correctly divined Lincoln's utterances as revealing his program "by driblets" but did not label them as such since he could not be certain. Another crystal-ball gazer was the *New York Herald.* Editor James Gordon Bennett himself likely penned the caustic editorial (he was then anti-Lincoln) titled "Drippings from the Inaugural" in which he said among other things, "Mr. Lincoln, on his way to the national capital, drops here and there choice morsels from his approaching inaugural."

That is precisely what the President-elect did. By comparing the major journey speeches with the 1860 Chicago platform and the First Inaugural Address the proof is easy to come by. The speeches clearly erect a bridge between platform and inaugural. Political pros would concur that the speeches were just what they should have been. There was nothing mysterious or unusual about the connection insofar as "Honest Abe" was concerned, although it is true that party platforms often are treated callously by the candidate. Lincoln hewed to the line.

When he wrote the chairman of the convention accepting the nomination, he said, "The declaration of principles and sentiments [the platform] which accompanied your letter meets with my approval; and it shall be my care not to violate or disregard it in any part."

Reporting on his Pittsburgh address the *New York Times* observed that "to these remarks too great importance can hardly be attached"; making the point that Lincoln intended "to redeem all the engagements of that platform." And nowhere could this be more appropriately promulgated, the *Times* went on to say, "than on the spot where the Republican organization originated," referring of course to the formation of the *national* Republican party here five years before.

As to the quality of the journey speeches, some stand with Lincoln's best. The Farewell to Springfield takes rank next to the immortal Gettysburg and the Second Inaugural Addresses. Notable were his extemporaneous remarks in Independence Hall. Also noteworthy were those at Indianapolis (from the train platform particularly), Cincinnati, Columbus (both), Pittsburgh, Cleveland (the most revealing), Philadelphia (three), Trenton (two), and the one he did not utter but wrote out, his "Address to Kentuckians." The reply to New York City's wily mayor was a fine example of Lincolnian diplomacy. His speeches at Lafayette, Steubenville, Buffalo, and Albany (two) directed attention to specific subjects and the two at Harrisburg especially to the subject of peace. Under circumstances never encountered by a President-elect before, Lincoln turned in an outstanding performance.

Thousands of Americans saw and heard him for the first time; millions read what he was saying. For two weeks he dominated the news and inspired his countrymen. At the same time that he was making patriotic appeals to the people he was privately carrying out political chores with local and state leaders; meeting other public officials, newspapermen, railroaders, industrialists, business and professional men, and leading citizens.

He sought close contact with the governors. He breakfasted with Indiana's Governor Morton, stayed overnight in the mansion of Ohio's Governor Dennison, dined with New York's Governor Morgan, took buffet lunch with the New Jersey legislators, and suppered with Pennsylvania's Governor Curtin.* These states had

---

* The governor of New Jersey, Charles S. Olden (Republican), was in Washington attending the Peace Conference. Lincoln saw him there.

been critical in his election and he was now personally acknowledg-
ing their support. Moreover, it was these states together with those
of old New England and the new Northwest that would with his
home state stand as the bulwark of the Union and provide the
men and materials to free the nation.

Of his travel to Washington Lincoln made a master political
stroke. By it he assumed leadership of the party and helped to unify
a fractionated political organization only five years old, made up
of dissidents from all other parties and operated more on a local
and state basis than as a national unit. Elevated into control of the
federal government for the first time, the swaddling party represented such a conglomeration of personalities—crusaders, theorists,
and practical pros—that it could easily disintegrate and join other
defunct parties, which included Whigs (twice), Tories, Federalists,
and other "splinter" groups like Free-Soilers, and Know-nothings.
Welding the discordant factions into a cohesive whole, holding
them to steady goals under the devastating blows of a civil war,
bequeathing to posterity political ideals that ensured a strong party
for a century, these alone certify that the sixteenth President was
the master statesman of American history. His journey to the
nation's capital was the initial demonstration of his political skill.
It witnessed his entrance upon the world stage; it was the curtain-
raiser to all that followed. It was his journey to greatness.

It also represented one of a long list of his achievements gained
against active opposition. He undertook the extended route over
objections of friends who held it unnecessary. One such was Judge
David Davis who wrote Simon Cameron he had just returned
from Springfield, and was preparing to leave with Lincoln but felt

"the fatiguing trip ought not to have been taken. I am sorry for it,"
he said. "It could have been prevented. Mr. Lincoln invited me to
accompany him and although at great personal inconvenience, I
will try . . . to continue with him to Washington." Senator Seward
wrote Lincoln advising him to call off the long trip or at least to
step up the schedule in order to foil assassination plots, of which
there was much talk. Disregarding these counsels and despite the
dangers involved, Lincoln went ahead on the strength of his own
carefully thought-out convictions.

Time and again his foresight proved out. There was his "House
Divided" speech delivered in the Illinois Hall of Representatives.
The night before, he read it to a group of party leaders gathered in
the State Library. Almost to a man they objected to the theme;
and when he lost the senatorial election, they claimed it was largely
due to this controversial speech. Douglas pounced on it and
denounced it as a call to war. This Lincoln denied. He explained
that it was not a wish but an expectation. "I have often expressed
an *expectation* to die, but I never have expressed a *wish* to die,"
he said. Similarly with slavery. Its opponents would arrest its
further spread and place it in the course of ultimate extinction, or
its advocates would push it forward until it became lawful in all
states. One or the other must prevail, he declared; that was the
expectation. Subsequent events, everyone knows, redeemed his
prophecy. The address has grown to be among his most famous
utterances.

There was his decision on Fort Sumter. Lincoln requested that
Cabinet members give him a written opinion on measures to be
pursued. All but one were against sending reinforcements to or
holding this isolated federal stronghold in Charleston harbor that
had become a symbol of federal strength. Again Lincoln, despite
Cabinet opposition and the covert machinations of his Secretary of
State, had to make the determination. He ordered food sent to the

starving garrison, a humanitarian act, notifying South Carolina's governor he was doing so. The rest is history.

So it went throughout his presidency, from withholding the privilege of habeas corpus to reappointing McClellan that secured the victory of Antietam. His foresight, insight, clear sight, or combination thereof, or intuition if you prefer, demonstrated he saw more clearly through the darkened glass; that he possessed a measure of prescience eclipsing lesser minds; and that he had an inner strength to act upon his convictions in the face of contrary counsel.

John Hay wrote Herndon that "it is absurd to call him a modest man. . . . It was his intellectual arrogance and unconscious assumption of superiority that men like Chase and Sumner never could forgive." Chase and Sumner were notorious egotists. Chase never was able to realize why he should not be President instead of gawky fumbling Lincoln. To gain his objective, after Lincoln had appointed him Chief Justice of the Supreme Court, he deserted the Republican party and in 1872 ran as a Democrat for the presidency. Sumner was more than a "proper Bostonian." He considered himself a superior person. He fought Lincoln on the administration's restoration program—and defeated it. Though Chase and Sumner were able men, they would have receded into comparative obscurity had it not been for their association with the backwoodsman from Kentucky. The youthful Hay (twenty-six at the time) could not have selected a more potent example of Lincoln's ability to manage men than these two prima donnas.

What young Hay did not realize was that Lincoln was so often right over their contrary views that they resented his irritatingly good judgment. Nothing is more hurtful than a bruised ego. Chase's and Sumner's were supersensitive. For not only did the Chief Executive exhibit better judgment in the face of their opposition but frequently outmaneuvered them. For a politician to be out-

maneuvered is devastating. The record shows Lincoln handled
them with exceptional consideration. Their tactics against him
were mean and petty, and maddening to read about today. From
this distance their acts bear all the marks of professional jealousy.
A lesser character would have given them short shrift; they were
fortunate in having as their superior the most perceptive and
patient President ever to occupy that office. He went to extraordinary lengths to secure political harmony.

Suave Seward, older, shrewder, more experienced in men and
their wiles, early grasped Lincoln's capabilities. He saw what
others could not. "He is the best of us all," Seward wrote his wife
after watching the work of the man who had taken the presidency
away from him. Four years later when he cast his ballot for
Lincoln's reelection he responded to serenaders gathered in front
of his Washington residence: "Henceforth all men will come to
see him as you and I have seen him; a true, loyal, patient, patriotic
and benevolent man. . . . Abraham Lincoln will take his place
alongside Washington, Franklin, Adams, Jefferson and Jackson,
among the benefactors of the country and of the human race."

Hay really was not far behind Seward in his admiration of
the "Tycoon," as he affectionately if irreverently nicknamed the
President. He concluded his letter to Herndon—written from Paris
in 1866—"I believe Lincoln is well understood by the people. . . .
I consider Lincoln Republicanism incarnate, with all its faults and
virtues . . . and Lincoln, with all his foibles, the greatest character
since Christ."

The assembly chamber at Albany was opened to an impatient
public at 1:15 A.M. The pushing and hauling of so many people

straining to get in at that unusual hour and for the somber purpose
was wholly unexpected. Police and militia were present in small
details only. The military units had returned to dispersing areas
from where many made their way back to the capitol as individuals
to swell the already oversized crowds. At better than sixty a minute
the anxious multitude trooped through the hushed chamber without
let-up.

The sixth day of the homeward trek dawned bright and clear;
such a day, proclaimed a local reporter, as heaven grants on rare
occasions. The sky was blue; the sun was warm; the air was touched
by a light breeze from the south. Before daybreak, excursion
trains, boats, stages, and all manner of horse-drawn vehicles began
arriving with overflow loads from Burlington on Lake Champlain,
from Brattleboro on the Connecticut River, from Springfield in
Massachusetts, from the Catskills, from Troy, Schenectady, Saratoga Springs, Glens Falls, and the high Adirondacks. Fifty thousand
persons viewed the remains, the New York papers said, the greatest
multitude yet seen in the state capital.

By ten o'clock State Street, a hundred feet broad, was filled
with visitors, and at noon the thoroughfare was a living mass of
people. So were Broadway and side streets. At 1:30 P.M. state
house doors were closed and thousands were left standing four
abreast in a line a mile long. At two the procession to the depot got
under way. All marchers except the hearse itself were on foot
including the governor, mayor, public officials, and all delegations.
No banners or other devices were permitted, only the national
colors, black-bordered, held in the horizontal position. At quarter
to four the railroad station was entered and the casket transferred
to the railroad conveyance, and at four o'clock the New York
Central's Lincoln Special steamed out of the capital city of the
Empire State.

Governor Reuben E. Fenton could not accompany the train; the

close of the legislative session and the signing of recently passed
bills with pressure of other state business kept him at his desk.
This was a great sorrow to him since he held the late President in
great esteem, having known him personally and cordially.

Now commenced a fifteen-hour pilgrimage across the center of
the state, through the storied Mohawk Valley, along the water-level
Erie Canal, in and out of growing cities and towns, past prosperous
farms and villages, reaching at seven in the morning the terminal
port of Buffalo on Lake Erie, gateway to the west. "The Knickerbockers of Albany, the Cosmopolites of New York, the Quakers of
Philadelphia, the Dutch of Harrisburg, the Emotional Children of
Baltimore, had all manifested in appropriate forms their great bereavement." Now the rural folk were revealing a unanimity and
depth of feeling that would last for generations.

The multitude gathered at Schenectady stood stock still with
uncovered heads as the cars slowly moved by. At Canajoharie
the decorated Palatine Bridge was filled with women weeping on
one another's shoulders, one fainting as the train passed. A colla-
tion (buffet-type meal) was served at St. Johnsville, sixty-four
miles from Albany, the twenty-two comely young ladies acting as
volunteer waitresses being privileged to file through the hearse
car in acknowledgment of their services. At Little Falls a committee
of ladies accompanied their tribute of flowers with a note explaining that the cross was a symbol of his ever-faithful trust in God, the
shield an emblem of the protection he had given to the liberties of
the people, and the wreath a token of the "mingling of our tears
with those of our afflicted nation." At Herkimer a group of thirty-
six ladies, symbolizing the states of the whole Union, each in a
white dress with a black sash from left shoulder to right hip, held
national flags edged in sable. Twenty-five thousand gathered at
track-side in Utica though it was raining. At Syracuse, reached ten
minutes before midnight, thirty-five thousand paid their respects in

a driving downpour. Rochester was entered at 3:20 A.M. Though the hour was unconscionable and the weather inclement, the Fifty-fourth Infantry regiment, a company of Veteran Reserves, the Union Blues regiment, a battery of the Twenty-fifth Brigade, and several bands were surrounded by a solid sea of citizens.

"A pillar of fire by night" guided the cortege not only in cities and towns but through the countryside. The rains came and went but the light never faltered; a ribbon of fire stretched across the Empire State from Mohawk to Niagara.

Dawn broke at five o'clock, and Batavia presented former President Millard Fillmore. He and other western New York notables boarded the train here as escort into Buffalo. The pause was for ten minutes to change engines and crews, the locomotive attached being the same one that had pulled the inaugural special four years before, and was manned by the same crew.

Buffalo ceremonies were admirable. The Associated Press reported the arrangements were "better than elsewhere along the route." The *Rochester Union* graciously complimented her neighbor by quoting General Dix in similar vein, saying that "the arrangements were far ahead of anything which had been attempted in any other place through which they had passed." *

These were sweet words to Buffalonians eager to redeem the good name of the city from the obloquy of four years before when the lives of *two* Presidents had been endangered in their city. That was when former President Fillmore and President-elect Lincoln had greeted each other in the railroad station upon the latter's entrance into the city. Both had been overwhelmed by an over-enthusiastic mass of humanity. The incident unfortunately was followed by another that multiplied the dishonor. Lincoln had his speech marred by wood being sawed, in payment of an election bet,

---

* Since General Dix had boarded the Special at Philadelphia he was in a position to judge.

under the hotel balcony from which he was speaking. The dis-
courteous incidents, due to faulty planning and poor policing, were
humiliating to the loyalists of the Niagara frontier. Buffalonians
made sure this time nothing would go amiss—and nothing did.

From the moment the train pulled into the Exchange Street
depot at seven o'clock and the weary travelers partook of a hearty
breakfast in Bloomer's Dining Saloon until departure for Cleveland
that evening, everything went off smoothly and quietly. The procession escorting the remains from the station to St. James Hall in the
Young Men's Association building was not a lengthy one. The city
had held an imposing commemorative procession on the day of the
White House obsequies. By curtailing the march now more time
was available for the people to view the martyred dead, and for
eleven hours the public moved past canopied catafalque and blos-
som-strewn casket.

"The face wore the same kind, benign look that characterized
the 'People's President' when alive," noted the editor of the
Buffalo Express, who had been personally acquainted with the deceased. The face was only slightly discolored, he said, and not as
much as one had been led to expect; in fact, the lifetime expression
of the features was striking. "The thought would arise as we gazed
upon his quiet smile," observed the editor wistfully, "that he had
found the rest for which he must have so often sighed."

"Rest, Spirit, Rest," sang the St. Cecilia Society as their floral
tribute was laid at the head of the bier while at the foot the ladies
of the Unitarian Church, which the deceased had attended on his
inaugural passage, laid an anchor of flowers on which was inscribed: "Truth crushed to earth shall rise again, The eternal years
of God are hers, While Error, wounded, writhes in pain, And
dies among his worshippers."

Buffalo crowds were immense yet courteous, yielding readily to
volunteer officers and city police to prevent disorder and con-

fusion. Company D of the Seventy-fourth Regiment served as honor guard with distinction and wholly redeemed their unfortunate involvement in the previous difficulty. General Townsend in his account noted that "everything passed off without the least incident."

The general also noted receiving here first news of the capture and death of the assassin.

12

TO relate the details of Lincoln's assassination would be like re-
peating yesterday's newspaper; it is a universally known event
of American life. The capture of the assassin was also headline
news.

Identity of the culprit was established the night of the crime by
a board of inquiry set up in the room next to where the President
lay dying. The assassin escaped detection for eleven days and was
killed in the process of capture. That a single individual had committed the praesidicide was too fantastic to be believed. The ac-

cepted fact was that it was a rebel conspiracy. The only question was who were responsible higher up. Even when the conspirators were caught, exhibiting a sorry lot of marginal mentality, the operation could only be viewed as rebel inspired. The simultaneous attempts to murder Vice-President, Secretary of State, and Commanding General were considered prima facie evidence of a master plot. The character of the assailants mattered little; governments make use of anyone willing to do a dirty job regardless of background.

To adjudicate the crime a military tribunal was set up. The victim being the Commander-in-Chief, the war not ended, and the site of the deed Washington, center of the war zone, there was no question of the jurisdiction of a military commission; although its exclusive jurisdiction was questioned by defense attorneys.

General Hunter was detached from the traveling cortege by telegraph and designated president of the court; eight additional general officers were appointed by President Johnson. Brigadier General Joseph Holt (former Secretary of War in Buchanan's Cabinet) was named judge advocate and recorder, aided by two assistants. Hearings began May 9. Testimony was taken continuously until June 28. Findings were read and sentences pronounced June 30. Four conspirators were hanged; three sentenced to life imprisonment, one to six years, all at hard labor.

The proceedings were recorded in shorthand by Benn Pitman, the brother of the originator of a famous stenographic method, and printed for all to read. The testimony failed to connect the deed with Confederate officials. (One witness turned out to be a perjurer.) There were good reasons for lack of such evidence; it was highly self-incriminating. Those who had known the assassin hastened to deny all knowledge of him and destroyed anything having to do with him. Everybody ducked for cover. Public feeling ran high.

The military tribunal was castigated by political opponents as prejudiced and charged with covering up the real facts, namely, that the murder had been engineered by Republican radicals, specifically by Secretary Stanton and his coterie. Since the radical wing of the Republican Party did gain control of the federal government after Lincoln's demise the charge was given ex post facto impetus, and it has continued to simmer along to this day. The accusations created confusion and suspicion. This was a distinct gain for the opposition since they could not afford to remain silent and accept the entire onus of the crime. It is always good politics to derogate opponents, and no matter how fantastic the charge some of it will be believed by some people. That is standard political technique the world over. Stanton, target of the political opposition for his vigorous prosecution of the war, was even denounced as being responsible for the deed to further his own political ends. This was a vindictive accusation without the slightest foundation in fact, a smear in the worst (best) political manner.

To develop espionage and sabotage activities against the Union the Confederacy sent three high commissioners to Canada. They were given instructions by President Jefferson Davis, partly verbal and partly written. His letter to Jacob Thompson, ablest of the three, cited in *The War of the Rebellion; Official Records*, reads: "Confiding special trust in your zeal, discretion, and patriotism, I hereby direct you to proceed to Canada, there to carry out such instructions as you have received from me verbally in such manner as shall seem most likely to conduce to the furtherance of the interests of the Confederate States of America which have been instructed to you." Just what Davis' instructions to the commissioners were and what they in turn transmitted to those who assassinated Lincoln will ever remain unknown.

The deep passions involved will prevent objective evaluation of the origin and development of the Lincoln assassination plot, but what cannot be overlooked is that much evidence is yet to be brought to light. The Civil War records of the National Archives in Washington, for example, are now fully available to qualified researchers. Certain files were withheld from the public until recently so that no living person would be hurt. These records have not been fully explored.

Here is a huge leather-bound ledger stamped "Register of Records Relative to the Lincoln Assassination," which offers specific starting points. Here are three long file boxes stuffed with century-old documents, letters, reports, and memoranda labeled "Lincoln Assassination Suspects." And here are more than a dozen files marked "Scouts, Guides, Spies and Detectives." Yonder are shelves crammed with "Turner-Baker Papers" that have a special index, so voluminous are the records of Lafayette C. Baker, head of the United States Secret Service during the war, and of Major Levi Turner of the Judge-Advocate Department; a veritable treasure trove of cloak-and-dagger drama.

Much of the Archives' Civil War material must be sorted and inventoried before it can be indexed. A beginning has been made; there is a "Preliminary Inventory of the Records of the Adjutant-Generals Office, 1775-1948" and a "Preliminary Checklist of the Records of the Judge-Advocate General, 1805-1942." An unsorted mass of miscellaneous documents such as accounting records of secret service funds, correspondence with the Confederate commissioners in Canada, documents in cipher and code, can be brought to life only by trained researchers and knowledgeable scholars capable of fitting together the bits and pieces of the intricate puzzle.

Vast as it is, the collection represents a fraction of the activities of Union and Confederate spies, undercover agents, and intelligence operators. Who knows how much went unreported? Fragmentary documents have come to light revealing a connection between the presidential assassin and a Confederate commissioner in Canada; Montreal bank transactions point an accusing finger. Until loose ends are fitted together much will have to remain conjecture.

There is nothing conjectural about Confederate undercover activities greatly intensifying in 1864 and reaching the awful crescendo of April 14, 1865. The secessionists realized they were losing the war and stepped up last-ditch attempts to retrieve their waning fortunes. Grasping at every desperate straw nothing appeared too foolhardy to try. Abetted by disloyal Copperheads of the North and supervised by the commissioners in Canada they conspired to detach the northwestern states of Ohio, Indiana, Illinois, Wisconsin, and Minnesota to form a Northwest Republic that would cooperate with the South and oppose the North. "The Great Northwest Conspiracy" did not come off, but concurrent agitation among Sioux Indian tribes domiciled in Minnesota brought about an uprising that cost the lives of more than four hundred settlers and soldiers before the massacres could be halted by Union troops.

The troops had to be sent to Minnesota from other fronts as the Confederate plan had envisaged, and recruits in the area had to be organized and put into action on the spot, further weakening the Union war effort. Thirty thousand settlers fled the Red and Minnesota river valleys. Immigration came to a dead stop. John Pope, ill-starred Union general of Second Bull Run, was detailed to St. Paul to establish a military district of the Northwest. In fomenting this Indian uprising the Confederates did achieve a measure of success, for the Federals had to remove the Sioux to reservations in Dakota Territory and set up a chain of military posts to safeguard the frontier. To make it as expensive in manpower as possible the rebels restricted paroles, stipulating that a parolee was not to engage in military action against the Indians, a practice the Union had been following.

The rebels were successful in another piece of derring-do. They raided the St. Albans (Vt.) banks and netted $100,000 in sorely needed gold specie.* It was stolen by raiders at gunpoint just like common thieves, killing one citizen in the process. Fleeing back to Canada fifteen miles away they were arrested and tried in a Canadian court which had to release them as not having committed a crime within the court's jurisdiction. Relations with the British North American Colonies, as Canada was then known, already strained by the nest of rebel spies and saboteurs headquartering there, were greatly intensified by this incident. Little could be done under existing treaties. Pressures had to be exerted unofficially. The Canadian government did reimburse the banks for $50,000 as a gesture of goodwill.

From Canada too came a Confederate guerrilla band plotting to release ten thousand rebel prisoners held on Johnson Island in Sandusky Bay, Ohio. Recruited from General Morgan's Kentucky raiders and led by an acting master of the Confederate navy, John Y. Beall, the plot misfired. Beall was caught. Great influence was brought to bear on President Lincoln to commute the culprit's death sentence but in view of Beall's unsavory record, he refused. Beall was hanged February 24, 1865.

Confederate agents were also held responsible for inciting the New York draft riots; one John A. Andrews, as an example, was arrested while agitating a mob to commit unlawful acts. He also had been directing the activities of a mob on the loose. Imprisoned on Blackwell's Island he mysteriously disappeared, likely spirited away by sympathizers in the local government.

Following the draft riots Confederate agents attempted to destroy Manhattan by fire, the plot scheduled for election day. Ten thou-

* The amount is variously reported up to $200,000.

sand Union troops under redoubtable General Benjamin F. Butler
were stationed around the perimeter of the city and on ships in
the harbor, ready for any election-day trouble. The incendiarists
deferred their operation until November 25. The full details were
disclosed around the turn of the century when "I-was-there" books
on the Civil War achieved popularity. Arsonist John W. Headley
of Kentucky said two things saved New York from a terrible holo-
caust; one was the prompt response of firemen and the other that
the Greek fire bombs failed. The fires were extinguished without
doing much damage, though causing great excitement.

Headley, a young Kentuckian from near Hopkinsville who had
ridden with Forrest and escaped with him when Grant took Fort
Donelson, related that a fellow arsonist was caught in this New
York operation. He was Robert C. Kennedy who gave a signed
confession to the *New York Times* contingent upon his being con-
victed. He was; then hanged. The judge said in sentencing him:
"To attempt to set fire to the city of New York is one of the greatest
atrocities of the age. There is nothing in the annals of barbarism
which evinces greater vindictiveness. It was not a mere attempt
to destroy the city but to set fire to crowded hotels and places of
public resort in order to secure the greatest possible destruction
of human life." Kennedy had fired four hotels and Barnum's
Museum. All fortunately were saved.

The Niagara frontier was a center of espionage activities, a
Confederate commissioner being stationed in Toronto. Late in 1864
their spy network learned that seven Confederate generals were to
be transferred from Johnson's Island to Fort Lafayette, New York.
Commissioner Thompson proposed that the train be held up, the
generals freed, and conducted back to their commands. A party
of ten agents headed by the soon-to-be-caught Captain John Y.
Beall filtered across the Niagara Falls Suspension Bridge to Buffalo.

They did not know which train the generals would be riding and to scout the situation nine went to Dunkirk, one to Erie.

They learned the generals were yet to come but could not find out when. Returning to Buffalo, where they would be less noticed in a large community, they decided to derail the train east of the city a few miles. "We reached the appointed place on the road and secreted our conveyance in a woods nearby," recounted Headley. They dragged an iron rail across the track should they be unable to flag the train with a lantern and started to cover it with snow. "But before we could get everything ready," complained the young Kentuckian, "the train went by without trouble." Throwing the impeding rail fifty yards, the cars drew to a stop and the crew came looking for the trouble with lanterns. The conspirators beat it back to Buffalo. The generals, none the wiser, continued on to Fort Lafayette. Beall was arrested while asleep in a lunchroom in Niagara Falls. Headley escaped, walking across Suspension Bridge to Canada and safety.

Not only riots, arson, and kidnapping but revolution was plotted for New York. With the aid of local Copperheads the plan was to seize the Sub-Treasury, release Confederate prisoners from Fort Lafayette, set fires to distract attention, and flee back to Canada. The enterprise failed, due, so it is said, to backing down by the leading agitator, James A. McMasters, editor and owner of the antiadministration *Freeman's Journal*, even though the governor was reported to have given his unofficial promise of official neutrality during the operation.

Boston, Cincinnati, Philadelphia, and other large cities were set on fire but escaped with little damage due to rebel ineptitude and alert fire departments. Chicago was made the target of an insurrectionist plot that failed to come off. Another rebel plot was to release the nine thousand prisoners of war held in Camp Douglas on Chicago's Southside while the Democrats held their national nominating convention in the city during the week of August 29, 1864. Alert counterspies ferreted out the conspiracy and put camp authorities on guard. "Sons of Liberty," "Knights of the Golden Circle," and the "Order of American Knights," all wilted when the hour of decision arrived. One of the undercover agents, Captain Thomas Hines of Kentucky, was so disgusted at the lack of courage he vowed Chicago Copperheads were not entitled to wear a copper penny in their lapels but should wear a white feather.

Out of National Archives' records steps one Edward Frazer, who while testifying before the St. Louis provost marshal on boat burnings told that steamers were burned to the water's edge, that large sums of money were paid by the Confederate government for the work (he had taken some), and that Jeff Davis and Judah Benjamin were offering $400,000 to destroy the Long Bridge at Nashville so as to cut off soldiers and supplies funneling through that base.

And there is Felix Stidger, loyal Kentuckian, who infiltrated the disloyal "Sons of Liberty" and rose in their inner councils. He was elected Grand Secretary of the Indiana chapter. Stidger singlehandedly shattered the Confederate Northwest Conspiracy. His evidence also helped put down the Northeast Conspiracy—an equally devastating plot seldom mentioned in Civil War history— designed to take New England out of the Union and make it an independent republic cooperating with the South.

The immediate goals of Confederate undercover activities were to halt inflow of manpower to Union armies, to secure return of sorely needed men and officers in Union hands (Grant had halted prisoner exchange and rebel manpower was running dangerously low), and to sabotage the Union war effort in every way possible. The final years of the war were filled with their train and bank robberies; they raided farms and villages and committed other nonmilitary acts of terror on the civilian population. It is now clear

their final purpose was to overthrow the federal government and
in pursuit of that objective even attempted to kidnap Vice-Presi-
dent-elect Andrew Johnson before he could reach Washington.

The question properly arises: Did they also conspire to assassinate the head of state as the supreme effort of their desperation?

Those disinclined to accept the affirmative should consider not
only the unexplored public records noted above but also private
files. For instance, only in this decade has it become known that
the would-be dictator and presidential candidate, General George
B. McClellan, hired (at public expense) Allan Pinkerton and his
detective agency to spy on President Lincoln, to report his activities, visitors, conversations, attitudes, and habits. One shudders
at the near-miss this nation had from domination by this self-in-
flated militarist who never won a major engagement and who in-
sinuated himself into top command of the military forces by depos-
ing loyal and able but aging General Winfield Scott. One shudders
when looking at the photographs Matthew Brady took on the
Antietam battlefield showing Lincoln, McClellan, and Pinkerton
together.

In one view the tall Kentuckian stands between "Little Napoleon" McClellan and Major E. J. Allen, which was Pinkerton's
military undercover name. Then there is the widely known pose
of the President and the general sitting together in the latter's tent.
All the while the Chief Executive was under close surveillance by
private detectives on the public payroll.

Pinkerton informed McClellan he rode with the President
on the train back to Washington and had considerable conversation
with him. "He spoke very freely and was very friendly when
speaking of you," reported the famous Chicago railroad sleuth
well known to Lincoln. The detective informed McClellan that he
also had a private conversation with Mr. Hatch of Springfield
"who told me he knew the President believed you to be the ablest

general in the country and the only one capable of fighting a large army." *

What action toward the office of the President of the United States was being contemplated by this reincarnation of a feudal militarist who wrote his wife that only he could save the nation and whose peculiar actions in the war demonstrated time and again he was playing his own political game? Was he another "man on horseback" watching and waiting for the right moment to take over the government? The answer is beyond proof, but not beyond conjecture. The incontestable fact is that the sixteenth President was cut down by forces opposed to him and his policies; forces of which he was aware and which he characterized as "the fire in the rear."

The somber fate that would be Lincoln's as President lay ahead of him, hidden in the mists of time, the day he reached Buffalo on his journey to take office. The same day fate deposited Jefferson Davis in Montgomery, Alabama. Davis had left his Mississippi plantation at the telegraphed invitation of thirty-eight delegates from six cotton states (Texas came later to make seven) who were appointed by their state legislatures or by state conventions. The delegates voted to set up a new national government to be called "The Provisional Government of the Confederate States of America" and agreed on Davis to be President. Lincoln, speaking from the American House balcony, told his Buffalo audience it was natural to expect something of him in view of the threatened difficulties. As to what should be done he pointed out the troubles

* Ozias M. Hatch, Illinois secretary of state, was visiting the President in Washington and was invited to come along to Antietam. Neither he nor Lincoln were as gullible as Pinkerton reported to McClellan. A light sleeper, the President arose early one morning and meeting Hatch already up took him to a point overlooking the vast Union army asleep on the hills and valleys of the battleground. Sweeping his arm in their direction he asked Hatch who he thought they were and replied to his own question: "McClellan's bodyguard!"

were without precedent. He said that as they had "never been
acted upon by an individual situated as I am, it is more proper that
I should wait, see the developments, and get all the light I can so
that when I do speak authoritatively [at inauguration], I may be as
near right as possible."

His advice was received with wide acclaim over the country; it
was prudent, logical, sensible. Those who urged he "do something"
overlooked that he had no power to do anything; he was as plain
as John Doe. Yet he was accused of temporizing. He had prepared
his inaugural address, they charged, and knew what he was going
to propose. If he did not intend to disclose his decision for war or
peace he should have remained silent and reached Washington
without fanfare and pageantry, they said. Lincoln had cogent
reasons for wanting to talk to his countrymen.

His journey to Washington was a mission of peace. He counseled
Buffalo listeners to keep their composure. "Stand up to your sober
convictions of right," he said, "to your obligations to the Constitution; act in accordance with those sober convictions and the clouds
which now arise on the horizon will be dispelled and we shall have
a bright and glorious future." At the first major stop after leaving
Springfield, he had sounded the theme of his trip. "While some of
us may differ in political opinions, still we are all united in one
feeling for the Union," he asserted at Lafayette, Indiana; and declared, "We all believe in the maintenance of every star and every
stripe of the glorious flag."

At Cincinnati he had stressed the free institutions "which we
have increasingly enjoyed for three quarters of a century," re-
minding the audience there was no other country where the people
could turn out and enjoy the day precisely as they pleased "save
under the benign influence of the free institutions of our land"
which he hoped to see repeated every four years. At Pittsburgh he
had advised a sea of hearers to "keep cool," that if people on both

sides of the line would keep their temper the troubles would come to an end. "The question which now distracts the country will be settled," he explained, "just as surely as all other difficulties of like character which have originated in this government have been adjusted. . . . Let the people of both sides keep their self-possession and just as other clouds have been cleared away in due time, so will this great nation prosper as before."

To New Jersey's General Assembly he had proclaimed, "The man does not live who is more devoted to peace than I am. None would do more to preserve it." In Independence Hall he found himself "standing in the place where were collected together the wisdom, the patriotism, the devotion to principle, from which sprang the institutions under which we live," and he told the audience, "There is no need of bloodshed and war. There is no necessity for it. I am not in favor of such a course . . . and there will be no bloodshed unless it be forced upon the Government."

At Harrisburg he had pleaded with the people gathered in the public square and then with the Legislature in joint session. Referring to the military display that had greeted him, he said he was proud to see them but hoped their services would never be needed "especially in the shedding of fraternal blood." "It shall be my endeavor," he avowed, "to preserve the peace of this country so far as can possibly be done consistent with the maintenance of the institutions of the country"; and concluded this final speech before reaching his destination, "I most sincerely hope that we shall have no use for them. . . . I promise that, insofar as I may have the wisdom to direct, it shall be through no fault of mine."

Abraham Lincoln failed in his self-imposed, cross-country peace mission; yet no sensible American would have had him do otherwise and earnestly hoped he would succeed. No one hoped more fervently than he himself for he knew apprehension existed "among the people of the Southern States that by the accession of a Republican Administration their property and their peace and personal security" would be endangered. He pledged that in no way would he interfere with their institutions. More was involved than only the southern states, however, and he reminded everyone in his Message to Congress in Special Session, July 4, 1861, that the very life of the American form of government was at stake. "Our popular government has often been called an experiment," he said. "It is now for them to demonstrate to the world that those who can fairly carry an election, can also suppress a rebellion—that ballots are the rightful and peaceful successors of bullets—and that there can be no successful appeal except to ballots themselves at succeeding elections."

There was more. "This issue embraces more than the fate of the United States," he testified. "It presents to the whole family of man the question whether a constitutional republic or a democracy . . . can or cannot maintain its territorial integrity. Must a government of necessity be too *strong* for the liberties of its own people," he asked, "or too *weak* to maintain its own existence?"

The answer came only after four years of sanguinary fratricide and he had been reelected by popular vote in the midst of the storm. He told a serenading audience the election demonstrated beyond doubt that a people's government can sustain a national election during a great civil war. "Until now," he emphasized, "it has not been known that this was a possibility. It also shows how *sound* and how *strong* we still are." Thus his prophecies were fulfilled. The government of the people by those same people proved it could live and flourish under the most extreme difficulties, a new achievement in the world. The people said Lincoln did it; he said they did it. The stark truth is that neither could have done without the other. Such was a lesson of the war: A successful republic requires a great body politic and a great leader from among them acting in concert to achieve a great moral goal.

13

TO Cleveland was another all-night run, leaving Buffalo at ten minutes after ten and pulling into the Forest City at seven o'clock in the morning. The weather was good. Wayside fires, guns, bells, bands, and uniformed groups greeted the entourage along the 183-mile Lake Shore route across three contiguous states.

"The intensity of feeling seemed, if possible, to grow deeper as the President's remains went further westward where the people more especially claimed him as their own," reported General Townsend. Nor did the crowds diminish as the night grew later. Dunkirk, reached after midnight, displayed the favorite tableau of thirty-six young ladies dressed in white robes, grouped on a platform lighted by kerosene lamps. At one o'clock wood and water were taken on at Westfield. A party of five ladies including one whose husband had been killed at Cold Harbor, boarded the Lincoln car and laid a floral wreath on the casket inscribed "Ours the Cross; Thine the Crown." News dispatches related that all were affected to tears and "considered it a sacred privilege to kiss the coffin."

Nowhere, however, was there a sign of the young Westfield miss who had written the famous letter advising the presidential candidate to grow whiskers. That incident had created a sensation on the inaugural journey and has since become Lincoln lore. Everyone knows that when the train halted here Lincoln called out for his youthful correspondent and twelve-year-old Grace Bedell stepped forward. The newly bewhiskered President-elect took her in his strong arms, kissed her, and reminded her of her letter. Grace would be sixteen now. Surely she and her Lincoln-admiring family were among those present paying their respect to their departed friend. Yet nothing was reported in public prints. Family legends are silent. Two years later, the records show, Grace married a Civil War sergeant and they homesteaded near Delphos, Kansas. Lincoln's letter to Grace is a cherished heirloom and still in the family's possessions.

Something of her sweet spirit was remembered a few miles further on. At the New York-Pennsylvania line the train stopped to permit New York officials to turn over their responsibility to Keystoners. A twelve-year-old lass, Leonora Crawford, from the nearby town of Northeast, entered the hearse car and placed on the bier a bouquet inscribed, "Rest in Peace." The brief ceremony was lighted by lanterns along the track and by huge fires that reddened the sky.

The mayor of Erie and other Pennsylvania dignitaries boarded the cars here. At Erie the reception was marred by a misunderstanding. Train officials had sent word there were to be no ceremonies from Buffalo to Cleveland that would disturb the escort's much-needed rest. The report proved erroneous. Erie citizens were mortified at the failure to offer proper recognition of the distinguished remains. Though it was three o'clock in the morning when the cortege arrived they managed to extemporize a torchlight procession, but it was not as elaborate as they would have liked.

The Ohio-Pennsylvania line was passed at 3:45 A.M. and the slow-paced train puffed through northern Ohio towns until half past six when a stop was made at Wickliffe. Governor Brough, ex-Governor David Tod, General Joseph Hooker commanding the Department of the Ohio, their staffs, officials, and leading citizens joined here and rode the fourteen miles into Cleveland.

The green slopes at lakeside were carpeted with Clevelanders viewing the scene as if in a huge amphitheater. Atop the plateau under an arch draped in mourning stood a woman dressed in horizontal bars of red, white, and blue, a black-trimmed Liberty cap on her head, holding a black-edged national flag. She represented Liberty-in-Mourning. The train entered the downtown union depot and a locomotive of the Cleveland and Pittsburgh line hooked onto the cars in reverse, hauling them to the Euclid Avenue Station at Seventy-ninth Street. It was from here that President-elect Lincoln had made his previous entrance into the city amid wildly enthusiastic crowds. Now he was received in respectful silence. The hushed spectators bared their heads as his remains were placed in the ornate vehicle and borne through the same streets as before, this time to the Public Square.

At the center of the Public Square he was laid on a flower-banked dais in a pavilion constructed for the occasion and open at both ends to permit passage of two double lines. Along the pagoda-like roof stretched a banner proclaiming the city's memorial message, a quote from Horace: *"Extinctus Amabitur Idem."* *

A brief service was conducted by the bishop of Ohio, Charles P. McIlvaine, who read from the Episcopal burial ritual and closed with a touching prayer. Marchers in the procession passed through first, followed by the general public. At half-hour intervals guns thundered. Bands stationed on hotel balconies around the square evoked requiems. Visitors packed the streets; five hundred from Detroit were accompanied by two bands; two hundred from Meadville were headed by Captain Derrickson of the Pennsylvania Bucktail Brigade whose company had guarded the President at the White House. To give visitors the advantage local citizens held back in the early part of the day. Cleveland was the first city to erect a special building to provide the people with the best possible accommodation and at the same time honor the heroic corpse with a distinctive setting.

The drizzle that commenced about noontime turned into rain during the afternoon but attendance did not lessen; thousands were still in line when, an hour before midnight, the casket was borne to the union station in a driving downpour.

Rain had accompanied Lincoln on his prior visit. "We have been marching for two miles through rain, snow and deep mud," he had begun his remarks from the balcony of the Weddell House and complimented the people on their turnout. "Your large numbers testify that you are in earnest about something; something worth more than any one man or a thousand men or ten thousand men. You have assembled to testify to your devotion to the Constitution, to the Union, and the laws, and to the perpetual liberty of the people of this country."

* "Dead, He Will Be Loved the Same."

Then he pulled open the curtain that too often cloaks political operations. "I think the present crisis is altogether an artificial one," he told the attentive audience. *"What they fear who seek to destroy the Union is altogether artificial,"* he said and drove home the point by asking: "What is happening to hurt them? Have they not all their rights now as they ever had? Have they not the same Constitution and laws that they have lived under for seventy-odd years; and have we any power to change them? Why all this excitement? Why all these complaints?" He repeated the charge that "the crisis is altogether artificial" and asserted that it had *"no foundation in fact."*

To professional politicians Lincoln's meaning was clear. To the uninformed it came as something of a shock. The average citizen's concept of the dramatic events was that his country was breaking apart, and that Lincoln's job was to save it. Was he *too* honest in drawing aside the political curtain? Should he have told his countrymen the political facts of life? If not, what should he have said en route to Washington?

His disclosures presented a heaven-sent opportunity for political opponents to denigrate and demean him; to call him stupid, a "simple Susan," and other epithets. And some did who should have known better.

Not only in Cleveland did Lincoln reveal the facts about political manipulation; he introduced the vital topic on the first day of the journey. At Indianapolis he quoted Solomon about there being a time to keep silent when men "wrangle by the mouth" using the same words but not meaning the same thing. "Now I ask the question," he said, "where is the mysterious original right for a certain district . . . called a State, to play tyrant over all its citizens and deny the authority of everything greater than itself?"

In Columbus he made the "nothing-going-wrong" charge to those who would understand him: politicians like himself. "It is a good thing," he remarked to the Ohio Legislature gathered in joint session, "there is no more anxiety for there is nothing going wrong. It is a consoling circumstance that when we look about, there is nothing that really hurts anybody."

That morning in Pittsburgh he told the largest crowd to assemble in the Golden Triangle, motioning across the Monongahela, "Notwithstanding the troubles across the river, there is really no crisis springing from anything in the government itself. In plain words there is no crisis except an artificial one." He emphasized the statement by putting the query, "What is there now to warrant the condition of affairs presented by our friends 'over the river'?" He replied, "Take their own view of the questions involved and there is nothing left to justify the course they are pursuing. I repeat, there is no crisis; except such a one as may be gotten up at any time by turbulent men aided by designing politicians."

At Philadelphia the mayor welcomed Lincoln, mentioned the upset condition of the country, and said he hoped the new President would do something about it. Lincoln responded it was true "there is great anxiety amongst the citizens of the United States at this time" but held it a "happy circumstance" that the dissatisfied part of the nation could not point to anything in which they were actually being injured or about to be injured. He said he felt justified in concluding that "the crisis, the panic, the anxiety, of the country at this time is artificial." To tremendous applause he challenged, "If there be those who differ with me upon this subject they have not pointed out the substantial difficulty that exists."

Obviously what Lincoln meant was that the seven states breaking away from the Union did so without warrant and the reasons were contrived. In this he was not alone. "The truth is that the grievances complained of by the cotton states are either not material or remediable," declared Associate Justice of the Supreme Court John A. Campbell, Georgian by birth and Alabamian by residence,

Campbell pointed out that by the Kansas-Nebraska Act of 1854 and the Dred Scott decision three years later "every act of Congress that places any prohibition upon slavery was removed from legislative and juridical authority of the United States"; and said he knew of not a single statute on the books that a Southern man could complain of. "But this does not satisfy the politicians," remonstrated the bewhiskered justice before he went south to become Davis' assistant secretary of war. "They are brought to insurrection and disunion because a President-elect holds contrary political or social opinions."

Lincoln summarized the intransigent situation in the Second Inaugural, stating that slaves constituted "a peculiar and powerful interest" and that "this interest was, somehow, the cause of the war."

Why do men desperately crave freedom and yet enslave one another? Why do they fight to the death for liberty yet will not yield it to others? Is it because of a ruthless drive for personal power? To prove the self to oneself by dominating fellowmen?

Slavery was in the world when man put his first marks on stone and clay and parchment and likely was coeval with his emergence into human consciousness. All ancient civilizations were founded on some form of human bondage. It was a way of life for untold millenia. The glory that was Greece and the greatness that was Rome were slave-based. Kings and queens owned slaves by the thousands. Subjugation of whole races was not unusual such as Helots by the Spartans.

When the Israelites were few in number and starving they sold themselves into bondage to the Egyptians. Multiplying, they grew to be a threat and their masters attempted to slay newborn males to halt the increase. Moses was hidden in the bulrushes to save him from extinction. The Jewish God, Jehovah, retaliated by visiting plagues "to let my people go." When they got away Jehovah parted the Red Sea to aid their escape. Entering the land of milk and honey they did not forget their experience in racial antagonism and determined to exterminate the tribes residing in the Promised Land. Moses announced that the inhabitants, whose land they were taking, were to be killed off. The tribes heard of their coming extinction and devised a "wily" plan. They offered to become slaves. So the Israelites took the land and doomed the inhabitants thereof to perpetual bondage as "hewers of wood and drawers of water." (Joshua 9:1-27.)

Stripped to its roots, human slavery is nothing more than exploitation of the weak by the strong. "Slavery is grounded in the selfishness of man's nature," asserted Lincoln. He said that opposition to it was due to man's love of justice. "This is a world of compensation," he observed, "and he who would be no slave must consent to have no slave."

By the time he arrived in the world the worst practices had been deposed over most of the globe. Nowhere was it brought to such dramatic and bloody halt as in America during his presidency. For that reason Abraham Lincoln stands as the symbol of freedom the world over. The Emancipation Proclamation has been linked with the Magna Charta and the Declaration of Independence as the three greatest documents in world history relating to human liberty.

From boyhood he grew up under legislation that gave every appearance and the distinct hope that slavery was on its way out in the United States. The Constitution contained a provision abolishing the slave trade by 1808, the date coinciding with similar abolishment by the English. Slaveowners were appeased by giving them greater political power in the new nation. Their slaves were counted as three fifths of a vote, thus adding to the total representation of slave states over "free" states. (The clause was nullified by the Fourteenth Amendment.)

Where he stood on the slavery question Lincoln made clear in his first term as state legislator. He and Daniel Stone, fellow legislator from Springfield, entered a vigorous protest to the "resolutions upon the subject of domestic slavery" that were passed in the Illinois General Assembly. The protest, dated March 3, 1837, summarized his slavery position; and its style indicated it was his composition. One, "the institution of slavery is founded on both injustice and bad policy." Two, Congress had no power under the Constitution to interfere with the institution in the different states. And three, it was not always politically wise to do what was legally permissible.

The latter pertained to agitation bringing radical overtones to the word "abolition." The Lincoln-Stone protest stated that "promulgation of abolition doctrines tends rather to increase than to abate the evils." Lincoln was no abolitionist in the sense the word was then being employed, namely, immediate emancipation regardless of consequences. To that drastic course he would not subscribe although he was wholeheartedly for emancipation. "Those who deny freedom to others," he observed, "deserve it not for themselves; and under a just God cannot long retain it."

Abolitionists charged Lincoln was complacent about slavery, basing their charge on his lack of all-out support for their radical measures and giving the impression he was remiss in his obligations to the public. To put the subject into proper perspective requires reviewing Lincoln's political life from 1830 to the outbreak of rebellion, the period in which the slavery issue took hold of the populace and reached a climax.

Just as railroad, telegraph, and steam engine were remaking the economy of America, so the subject of Negro slavery was developing in American consciousness. Up to then it had not been of much public concern, North or South. The tempo of agitation increased in this thirty-year period. Southerners cried out that the drum-

beating of yankee antislavery radicals would make a bloody encounter "irrepressible." They demanded it be stopped. Horace
Greeley, founder and editor of the widely read *New York Tribune,*
took his quill in hand and charged it was just the opposite. He said
men who should have seen but would not, that slavery never left
the North alone nor even thought of so doing.

A great reform wave had inundated young America of which
antislavery was a part. The movement was aimed at improving
the lot of mankind; a compound of idealism, humanitarianism, and
liberalism, extending to religion in the form of transcendentalism
and unitarianism. It was a resurgence of the long rolling tide that
had brought to the American people the great social and political
advances embodied in the Articles of Confederation, the Declaration of Independence, and the Constitution. It was a nineteenth
century rebirth of doughty Pilgrim pioneering, Puritan dynamism,
and Cavalier spirit, all seeking to build a better way of life.

Now more people were being touched more deeply than ever
before by agitation on public education, freedom of speech, freedom
of religious worship, temperance, women's rights, penal reforms,
mental hospitals, and other programs of social betterment including
freedom for bondsmen. The widespread revival, aided by economic
and technological factors, was an explosion of human yearning, a
renaissance typically American in its manifestations—manifestations which have not, even to this day, run their course.

Too many searchers for causes of the Civil War do not take into
account that the great conflagration could hardly have been ignited
by rational reasons. The reasons were rational enough but the
people's reactions thereto were highly emotional and the power so
generated could not be contained within reasonable bounds. Something had to give. Until that fundamental fact is appreciated, one
gropes in a twilight of confusion trying to comprehend the cata-
clysmic conflict. Those who indulge in wordy histrionics and call

it a "needless" war overlook that man does not live by reason
alone.

When Lincoln reached Washington with his family on December
2, 1847, he found, in contrast to his own rather uneventful campaign, that at the federal level abolition of slavery was a growing
political concern. In his Seventh Congressional District the antislavery vote had not been of consequence. His constituents were
for the most part, like himself, conservative Whigs of southern
birth or antecedents.

Lincoln's voting record in the Thirtieth Congress revealed a
puzzling pattern. He voted favorably on all antislavery petitions
from citizens but opposed abolitionist bills and resolutions, then
voted many times in favor of the Wilmot Proviso. The latter, tacked
onto money bills by David Wilmot of Pennsylvania, provided that
"neither slavery nor involutary servitude shall ever exist in ter-
ritories acquired by means of the money appropriated." On the
subject of slavery itself Lincoln said nothing; his speeches were on
different topics. Then in the second session (1849) he burst out un-
expectedly with an amendment to a resolution before the House
abolishing the slave trade in the District of Columbia. Debate
waxed loud and prolonged (slave pens were visible from government offices) but both the amendment and resolution failed to pass.

The Whig party had taken no official stand on slavery for the
plain reason it was a national party with members South and
North. (Three fourths of the slaves were said to be owned by
Whigs.) Though untrammeled by party policy Lincoln was subject to the will of the voters. Personally he held that human servitude was a great moral wrong. Thus he was caught between a
moral principle and the constituents of his district. The dilemma
was also within himself (as with all southerners) for he too was

of the South. He was a victim of the age-old quandary that besets mankind with never a clear solution: love versus duty.

Which way should he turn? To the stern duty of moral right and his own conscience? Or to the people whom he represented? How resolve the question? Temporarily he was saved by Congress putting through the 1850 Compromise. This appeared to abate the vexing issue. The great Henry Clay, Lincoln's political hero and like himself a Whig and a Kentuckian, had done it again.

Again the geographical limitation was fixed beyond which slavery could not go. For thirty years, from 1820 to 1850, the two Missouri Compromises had halted the spread of slavery by federal legislation. Slavery appeared to be on the way out for climatic and economic reasons also. Quite naturally Lincoln, along with many others in public and private life, rested in the belief that slavery was, as he often said, "in the course of ultimate extinction."

Returning from Washington in the summer of 1849 he seemed to be at the end of his political career. His position on the Mexican War contributed largely to his district's going over to the opposition (Herndon had warned him of the consequences), and he had lost out as commissioner of the General Land Office. To obtain that appointment he had made determined efforts, expecting it in recognition of his effective campaigning in behalf of the Whig presidential candidate, General Zachary Taylor. "Old Zach" got elected but Lincoln came away empty-handed, his outspokenness on the "spots" still hurting him. A few months later he was offered the secretaryship and then the governorship of Oregon Territory; both of which he declined.

He resumed law practice, devoting himself to the Eighth Judicial Circuit and higher court work, almost abandoning politics, rebuilding the income he had lost during his political service. At this juncture of his life, from fortieth to forty-fifth year, Lincoln appeared little different from a thousand other small-town lawyers who enter politics and alternate with law as the chips may fall; a way of life that combines good living with an ever-widening circle of friends. He was typical too of the many Americans of that day born in humble circumstances, nurtured in sturdy frontier life, making their way through initiative and force of character. He gave little hint of the greatness to come. But when seen in retrospect the solid foundation he built in this formative period bears significance.

Applying himself to his practice he became a lawyer's lawyer, the local attorney preparing the case and calling upon him as trial counselor when court convened in town. Lincoln knew the court, and juries liked him. His practice embraced all legal categories among which must be noticed two cases involving slaves. Early in his legal career (1841) he was able to set free a slave girl named Nance, the case turning on the fact that the sale was illegal in Illinois. The other case came after his election to Congress. Acting for a slaveowner he sought to send back south a slave family brought to Illinois as seasonal workers. Lincoln presented good legal grounds for his client but lost the case, probably for reasons of public policy. The slave family was set free. The disgruntled slaveowner skipped town and Lincoln was stuck for his fee. The case is seldom mentioned by guardians of the Lincoln legend; and when it is, is smoothed over by platitudes. These cases are cited to indicate that the great moral, political, and humanistic elements of human slavery had not yet taken hold of American hearts. Like most attorneys Lincoln accepted cases as they came along, and since slavery was part and parcel of everyday life it was all in a day's work.

A drastic change occurred in 1854. The full realization that *human* slavery was now *legal* in all of *free* America hit him, and the nation, with passage of the Kansas-Nebraska Act. Designed to create two new states out of Indian territory that stood in the way of building a transcontinental railroad, the act repealed the Missouri Compromise. The repeal provision had been inserted in the bill to secure southern votes necessary for passage. Explained Lincoln in his detailed autobiography using the third person: "In 1854, his profession had almost superseded the thought of politics in his mind when the repeal of the Missouri Compromise aroused him as never before." The nation was roused likewise.

Anti-Nebraska groups sprang up in every part of the North and in the next two years these spontaneous gatherings coalesced into a national political party, adopting the name Republican. The coalition was cemented not only by the Supreme Court's Dred Scott decision in 1856 that a Negro had no human rights and which also nullified the Missouri Compromise thus making slavery operable nationally but also by the strife in "bleeding Kansas" incited by the doctrine of "popular sovereignty"; by John Brown's raid at Harper's Ferry; by *Uncle Tom's Cabin* and *The Impending Crisis*, two incendiary books read by millions; and by other incidents that fanned the fire of public indignation.

"We find ourselves," Lincoln reminded a young men's Lyceum in Springfield, "under the government of political institutions conducing more essentially to the ends of civil and religious liberty than any of which the history of former centuries tells us." All this was bequeathed us, he pointed out; a legacy of hardy, brave, and patriotic ancestors. "The task of gratitude to our fathers, justice to ourselves, duty to posterity, and love for our species in general, requires us faithfully to perform."

So Lincoln took to the hustings and there followed his famous polemics: the "House Divided" Speech, the so-called "Lost Speech," the address at Cooper Union, those made on the New England tour, and the memorable debates with Senator Douglas. A new Lincoln emerged. From a rudderless small-town lawyer and self-seeking politician arose a dedicated American, infused with ardor and purpose that metamorphosed him into The Man Everybody Knows. Evidence of greatness appeared. Twice defeated for senator, his purposes were now unflinchable. The moral goal of his political course was unshakable. The people were like-minded.

It was the unity of moral purpose between Lincoln and the majority of the American people that the greatness of both took substance and sanctified The War That Unified the Nation. For, as he so ably articulated the thoughts of his fellow countrymen, "In giving freedom to the slave we assure freedom to the free; honored alike in what we give and what we receive."

14

SHOWERS fell during the run from Cleveland to Columbus, sometimes a heavy cascade. As with their preceding compatriots Ohioans were not deterred by the spring rain and they ribboned the track with lanterns and torches. Toward morning the rain abated and a warm sun pushed through scurrying clouds, caressing the lilac bushes blooming in dooryards. Five miles above Columbus an aged woman at trackside held in one hand a sable scarf and in the other a freshly picked bouquet of wild flowers that she stretched imploringly toward the moving train.

218

Ohio's capital city was entered at half after seven. The train halted in union depot so that the Lincoln car lay across High Street and the casket could be removed directly to the hearse. To get a better view of the proceedings women and children as well as men crawled under the cars, remaining there watching until warned by police to save their lives.

Up High to Broad and around the business district, the catafalque was escorted by an imposing procession of civic and military organizations. Passing Soldier's Home it was sprinkled with flowers by the invalid and crippled veterans, many on crutches, who had strewn the street with lilacs. The air was filled with the fragrance of lavender blossoms.*

The procession halted at the capitol's west entrance. Ohio's Eighty-eighth Volunteer Infantry, the honor escort, formed facing lines from street into rotunda. Into the circular chamber the veteran sergeants from Washington carried the casket to a mound of green moss dotted with white flowers atop a platform ascended by five steps. At the corners of the steps emblematical amaranth and stately justitia reached to the top of the bier and between them vases of forget-me-nots, lilacs, roses, violets, and honeysuckle alternated with wreaths of ivy and laurel.

The base of the rotunda was margined in flowers; three wall panels contained collections of war-torn battle flags, draped in black, mute testimony of Ohio's patriotic dead. The fourth panel held William H. Powell's huge canvas, "Perry's Victory on Lake Erie." ** From the lofty dome columns of sunlight streamed down-

---

* In his annual lecture on Lincoln Walt Whitman would say: "I remember the season being advanced and there were many lilacs in full bloom. By one of those caprices that enter and give tinge to events without being at all a part of them, I find myself always reminded of the great tragedy of that day by the sight and odor of these blossoms." As everyone knows, Whitman wrote "When Lilacs Last in the Doorway Bloom'd" which together with his "O Captain! My Captain!" rank as the classic expressions of the Lincoln tragedy.

** Now in the U. S. Capitol, east stairway, Senate wing.

ward on the historic scene, etching it with unforgettable clarity.

The public approached the carpeted platform four abreast and divided as they mounted the steps. From half after nine in the morning until sunset they honored the first President to be born west of the Appalachians; one who was like themselves, a prairie pioneer; who had shaken their hands and returned their greetings in the same place four years before. Outside on the east terrace in front of closed doors commemorative ceremonies were conducted beginning at three o'clock. An eloquent panegyric was delivered by the state senator from Chillicothe; familiar hymns were sung; eminent ministers uttered touching prayers; and an augmented choir rendered Bryant's "Ode on the Burial of Abraham Lincoln." * At six o'clock the cortege moved to the Great Central Railway Station and in the long shadows of a setting sun Abraham Lincoln passed forever from the capital city of the Buckeye State.

The flowers that adorned casket and bier were sold at auction at the request of the donors, the Cincinnati Horticultural Society. Funds so collected were turned over to the Ladies Aid Society for distribution to needy families of soldiers and sailors. To keep the memorial open for those who had been unable to get in, city authorities appealed for replacement flowers and Columbians responded nobly from their vernal gardens.

"This funeral journey will form one of the most intensely impressive chapters of the history which some future Macaulay will write of the momentous events through which our nation is now passing," commented the *Ohio State Journal*, claiming it would stand among other observances of the death of a statesman "as Bunker Hill monument would among the unpretending markers of a country churchyard."

The homeward route from Columbus lay directly westward to

* This was the composition read Tuesday in Union Square, New York. See the close of Chap. 8.

Indianapolis, by-passing Pittsburgh and Cincinnati which had been visited on the inaugural route, shortening the trip by some two hundred miles. Again the all-night trek commenced in a downpour the constant repetition of which made it seem like a cue in a stage play. Toward midnight the rain slackened, the sky cleared, and stars stippled the heavens the rest of the way to Indiana's capital. Whether starlight or showers, the night was filled with the sights and sounds of a martyred hero moving toward apotheosis. At the state line the cortege passed through an evergreen arch.

Arches dotted the route through the Hoosier State. The first town reached, Richmond, presented a handsome one built by the Airline Railroad which crossed at this point. Atop the arch a woman attired as Liberty knelt beside a coffin attended by a boy soldier and sailor. Locomotive headlights and great fires lighted the somber scene. Much in evidence were the broad-brimmed hats and dark bonnets of Quakers among a concourse of fifteen thousand persons, the total greater than the town's population. Proportionately, the Society of Friends were more numerous here than in Philadelphia. Several ladies came forward bearing wreaths; one for son William was inscribed, "Like the early morning flower, he was taken from our midst." Indiana's intrepid war governor, Oliver P. Morton, and the Indiana escort committee, boarded the cars. The time was early Sunday morning, beginning the tenth day of travel.

The little town on the western edge of the county, Dublin, was passed at 4:20 A.M. The loyal community had dressed its depot with portraits of Lincoln, Grant, Sherman, Sheridan, and Morton and had built a neat arch over the track. Dublin was also a Quaker village although there was little outward evidence. What was in their hearts was indicated by the large proportion of menfolk they had sent to help the Union effort despite their opposition to war.

The scheduled demonstrations at Indianapolis had to be canceled upon arrival because of the heavy downpour, disappointing alike the City Councils and trainloads of mourners that had come from Cincinnati, Louisville, Covington, and including the governor of Kentucky. Instead all went to church and listened to sermons the clergy had prepared for the occasion.

In union station the casket was transferred to the special conveyance drawn by eight white horses. Six of the horses and the driver, Elijah Hedges, had taken Lincoln through shouting throngs on his inaugural visit. Now a band discoursed "Lincoln's Funeral March." * From depot to State House between solid lines of soldiers standing at present arms the abbreviated procession marched up Illinois Street to Washington and west on Washington to State House Square, passing under evergreen arches at each corner. Sidewalks, housetops, windows at all levels were choked with spectators despite the deluge. Bringing up the rear a rain-soaked group of Negro Masons in full regalia carried banners that read: "Lincoln, Martyr of Liberty"; "He Lives in Our Memories"; "Colored Men, Always Loyal!" and an enlarged facsimile of the Emancipation Proclamation.

From Washington Street the cortege entered the capitol through a forty-foot-long structure, the carriageway up the center flanked by six-foot aisles. The remains were deposited in capitol hall on a canopied catafalque banked with flowers and wreaths. At the head of the casket on a draped pedestal stood a marble bust of the deceased, the brow encircled by a laurel wreath.

Five thousand Sunday school children passed the bier first. Then all day until ten in the evening a steady stream flowed by at better than a hundred and fifty persons per minute; altogether a hundred thousand were estimated by police to have paid their final respects

* Composed by Charles Hess of Cincinnati and presented for the first time.

to the embalmed Hoosier boy on this sabbath. Indiana had never seen such a sight.

The general public was accorded all the time possible; there were no memorial exercises. After the closing hour visiting dignitaries, prominent citizens, and other official personages were given a special viewing. Then through double lines of military standing at salute, the mortal coil was returned to the train, the march illuminated by torchbearers. Flowers from casket and dais were collected by the state librarian for preservation. The other memorials were left intact for thirty days to accommodate the public unable to attend the lying-in-state.

The train left at midnight, and by the same railroad line, the Lafayette and Indianapolis, over which he had traveled as President-elect on the way to Washington. On that occasion, instead of going into union station, the inaugural special had halted where the Lafayette tracks crossed Washington Street. Here Lincoln had been greeted by the governor and an ebullient throng of well-wishers. The governor delivered a speech of welcome to which Lincoln responded at once from the rear platform of the train.

His response (impromptu as far as can be determined) represented his first extended remarks since leaving Springfield. As such they warranted special attention and careful evaluation but received neither. The press paid scant heed, concentrating instead on the address from the Bates House balcony given immediately upon his arrival there. The latter has become known as the Indianapolis speech; yet the former was so finely phrased as to seem prepared; and so sound in principles enunciated as to stand for American political doctrine. That the remarks offered a master key to Lincoln's political thinking has almost escaped notice.

Expressing thanks for the magnificent reception Lincoln said that he could not take to himself any share of the compliment thus paid "more than that which pertains to a *mere instrument,* an *accidental instrument,* perhaps I should say, of a great cause." His reliance, he said, would be placed upon them, the people of the United States, in the many trying positions in which he would be placed. "I wish you to remember now and forever," he emphasized, "that it is your business and not mine that if the union of these States and the liberties of this people shall be lost; that it is but little to any one man of fifty-two years of age but a great deal to the thirty millions of people who inhabit these United States. . . . I, as already intimated," he repeated, "am but an *accidental instrument,* temporary, and to serve but a limited time."

Indianapolis was first to hear him state this concept of himself and his situation, and which he would reiterate with variations throughout the journey, saying at Lawrenceburg, "I have been selected to fill an important office for a brief while and am now in your eyes invested with an influence that will soon pass away"; to the legislature at Columbus, "I cannot but know what you all know, that, without a name, perhaps without a reason why I should have a name, there has fallen upon me a task such as did not rest even upon the Father of his country"; at Cleveland, "Do I desire that you should think this extreme earnestness is about me? . . . But I know it is paid to something more than to any one man or any thousand or ten thousand men"; at Albany, "It is much more gratifying to me that this reception has been given to me as the representative of a free people than it could possibly be if tendered as evidence of devotion to me"; at Philadelphia, "The reception you have given tonight is not to me, the man, the individual, but to the man who temporarily represents the majesty of the nation"; and in the last speech before reaching Washington, to the Pennsylvania Legislature, referring to the flag-raising at Independence Hall that morning, "In the whole transaction I was in the hands of the people who arranged it, and if I can have the same generous co-operation of the people of this nation, I think the flag of our country may yet be kept flying gloriously."

Did Lincoln mean he was an instrument of the American body politic? He certainly was such an instrument as is every President. Did he mean he was an instrument of the great cause then occupying the forefront of American attention, human slavery? He could have meant that too. Both were included in his whole meaning although neither reached the heights to which he projected his position and his responsibility.

Consider first what he said at the beginning of the journey, his initial communication to the people following nine months of complete silence, telling his neighbors gathered in the winter rain to see him off, "Without the assistance of that Divine Being who ever attended him [George Washington], I cannot succeed. With that assistance, I cannot fail. To His care commending you as I hope in your prayers you will commend me, I bid you an affectionate farewell."

Again and again on the way to Washington he emphasized that reliance on the divine will represented the nation's real strength, that *he and the American people were instruments of the God of history.* Looking across the Ohio River to his native Kentucky, he told the Cincinnati audience that "under the Providence of God, *who has never deserted us,* we shall again be brethren, forgetting all parties, ignoring all parties"; and in Columbus that "all we want is time, patience, and a reliance *on that God who has never forsaken his people.*" At Albany he exhorted, "I still have confidence that the Almighty, the Maker of the Universe, will, *through the instrumentality of this great and intelligent people,* bring us through this as He has through all the other difficulties in our country." At Trenton, "I shall be most happy indeed *if I shall be an humble instrument in the hands of the Almighty.*"

These concepts one sees developed in his state papers, in Thanksgiving Day proclamations, inaugural addresses, messages to Congress, and in personal letters. His writings reveal that he viewed himself as having been *accidentally* taken from among the plain people to lead them in their hour of great peril; that *the American nation was God's instrument,* "the last best hope of earth" in the governance of mankind. He saw the fratricide as a testing whether "that nation or any nation so conceived and so dedicated can long endure." He realized he was in the grip of events even as were the nation and the lowliest private in the ranks.

He wrote Mrs. Eliza Gurney that "we hoped for a happy termination of this terrible war long before this; God knows best and has ruled otherwise. The purposes of the Almighty are perfect and must prevail, though we erring mortals may fail to accurately perceive them in advance." To a delegation of Friends, who called upon him in June of 1862 urging him to take action in freeing the slaves and that by doing so he would secure the blessing of God, Lincoln responded he was deeply sensible of his need of divine help and sometimes thought he might be an instrument in God's hand of accomplishing a great work, and that he was certainly not unwilling to be. "Perhaps, however," he said, "God's way of accomplishing the end might be different from yours."

The same course was urged upon him a few months later by a delegation from Chicago of various religious denominations who presented a memorial indicating they represented the Divine Will. "I hope it will not be irreverent," the President replied, "for me to say that if it is probable that God would reveal his will to others on a point so closely connected with my duty, it might be supposed he would reveal it directly to me." He told them that it was his earnest desire to know the will of Providence in the matter. "And if I can learn what it is, I will do it!" he concluded.

In Lincoln's time the "age of faith" was passing from exclusive control of religious rulers into the hands of the citizenry. The principle of consent of the governed inaugurated in the Declaration of Independence and made operational in the Constitution, had become firmly established. No longer did religion exert political dominion over the people as it had for many decades. Church and state were separated in the New World. Sovereign power resided in the electorate regardless of sectarian faith, national origin, or political sentiment. This was the great fact initiated by the American Revolution for all the people of the world.

Lincoln appreciated that the Declaration was more than a mere manifesto of colonial revolt. He recognized it was the foundation stone of universal liberty. The inalienable rights spoken of in the Declaration were not parochial or national; they were international in scope. "This was their majestic interpretation of the economy of our universe," he told a Lewistown (Ill.) audience in the campaign of 1858, referring to the Founders of the Republic. "This was their lofty, wise and noble understanding of the justice of the Creator to His creatures. . . . In their enlightened belief, nothing stamped with the Divine image and likeness was sent into the world to be trodden on, and degraded, and imbruted by its fellows. . . . You may do anything with me you choose, if you will but heed those sacred principles. . . . Do not destroy that immortal emblem of Humanity—the Declaration of American Independence."

Lincoln's moral resolutions combined with his spiritual awareness of the higher meaning of the fraternal struggle made him the almost perfect model of political ruler. His character brought together the treasures of a free civilization and spiritual insight, enabling him to serve his countrymen without embarrassing self-righteous stances. He could wield his tremendous power without being blinded by the certain traps of self-prestige into which so many leaders fall. His far-seeing perceptions laid a sound basis for his compassion, as are seen in his "with malice toward none; with charity for all"; and his response to Negroes who knelt to him in

Richmond. "Don't kneel to me," he told them sternly, "I am but God's humble instrument."

His high-minded interpretation of American goals and his tough-minded regard for statutes in force have caused him to be characterized as "a practical mystic," "the theologian of democracy," "the spiritual center of the Republic"; and his sublime faith in the nation, "the Union as religious mysticism." His philosophy of government presumed a correlation of worldly counterparts to supernatural principles, and he looked for applications of godly precepts to human endeavors. His strong feeling of law and order evolved from his legal training, and his close acquaintance with the Bible moved him to find correlations therein.

"It is said to be one of the admonitions of the Lord, 'As your Father in Heaven is perfect, be ye also perfect,'" he told an immense Saturday evening audience in Chicago during his senatorial campaign, saying it was set up as a standard and he who did most toward reaching it attained the highest degree of moral perfection. "So I say in relation to the principle that all men are created equal," he explained, "let it be as nearly reached as we can."

Politics deals with the proximate ends of human life, religion with the ultimate ends. The difference between the now and the hereafter had led to separation of the powers of the ancient priest-king rule, a separation implemented by the Founding Fathers based on the needs of the new nation. The impact of the early patriots upon Lincoln and the people of his time was much greater than it is upon the enormously expanded and greatly diluted America of today.

Lincoln could almost reach out and touch the heroes of the Revolution. Only a generation before he entered the world thirteen of the British North American colonies had declared themselves an American Confederation; and in his seventeenth year the second and third Presidents, John Adams and Thomas Jefferson, died. His political hero, Henry Clay of Kentucky, known as "gallant Harry of the West," was in Congress when he was. Through Lincoln's veins flowed strains of New England Puritans, middle state Quakers, Virginia planters, Kentucky settlers. Quickened among the knobs of Muldraugh's Hill in northern Kentucky, he grew to adolescence in the forests of southern Indiana and lived his manhood on the prairies of central Illinois; a typical American "out of the wilderness."

He had in himself the driving power of his forebears, whose moral and spiritual forces have provided such a pervasive factor in American life as to have become characterized as the American ethic, sometimes called the Protestant ethic.* Actually it is the spirit of early Americans gone national; a compound of diligence, frugality, temperance, reverence for law, and that extra touch of vitality termed "Yankee push." The first comers to bleak northern coasts regarded virtue as the basis of prosperity. Jefferson and his Virginians held that property was the foundation of virtue. Fusion of the two forces over the decades generated the greatest driving power the world has yet seen, crystallizing the national character of America and giving it the messianic mold that continues to this day.

Whether American spiritual heritage is traced through the first settlers of Massachusetts, the Cavaliers of Virginia, Dutch of New York, Quakers of Pennsylvania, Swedes of New Jersey, Germans of North Carolina, Huguenots of South Carolina, French and Irish of Louisiana, Welsh and Scots-Irish of the Appalachian frontier, or the English of the whole Atlantic seaboard; whether America is represented as a new start for mankind, an escape from the evils of the Old World or as God's promised land, the character of the

* "The work of the Plymouth emigrants was the glory of their age," Lincoln wrote Joseph H. Choate. "While we reverence their memory, let us not forget how vastly greater is our opportunity."

United States was foreordained in the concepts of the early Anglo-Saxon and Teutonic settlers, concepts that took firm root in the first two centuries and spread westward with migration.

And not to be overlooked in realizing the separateness of America from European ancestry is the softening of religious and racial bigotry. Every religious sect operating in the American Republic has had to broaden its parochialism and ameliorate its arrogant assumptions. All are welcome here. Every ethnic strain or color of skin living in the fifty states of the Union has had to recognize that there is no such thing as a master race. Pluralism is the way of American life. Yet the original drive for achievement continues.

Puritans deemed their daily chores to be part of their Christian discipline; they did not work merely for selfish gain but were doing the Lord's work. So they threw themselves into building God's community in the land of promise. The success attending their everyday tasks was divine grace made evident, they believed. Accumulation of goods and distinctions of station were signs of the Lord's favor. Within this climate of belief each event had meaning for the divine purpose yet at the same time was held in place by the weight of the universe.

Puritan drive for achievement also embraced the belief they were a chosen people. Like the Hebrews of antiquity they considered they had been entrusted by God to exemplify right living. Theirs was a holy experiment. Biblical texts set forth the guidelines. To be sure, the precepts of Holy Writ had been given more than two thousand years before to a small Semitic tribe wandering among barren desert hills. The Puritans deliberated. Was he more absent from men now than then? Were the olden Hebrews the *only* people to whom God spoke? Who would carry out his teachings and follow in his footsteps?

The Puritans would. They would establish a new way of life in a covenant with the Lord. Though his purposes might not be known in detail, they were willing to work them out as they must be worked out in the mundane world. So they founded a community of the Lord in the New World and their religious concepts gradually developed new governing techniques and better ways of living. The flowering of Puritan and Pilgrim dreams is the America of today.

Recognition of the primary position of religious belief as the great motivating force of that centennium—religious duty then being man's *first* obligation—clarifies the motivations behind early American colonization. The principal concern was "neither the rate of interest nor discovery of gold but the will of God." This is not to say that economic, political, and personal (such as a new start) factors did not enter into men's calculations. Altogether the first century of North American settlement represented the largest religious migration known to history.*

Out of the give and take of the divergent groups colonizing the New World has blossomed the world's most powerful nation of free people. America's pluralistic society—*e pluribus unum*—forms the strangest people ever to achieve great power. Not to conquer other lands or other peoples, not to rule as masters, but to make the world a better place for all men to live in peace with justice: this is the American ideal.

That the United States was ordained by God to perform a mission to mankind inspired A. Lincoln as it did his Puritan, Quaker, and

* Intense religious devotion marked *all* early groups of settlers—we would call it intolerance. Separation of church and state was *not* part of the general thinking. This came as an American achievement, and was brought about by the simple necessity of getting along with one another on a reasonable basis. Though the apparent motive for colonization might be economic such as with the first English settlement at Jamestown, the Virginia Company had been authorized by the king to establish the Church of England; Maryland to establish the Roman Catholic Church; Bay State colonizers (Puritans) to practice their "purified" form of the established church; and Pilgrims to worship as Separatists, free from orthodoxy.

Deistic forebears. "Understanding the spirit of our institutions to aim at the elevation of men, I am opposed to whatever tends to degrade them," he asserted; and declared that "nowhere in the world is presented a government of such liberty and equality."

After the fatal Battle of Second Bull Run when, for the third successive time, his generals had failed him and his spirits were so low Attorney General Bates noted in his diary that Lincoln "seemed wrung by the bitterest anguish and felt almost ready to hang himself," he endeavored to set his thinking straight on the inexorable march of events. Retiring within himself, he wrote a memorandum which his secretaries found among his papers after his death. They noted it was not written "to be seen of men" and titled the fragment "Meditation on the Divine Will."

"The will of God prevails," Lincoln began. "In great contests each party claims to act in accordance with the will of God. Both *may* be, and one *must* be, wrong. God cannot be *for,* and *against,* the same thing at the same time. In the present Civil War it is quite possible that God's purpose is something different from the purpose of either party—and yet the human instrumentalities, working just as they do, are of the best adaptation to effect His purpose. I am almost ready to say this is probably true—that God wills this contest, and wills it shall not end yet. By his mere quiet power on the minds of the now contestants, He could have either *saved* or *destroyed* the Union without human contest. Yet the contest began. And having begun, He could give the final victory to either side any day. Yet the contest proceeds." There the fragment ends disclosing an anguished soul endeavoring to bring itself into closer communion with its Maker and trying to understand his purposes amid the fury of the storm.

PART V

THE FIRST AMERICAN

15

THE return route from Indianapolis retraced the inaugural route only to Lafayette and then instead of proceeding westward to Springfield detoured north to Chicago. All night the line was alive with people; and it seemed the entire countryside had converged on the railroad. The train moved over the Louisville, New Albany and Chicago Railroad from Lafayette to Michigan City; west over the Michigan Central to Kensington, Illinois; and north over the Illinois Central tracks into the bursting metropolis.

An immense throng greeted the brief halt at Lafayette where

the locomotives were changed. This was at half past three Monday
morning. At eight o'clock the travelers were breakfasted at
Michigan City. Here occurred an impressive reception.

The track was spanned with a succession of arches spiraled in
black and white entwined with evergreens and spring blossoms. The
arches were adorned with portraits of the late President and
placards of mottoes: "The purposes of the Almighty are perfect
and must prevail"; "With tears we resign thee to God and History";
and others. Sixteen maidens in white shirtwaists and black skirts
assembled on a platform sang hymns. Another thirty-six attired
in all-white with black scarves held small national flags and
escorted a Liberty in Mourning. Still another group, headed by the
niece of Schuyler Colfax, entered the car and deposited wreaths.
Colfax himself, who was speaker of the House of Representatives
and whose home was in South Bend, boarded the train with the
Chicago escort committee of one hundred.

A gifted orator, he had delivered a stirring memorial address the
previous afternoon in Chicago's Bryan Hall. At its conclusion the
assemblage adopted a resolution and appointed a committee to
establish a monument in honor of the deceased. The monument was
to be called *The Lincoln Institute* and would function in the manner
of New York's Cooper Union; would contain a hall to accommodate
large gatherings; would have an Emancipation Hall for statuary
and portraits of patriots who had distinguished themselves in the
battle for freedom, including of course, the Great Emancipator; and
would also provide an art gallery, an art school, free library, and
other benevolent and cultural activities. The proposal was eminently
worthy of its namesake.

Michigan City was left at half past eight and downtown Chicago
reached at eleven o'clock, in accordance with the Washington
schedule. Instead of entering the passenger terminal at Water Street

near the Chicago River, however, the train halted about a mile
south where the present passenger station stands at Twelfth Street
and Park Place. The latter street marks the southern boundary
of the parkland that graces Michigan Avenue, known then as Lake
Park, today renamed to honor Illinois' other notable contribution
to the war that preserved the union, General Grant. A special
platform built at trackside received the cortege. The Veteran
Reserve Corps sergeants transported the remains to a triple archway erected over Park Place and rested the casket on a velvet-
covered dais under the main arch.

Chicago's obsequies were the most unique of the journey: no
speeches, no prayers, no eulogies, no talk of any kind. A band
evoked "The Lincoln Requiem" composed for the occasion by the
band leader. Thirty-six high school girls stepped around the bier
depositing an immortelle, one for each state. They were attired in
flowing white robes and wore black velvet wreaths over their
brows. Some had fair ringlets hanging loosely to neckline and
others had neat plaits touching the shoulders. Each was the picture
of love and purity.

The last wreath placed, the band continued the requiem, a handsome hearse was brought forward, the casket installed, and a
procession formed into line. Up Michigan Avenue the column
marched, over Lake to Clark Street, down Clark to the Courthouse.
Here a canopied dais received the illustrious remains. Marchers continued through the courthouse in the order of march. The casket,
inadvertently, was not opened and the escort could only glance at
the flag-draped, silver-trimmed black box, observe the surrounding
decorations of mourning, and move on to the beat of muted drums.

Just before the public was admitted at five o'clock, however,
embalmer and undertaker opened the lid and exposed the features
so well-known to these Westerners. "Illinois clasps to her bosom her
slain and glorious son," proclaimed the banner spread over the

doorway through which he had been borne. And over the inside the banner read, "He left sustained by our prayers; He returns embalmed in our tears."

The evening hours heard requiems by soloists and by groups, among them: "I Yield My Spirit"; "He That Endureth to the End Shall Be Saved"; "Happy and Blest"; and an original composition, "Farewell, Father, Friend, and Guardian," the words by L. M. Dawes, the music by George F. Root, both of Chicago. At midnight German singing societies assembled to chant their impressive choruses.

The drizzling rain that commenced at nine o'clock did not lessen the rate of passage through the courthouse. All Monday afternoon and evening, all day Tuesday and Tuesday evening until eight, the great Northwest paid tribute to the departed leader. Their unremitting and overwhelming presence confirmed their deep feeling: "Let the Heavens Be Hung in Black!"

In point of numbers Chicago could not compare with its eastern counterpart. But it did take credit for the fact that although New York and adjacent communities aggregated one and a half million people, the eastern turnout, Chicagoans claimed, was only one quarter as many as turned out in the Windy City in proportion to total number of inhabitants. The figures were not offered in a spirit of boasting—"which the solemnity of the occasion itself forbids"— but to show that in behalf of Illinois' noblest son, his own metropolis had, as he might have anticipated, surpassed all others in proof of devotion; a devotion that was even greater in death than in life.

Indeed the importance of the tremendous turnouts along the way was not merely in the numbers of spectators, or in the magnificent pageantry, or in the lengthy processions, but in the all-pervading sorrow of the masses, noted the *Chicago Tribune* and exclaimed, "Thank God, He endowed Americans with hearts alive for such a man as Abraham Lincoln. 'Behold how they loved him'!"

If the deceased ever had thoughts of public honor after he passed from earth, the *Tribune* went on to say, he never would have dreamed of such precious memories as these; for he had "conquered the hearts of his countrymen, and that priceless possession is assured him in all coming ages by the loving testimonials which attend his funeral."

Escorting the hearse to the Chicago, Alton and St. Louis Railway station were a thousand torchbearers, the Chicago Common Council acting as pallbearers, and an array of military organizations headed by General Hooker. At 9:30 P.M. to melodies chanted by singing societies, the special train moved away from the depot toward its final destination. This was the last lap of railroad travel and the twelfth day of the trip.

"Night was forgotten by the people in their anxiety to show all possible respect for him whom they were expecting," noted General Townsend in his report. "Bonfires and torches threw their uncertain light upon the emblems of mourning which were destined to stand in their places for weeks to come."

This was Lincoln land. This was the country he knew and these were the places he had trod; from the sands of Lake Michigan to the banks of the Ohio River, from Alton and Quincy to Danville and Charleston and Shawneetown, from Cairo to Jonesboro to Springfield to Galena, this was home territory. The fertile black loam and waving grasses, the trees along creeks and rivers, the Indians and wandering game and empty spaces were now changing to fat farms, thriving villages, busy cities. And here too were the old familiar Eighth Judicial Circuit, the village of New Salem, the house at Eighth and Jackson Streets; his wife, sons, and neighbors —"Here I have lived a quarter of a century and have passed from a young man to an old man. . . . To this place and to the kindness of these people I owe everything."

Scarcely three miles from Chicago's downtown depot, "back o' the yards," demonstrations began again. Summit, Willow Springs, Lemont, and at Lockport a banner across the station that struck the heart with the invitation, "Come home." Rain commenced at Joliet and a mixed chorus sang "There Is Rest for Thee in Heaven." Elwood, Wilmington, Gardner, and then Dwight where the Prince of Wales had been entertained. Odell, Pontiac, Chenoa, and Towanda, highest point between Chicago and St. Louis. Then Bloomington where he had uttered the "Lost Speech"—lost because he held the audience so spellbound no one thought to report what he said—the embellished archway admonishing, "Go to thy rest." Shirley, McLean, Atlanta, and then the town of Lincoln was entered at seven o'clock in bright daylight. White-dressed ladies voiced a requiem in memory of their neighbor who, when asked if the town had been named for him, replied, "Well, it was named after I was."

Beginning at Joliet arches frequently spanned the track inscribed with mottoes and heartfelt sentiments. At Williamsville, twelve miles from Springfield, the archway proclaimed a fitting summation of Lincoln's career: "He has fulfilled his mission."

Springfield was entered at 8:40 A.M. This was only forty minutes later than the time specified in the Washington schedule, an unusual record considering the twelve days of continual travel covering 1,654 miles without accident or untoward incident.* Into the hometown slowly steamed the nigrescent train between two solid lanes of neighbors, friends, associates, and relatives who had known him since he was a country lad. They had come to honor their distinguished friend who had been immolated for having made freedom a reality. He was home again and this was journey's end.

To enumerate the demonstrations of affection in Springfield would be to repeat what has been told and retold in preceding

* Itinerary and mileage detailed in appendix.

pages. Yet not to do so would make it appear they were not worth
telling. Springfield's ceremonies had been planned with care and
were carried out in an able manner. "The eyes of the whole nation,
which has been watching the grief-burdened cortege as it passes
from city to city, will soon be turned upon us," the *Illinois State
Journal* reminded its readers a week before the event and urged
that all possible efforts be exerted to secure its success, if for no
other reason than as a mark of respect for their returning neighbor.
The committee on arrangements published notices of how to care
for the visitors. "It is of the utmost importance that all our citizens
throw open their homes and exercise the most liberal hospitality
to strangers." The committee called upon farmers of the vicinity to
bring in provisions and quantities of "good dry straw" to be sold
at the marketplace and on the day of the burial to bring cooked
edibles to be sold from their wagons. The advice was well given.
"The city is so crowded," a newsman telegraphed the first day,
"that it is impossible to procure lodging in a bar-room or on a pool-
table." Not much sleeping was done the night the remains were
placed on view in the State House.* The community had become
patriarchal ground.

To cover expenses attendant upon the obsequies the Springfield
City Council appropriated twenty thousand dollars. Final audit
showed only fifteen thousand expended, an unheard of experience
with a public expenditure. The reason was plain. The martyr's
return was no profit-making venture to homefolks. It was an affair
of the heart. The people wanted to give of themselves. The mayor
of St. Louis sent a handsome hearse. Only the charges for shipping
it and six black horses were paid by the city. The Alton Railroad
offered to return the equipage without charge. Michael Doyle, local
nurseryman, donated two hundred vases of fresh flowers to grace
casket and catafalque. From Michigan City three carloads of ever-

---

* Now the Sangamon County Courthouse in everyday use.

green trees arrived to decorate the capitol and the burial vault.

Day and night Springfield folks labored to get ready, 150 working at a time on the State House. The whole of the exterior was draped in sable; and symbols of sorrow were put up in the rotunda, the Hall of Representatives, governor's room, library, and in other public rooms with which the deceased had been identified.

The ladies of Springfield did more than their share cutting and sewing fifteen hundred yards of black and white goods of various kinds, exclusive of the magnificent catafalque. This structure was designed by a colonel of the quartermaster department and consumed three hundred yards of black velvet, the same amount of silver lace and satin fringe, and quantities of silk and crape in black, white, and blue colors; the blue for underlining the star-studded canopy. The ladies also helped to fashion the floral festoons that adorned the walls and make the mottoes of which the most conspicuous was the quote from his Independence Hall address: "Sooner than surrender these principles, I would be assassinated first."

The Lincoln residence, the building that housed his former law office, the church where the family worshiped were embellished in black and were objects of intense interest to thousands of persons eager to see the places that had known him intimately but that would know him no more. The two railroads serving the city testified their regard by elaborately draping their depots; the Alton road (now the Gulf, Mobile and Ohio) which had brought him home; and the Great Western line (now the Wabash) on which he had departed.* Private dwellings and business establishments were given the same loving care, the whole community wearing the widow's weeds.

The State House was ready to receive the residue of the town's

* The same railroad station is still standing, the Farewell Address commemorated by a stone marker.

most renowned citizen and an hour after the arrival in Springfield
doors were opened to the public. For the next twenty-four hours
America directed a final look upon the silent features near where
he had stood on the evening of June 16, 1858, and enunciated advice
and prophecy that have since become classic. "If we could first
know where we are, and whither we are tending, we could better
judge what to do, and how to do it," he had begun his speech on
the polemic "house divided" theme. "I believe," he explained, "that
this government cannot endure permanently half slave and half
free." In three years the crisis he had so clearly foretold was reached
and in four more years it was passed—passed successfully due to
his skill and courage. Today we see, to use his own words, "the
home of freedom disenthralled, regenerated, enlarged and per-
petuated."

Billy Herndon, as he passed the form of his illustrious partner,
reported that "we who had known him in other days and before
the nation laid its claim upon him, looked for the last time upon
the silent, upturned face of our departed friend" and noted among
the mourners former colleagues of bench and bar, old New Salem
neighbors, crippled soldiers from battlefields, "and some were little
children who, scarce realizing the impressiveness of the event, were
destined to live and tell their children yet to be born the sad story
of Lincoln's death."

The President's face was discolored from the effects of the wound;
but "no more than we remember to have seen in similar gunshot
wounds," remarked a war-veteran reporter who declared that otherwise the face exhibited an extremely natural and lifelike expression, "more as if calmly slumbering than in the embrace of death."
It did not take a vivid imagination, he asserted, "to discover a
placid smile resting on that marble face." The metropolitan press
conducted a poll of what old neighbors thought of the corpse, questioning them in the manner of an inquiring reporter. They were

asked if they had looked upon him, and if so did he look natural.
The answer was always yes. "These gentlemen also said the general
contour and expression of the physiognomy was as natural and lifelike as could be expected under the circumstances."

All America, it seemed, was arriving in Springfield. A trainload
pulled in from Chicago, another from St. Louis, and one arrived on
the Great Western at midnight, the passengers proceeding directly
to the State House, filing past the bier, and returning to the cars
which departed without further ado. More trains arrived during
the day, bringing thousands who were unable to secure sleeping
accommodations and had to walk the streets all night. Residents
cooperated splendidly and opened their homes to total strangers;
but the town of twelve thousand could not handle the overwhelming influx. Local Masonic bodies hired a large hall and filled it with
tables, keeping them supplied with food cooked by families of the
members, making no charge. The service was intended for visiting
brothers of the craft but no needy or hungry stranger was turned
away.

Every thirty minutes, between rising and setting sun, a detachment of Battery K, Missouri Light Artillery, fired a salute and at
the close of day boomed a national salute of thirty-six guns. The
presidential cortege had been received at the depot by an honor
escort in full dress uniform, the One Hundred Forty-sixth Illinois
Volunteers; and Company E, Twenty-third Regiment of Veterans
Reserve Corps. The escort to the cemetery included also the Twenty-
fourth Michigan Volunteers, a company of Forty-sixth Wisconsin, a
battalion of Fourteenth Iowa, the Halleck Guards and City Guards
of St. Louis, and groups of officers and enlisted men too numerous
to identify by name and unit who had come on their own account.

Ten governors walked in the procession as did delegations from
Cleveland, Cincinnati, Indianapolis, Milwaukee, Louisville, St.
Louis, and Chicago, in addition to senators, congressmen, and

federal officials from Washington. There were groups of clergy-men, lawyers, politicians, members of the press—the latter a greater gathering than seen in one place before—delegations of university and school officials, religious and fraternal societies, firemen, municipal authorities, "citizens at large," and closing the proces-sional, the Negroes. All America was in town.

"We have followed the remains of President Lincoln from the place of his assassination to this former home," reported a cor-respondent, remarking that millions of people along the way had manifested "by every means of which they were capable" their deep sense of public loss and appreciation of his many virtues. "And now," concluded the account, "it becomes our mournful duty to escort the mortal remains to their last resting place. . . . All hearts seem to beat as one; and all have said, 'Bear him gently to his rest.'"

State House doors were closed at one o'clock. A choir accom-panied by an instrumental band, standing on the steps, rendered Paesello's "Peace, Troubled Soul"; and as the priceless burden was conveyed to the hearse sang Pleyel's beautiful hymn, "Chil-dren of the Heavenly King." Deadened drums took up the slow-timed beat and the march began. The sable-draped bands elicited dirges and requiems among which was the favorite soldier lament: "Then wrap the flag around me boys, To die were far more sweet, With Freedom's starry emblem, boys, To be my winding sheet." The veteran sergeants, marching with sabers drawn, were escorted by parallel lines of distinguished pallbearers. A horse fol-lowed the hearse, "Robin" or "Old Bob," now sixteen years old, that Lincoln had ridden on the circuit and in political campaigns, duskily caparisoned and led by a groom. From the State House Abraham Lincoln's final journey went by his home at Eighth and Jackson Streets, out to the city limits, then north past the Gov-

ernor's mansion to Fourth Street, and out Fourth to Oak Ridge
Cemetery.

A natural beauty spot, Oak Ridge Cemetery took its name from
two ridges running east and west covered principally with oak
trees. Between the ridges wound a valley with pleasing irregulari-
ties, watered by a quiet brook fed from rivulets that trickled out
of small ravines intersecting the valley. Skilled landscaping, con-
forming to the natural terrain, had made the tract a beautiful
haven for sepulture.

It was a city cemetery initiated by municipal authorities in 1855
when Springfield was emerging from its status as a village to a
one-mile-square city. The first seventeen acres had been purchased
from Archer G. Herndon, father of Lincoln's law partner. Ten
years later the grounds embraced seventy-six acres. When Mrs.
Lincoln decided that her husband was to be buried here (instead
of downtown where the present state capitol stands), the city
donated a plot of six acres. On this the present mausoleum was
erected, built from funds donated by the people of America. Here
he and his family now lie together.

Temporarily the presidential remains were placed in a receiving
vault on the south side of the brook, some forty rods in from the
main (eastern) entrance. From the entrance the valley descends
rapidly but levels off momentarily into a cove; and at this point a
structure was built into the hillside, the exterior of Joliet white
limestone. Inside, the brick walls and roof were covered with
black velvet adorned with evergreen and floral pieces, the brick
floor strewn with sprigs of evergreen. The brick foundation in the
center of the room that supported the casket was hidden in blossoms. Son William's coffin was placed nearby.

Having performed for the last time the service for which they had
been detailed, the veteran Washington sergeants who had never

left the body unguarded for a moment, now surrendered their trust.
They locked the iron grated door and confided the key to the Honorable John Stuart. Stuart, Lincoln's first law partner and later his
cousin by marriage, had been designated by son Robert to receive
the vault key. The transfer was effected in the presence of the official Guard of Honor, family and relatives, including Robert who
had come direct from Washington.

Thousands of persons clinging to the steep hillside watched the
proceedings and thousands more ranged along the opposite hill. "A
sea of sober faces and bared heads" covered the picturesque valley.
To the left of the vault entrance a choir assembled on a platform
and to the right clergymen gathered on a speaker's stand. Facing
the vault stood the audience of congressional and federal groups,
governors and staffs, state and city delegations. Nearer the vault
entrance clustered pallbearers and close friends; and next to the
entrance, on both sides, sat family and relatives. The whole was
encircled by the military.

The final ceremony commenced with a prayer. Assembled vocalists offered the new composition "Farewell, Father, Friend, and
Guardian." Scriptural readings followed and then the hymn "To
Thee, O Lord, I Yield My Spirit." Now came the most touching
part of the ceremony to the audience. This was the reading of his
Second Inaugural Address, making his very presence seem im-
minent particularly his unforgettable admonition, "Let us strive on
to finish the work we are in . . . to do all which may achieve and
cherish a just and lasting peace among ourselves, and with all
nations."

The choir voiced the hymn "As When Thy Cross Was Bleeding,"
then Bishop Simpson delivered the principal oration, offering an
impressive review of the deceased's life that consumed more than
an hour and received wide acclaim in the press. He was followed by
the choir singing "Over the Valley the Angels Smile," written espe-

cially for the occasion. The Reverend Gurley from Washington pronounced a moving prayer and the vocalists rendered a hymn for which he had composed the lyrics, the first stanza reading:

> Rest, noble martyr; rest in peace;
> Rest with the true and the brave,
> Who, like thee, fell in Freedom's cause
> The Nation's life to save.

The ceremony was brought to a close by audience and choir joining in singing the familiar "Praise God from Whom All Blessings Flow," all standing and the family pastor raising his hand and pronouncing the final benediction, every head bowed.

The sixteenth President was in his grave. Abraham Lincoln was home at last, resting in peace. Slowly, sadly, quietly, the mourners melted away, moving from hillside and valley into town, having witnessed entombment of America's man of the century.

16

A MILLION Americans, declared the working press, were able to catch a final glimpse of the familiar features as Lincoln lay in state for a few hours in various communities; and more than seven million congregated to attend the cortege and take part in the ceremonies. "More people," summarized General Townsend, "looked upon the remains of the late Commander-in-chief during this period than had ever before viewed the form of man from whom life had departed."

Public grief was beyond anything seen in all history.

Was it because the people, having enfolded him in their hearts, mourned his loss as a beloved father? Was it because he represented their dream for a better tomorrow and now that dream was shattered? Was it because he had come up from their ranks and had, with humility and compassion, held the bonds of brotherhood together throughout the bitter fratricide? Or was it because they were so shocked and shamed by the foul deed they felt a deep sense of personal guilt? Though a thousand such queries might be propounded, each question had to be answered by each person in his own individual way.

But there was no question that everyone recognized the extent of his loss. The depth of this recognition unconsciously gave great value to themselves; their tremendous turnout bore witness to the universality of their affection. Nothing in Lincoln's tragic death affords greater inspiration to posterity than the unprecedented demonstration of the generality of people—our forefathers—revealing the genuineness of their sterling character.

It is in this light that the long journey, endless processions, interminable eulogies, and elaborate ceremonies must be interpreted. The citizenry were making plain they appreciated the fallen chieftain's eminence and what he had wrought. This fact (that Lincoln's contemporaries were fully aware of his greatness) may appear of small significance to us today especially since he has become in our estimation The First American. We are too apt to take much for granted and to exclaim: Why shouldn't they have appreciated their martyred President, he was the greatest! Yet we must recall it was at his bidding they bled and died; it was under his administration they lost sons, fathers, husbands, and brothers; and it was he who ruled when they suffered, sacrificed, and paid, and paid. They experienced the agonies of the terrible ordeal. We cannot feel as they felt.

What made Lincoln great was not only that he successfully managed the war between brothers but the manner in which he conducted and resolved the irrepressible conflict. And what made the American people great was not that they fought one another but that for which they fought. The manner of both parties was based on character. Herein lies the touchstone of American success.

That the Cotton States with their gracious country living battled to maintain their way of life (the Jeffersonian agrarian ideal) which they called "state's rights" while federals fought for the abstract notion that the Union must remain indivisible and the starry flag inviolate seems beyond the bounds of rational comprehension. Only within the framework of the great American experiment can such political philosophies be understood as bringing men to the point of killing one another. These two great concepts of political and social philosophy collided head-on, abetted by other specific antagonisms that fanned the emotional flames.

"My paramount object in this struggle," wrote Lincoln in August, 1862, "is to save the Union, and is not either to save or destroy slavery. . . . What I do about slavery and the colored race, I do because I believe it helps to save the Union; and what I forbear, I forbear because I believe it would help save the Union." A month later he released the first draft of the Emancipation Proclamation and said he did so because he felt that "slavery must die that the Union might live."

To Lincoln the Union was no mere mechanical contrivance of governments and laws, of legislatures, courts, post offices, and armies. It was much more real and vital. Other peoples are held together by geography, language, racial, economic, and religious similarities; the American Union is cemented by a compelling idea. America's noblest possession is the moral basis of a free society; a spiritual union that embraces a common heritage, a common philosophy, and a common goal.

Yet the goal of equality for all men and the dignity of the individual is more than American; it is a universal aspiration. The United States stands as a trustee for humanity. That is what Lincoln perceived. He was determined to maintain the Union because its maintenance gave strength and permanence to the most fundamental principle of human existence. Without that principle upon which the union of states had been founded the nation was lost, and without the nation the principle was lost. Liberty and democracy are safe only in a society that is free.

Unionists agreed. Though they may not have understood the ethical principle as clearly as Lincoln did, they shared with him the heritage of the Founding Fathers and the inspiration of the barefoot patriots of Valley Forge, Saratoga, and Yorktown. They remembered John Paul Jones, "Old Ironsides," Andy Jackson, Patrick Henry, Tom Paine, Benjamin Franklin, Betsy Ross, Thomas Jefferson; the whole galaxy of patriots from first settlers to latest generation, all nurtured in the American way, giving of their best to advance and preserve their Republic. George Washington had nothing to fear from those who came after him; they would prove worthy of him and of the patriots who supported him.

This may sound like copybook maxims out of McGuffey's fifth reader or a Fourth of July oration by a politician running for office. The strange part is that it is all true. Americans today are as loyal to their Americanism as they were in Lincoln's time, and in Lincoln's time they were as loyal as in Washington's. We are as proud of our heritage as they, for we have marched in their footsteps. Or else we were fooling ourselves when a few million of us went overseas in World War I to make the world safe for democracy, and when another few million of the next generation went into World War II to stop Fascists from dominating mankind, and again when we went into Korea to make plain that no aggressor could violate the mandates of the United Nations. And today we give and give and give at confiscatory tax levels to help less fortunate peoples the world over reach toward a better tomorrow.

Some call it the American dream. At times it has appeared as a nightmare and exhibited bizarre manifestations. That is not unusual since all human endeavors can produce excesses. To call this outstanding characteristic of the American people a dream is less than realistic and overlooks its tremendous power. A dream is wishful yearning and carries no element of fulfillment; it is a lazy, shiftless, evanescent sort of thing. That is not America. America is energetic, practical, purposeful. From the very first settlers the way of America has been struggle. Liberty and democracy are never wholly secured. The conquest of nature is never wholly achieved. Understandings between men are in continual flux. The so-called American dream is a ceaseless reaching for perfection in human and natural relationships.

Of the American way Abraham Lincoln and his contemporaries stand as exemplars. They, along with their predecessors, are the showers of the way. These patriots represent landmarks in the American struggle for a better world in which to live. For America is more than a dream. Its essence is the will to do better.

As we come to these closing paragraphs we realize how much is left unsaid. Abraham Lincoln was a many-sided man. And America is a complex country. Both are unique; both are without parallel in human history; both have been, and will continue to be, the subject of attention in every part of the globe. For Lincoln was more than a President of the United States. He was more than The First American. He personified mankind.

When he stated in the First Inaugural Address, "Why should there not be a patient confidence in the ultimate justice of the people? Is there any better or equal hope in the world?" he was speaking to a specific situation but the application was unlimited. And when he declared, "This country, with its institutions, belongs to the people who inhabit it," he was verifying what kings and dictators and rulers including presidents know very well but seldom admit: that the voice of God speaks through the people.

Lincoln characterized his countrymen as "the almost chosen people." Modesty prevented him from placing them (and himself) in first place among mankind for that final choice was the prerogative of a higher power. But he made clear that his concern in saving the Union was to maintain for the world "that form of government whose leading object is to elevate the condition of men . . . to afford all an unfettered start and a fair chance in the race of life."

Seeing his fellow citizens as the almost chosen people and himself as their accidentally chosen instrument he walked with them hand in hand, each clinging to the other as they beat their way through the ordeal of a tempest, each looking to the other for support and each getting it, so that the triumphant victory was finally achieved.

Out of all the blood and gore, out of the fiercest civil conflict that ever wracked a people, the gentlest memory to emerge is of him who brought the conflict to a successful end. That is the outstanding fact of Lincoln's career. It is always easy for the unsuccessful to be pleasant and friendly, easy for the weak to be gentle and compassionate. Nothing discloses character like power. The supreme test is absolute power. Such power resided in Lincoln's hands and it rested also with the United States as then the most powerful military force in the world. Yet no man can accuse President Lincoln and no nation can accuse this one of abusing the tremendous power in their possession. Does his gentle spirit, his spirit of compassion and friendliness, still guide the American people although he has departed the flesh? Is he still alive in the hearts and minds of those who follow in his footsteps? Have his fellow countrymen been a credit to his precepts and to the sacrifices of those who died with him?

Belief in resurrection is as old as man himself. Men have never believed in the triumph of evil and the death of goodness. The good cause is never defeated; human good lives and blossoms again. By whatever name men may call him the risen Lord still walks this earth. Socrates is not dead nor Francis of Assisi nor Maimonides nor George Washington nor any of the saints and heroes who lived and suffered for humankind. Nor is any human dead, it is not irreverent to say, who has ever truly and unselfishly loved another person. Nor is Abraham Lincoln.

We will not say farewell to him; we will not say good-bye to those who went with him. They walk again at midnight in this land of Lincoln . . . our land.

> Thanks to all. For the great Republic—
> for the principle it lives by, and keeps alive—
> for man's vast future—thanks to all!

APPENDIX: NOTES AND SOURCES

Chapter 1

Page 13. Leading Washington dailies in 1865 included the *Morning Chronicle, National Intelligencer, National Republican,* and *Evening Star.* Proceedings of Congress when in session were printed daily in the *Congressional Globe.*

Page 14. Seward's and Stanton's speeches were carried in evening papers April 3 and again next morning. Quotations are from *Intelligencer.*

Page 15. "Official announcement of the fall of Richmond was given to the public in an extra from this office *in advance of all competitors* at about half-past eleven today," boasted the *Republican.* (General Weitzel had entered Richmond at 8:15 A.M.; the War Dept. issued its notice at 10:45; and the public had the news in less than an hour.) Headlines yelled: "EXTRA! Glorious News! Fall of Richmond! Captured by Black Troops!"

The *Chronicle* reported that "the announcement of the reduction of Petersburg and almost immediately thereafter of the entrance into Richmond of a portion of the 25th Corps of the Army of the James, colored troops commanded by General Foster under General Weitzel, well-nigh crazed our citizens and residents with joy."

Among the units entering the rebel capital was the Twenty-second Colored Infantry which would head the Lincoln funeral procession. See explanatory note Chap. 5. The Negro in Lincoln's time is studied by Professor Benjamin Quarles in *Lincoln and the Negro*.

Greeley's comment: *Greeley on Lincoln,* p. 75: " 'Perfect through suffering' is the divine law; and the tensions of mind and body through his four years of eventful rule had told fearfully upon his physical frame. When I last saw him some five or six weeks before his death his face was haggard with care and seamed with thought and trouble. It looked . . ."

Page 16. Lincoln to Sheridan: *Lincoln in the Telegraph Office* by David H. Bates, p. 166. Also *Personal Memoirs of Philip H. Sheridan,* II, 129 ff.

Pages 15-22. Firsthand accounts of City Point and "River Queen" incidents: U. S. Grant's *Memoirs;* W. T. Sherman's *Memoirs;* David D. Porter's *Incidents and Anecdotes of the Civil War;* Horace Porter's *Campaigning with Grant;* Adam Badeau's *History of Grant.*

Page 18. Lincoln's "unbeknownst" anecodote: Grant's *Memoirs,* II, 533; Petersburg remark, p. 459.
    Lincoln's telegrams were to Stanton who relayed them to the press beginning April 1. (See any anthology of Lincoln's works arranged chronologically.)

Page 19. Modestly signed "A. Lincoln.": Archivist Elmer O. Parker, Army and Air Corps Branch of National Archives, finds that on all documents bearing the Great Seal of the United States Lincoln signed his full name; but that his general habit (not exclusively) was to sign letters and similar items with first initial only.

Lincoln's reportorial skill was heralded by *New York Herald,* April 3.

The Richmond expedition was well documented by participants and eyewitnesses, north and south, both published and in manuscript. Authoritative is bodyguard William H. Crook's "Lincoln's Last Day," *Harper's Magazine,* June and September, 1907; and *Through Five*

Administrations. Admiral David Porter penned two articles and included the material in his book, *op. cit.* The *Richmond Evening Whig,* which had resumed publication, carried an account April 5. The war correspondent for *Boston Journal* who signed himself "Carleton" wrote April 4 that he was standing on the bank of the James River when a boat pulled by twelve sailors came up stream. "It contained President Lincoln and his son." He enumerated the others. "There was no carriage near so the President, leading his son, walked the three-quarters of a mile up to General Weitzel's headquarters in Jeff. Davis's mansion." "Carleton" joined the party. He reported General Shepley met them on the street and Major Stevens got a detachment of Fourth Massachusetts Calvary as escort.

Navy Captain Barnes contributed his version in two illustrated articles "With Lincoln from Washington to Richmond," *Appleton's Magazine,* May and June, 1907.

Page 20. Lincoln to Weitzel: *Battles and Leaders of the Civil War,* IV, 728, "The Fall of Richmond" by Thomas T. Graves, aide-de-camp to General Weitzel, who overheard the remark.

Conferences of the President and Campbell were controversially reported, varying with the medium's political complexion. The *New York Tribune* account (April 22) was challenged by Campbell. Discussion and bibliography in R. W. Patrick's *The Fall of Richmond.*

Page 21. Lincoln wired this to Grant, April 6. Together with his written proposals of the day before (not quoted or mentioned here), Lincoln's position was established beyond cavil. R. T. Lincoln Collection, Library of Congress, Manuscript Division.

Marquis Adolphe de Chambrun, "Personal Recollections of Mr. Lincoln," *Scribner's Magazine,* January, 1893; and his *Impressions of Lincoln and the Civil War.*

Page 22. Lincoln's speech: April 10, *National Republican.*

Page 23. Lincoln's feelings: sleepless nights, Nicolay and Hay, and Crook; would exchange places, Schuyler Colfax; paced the deck all night, Crook; tired spot inside, Brooks; eating my life out, Owen Lovejoy.

Page 24. "Lady of the Capitol": bronze statue, 19½ feet high and weighing 15,000 lbs., by Thos. B. Crawford atop the Capitol dome, facing east. Also known as the "Statue of Freedom" and "Armed Liberty." (A replica stands in the Smithsonian Institution). Erected December 2, 1863, amid fanfare of big guns around the city and no speeches. Work on the uncompleted Capitol was suspended at outbreak of war but Lincoln urged continuance and is reported to have told a White House caller that "if the people see the Capitol going up, it is a sign we intend the Union shall go on." Contractors continued to work without payment until Congress passed new appropriations. Noah Brooks said in *Washington in Lincoln's Time,* p. 9, "It is no metaphor to say that the sound of the workman's hammer was heard in that building even in the dark times when it was not certain Washington was safe."

Page 25. Lincoln's speech: April 13, *National Republican.*

Page 26. Eyewitness was Noah Brooks, *op. cit.,* p. 224. Bibb related his experiences in pamphlet form and in *Atlanta Sunny South* according to John W. Du Bose of Alabama in *General Joseph Wheeler and the Army of the Tennessee,* p. 457. An influential Unionist in the South, Bibb was introduced to the President by ex-Senator Browning: *The Diary of Orville Hickman Browning,* II, 17.

Pages 26-28. *Diary of Gideon Welles,* II, 182. *Recollections of Abraham Lincoln* by Ward Hill Lamon, p. 114 ff.

Chapter 2

Page 31. Dr. Leale's comparative obscurity is not hard to understand. Appointed Assistant Army Surgeon only the week before (April 8), he was in charge of the stricken President only until the family physician arrived (about twenty minutes after coming into Petersen house), declined to talk to newsmen (*New York Herald,* April 16), stayed away from the autopsy, gave no testimony at the trial of conspirators, and was reluctant to discuss the subject in civilian life. Yet he performed one of the most courageous and successful feats in medical history.

Leale's first written report accompanied his letter of July 20, 1867, that responded to former Maj. Genl. Butler, a Massachusetts congressman and chairman of the House Assassination Investigating Committee. His second report became known with publication of *The Medical and Surgical History of the War of the Rebellion, 1861-1865,* Surgical Volume, Part 1, p. 305. His third, and most complete, report was given in a speech to the New York State Commandery of the Military Order of the Loyal Legion on Lincoln's one hundredth birthday anniversary and was published next day in *Harper's Weekly.*

At the bedside along with Dr. Leale, the family physician, and the Surgeon General, were Drs. Charles D. Gatch, Albert F. A. King, and Taft (all of whom were in the audience and as army surgeons responded to the call for a doctor); also Dr. Charles H. Crane, Assistant Surgeon General, and acting surgeon Charles M. Ford, both having come with the Surgeon General; also Drs. F. J. May and C. H. Lieberman, local physicians who heard of the crime and offered their help; also Dr. Lyman B. Todd, Mrs. Lincoln's cousin from Lexington; and finally a local homeopath, Dr. Ezra W. Abbott, who also volunteered his services. What good a dozen doctors could do huddled in a seventeen-by-nine-and-a-half-foot room with a dozen other spectators is beyond comprehension or explanation.

Drs. Ford and King kept an official log, afterwards published in the medical press. Dr. Abbott also kept one that was released during the night to the press and that formed the basis for dispatches.

Death came to the President without a struggle, without perceptible movement, at twenty-one minutes and fifty-five seconds after seven o'clock, and the heart ceased beating at twenty-two minutes and ten seconds past the hour. "Every necessary act of love, devotion, skill and loyalty had been rendered during his helpless hours," reported Leale, and noted that prolongation of the President's life had helped lessen the shock upon the people; that the country had been given time to swear in another Chief Magistrate; and that "the grandeur of the continuity of the Republic was confirmed." His prompt and skillful ministrations added to the President's extraordinary vitality had kept him alive for nine hours and nine minutes after the fatal shot entered the brain.

Let it be noted also that Dr. Leale's meritorious acts did not go unrewarded. When he was honorably discharged in January, 1866, he was brevetted captain. A summary of his career is in *National Cyclopedia of Biography,* II, 52. The New York Academy of Medicine maintains an open file on him.

For further medical references see "Physicians to the Presidents and Their Patients: a Bibliography," July, 1961, *Bulletin of the Medical Library Association,* by Charles Roos, Reference Librarian, National Library of Medicine.

Dr. Taft's quote: "Abraham Lincoln's Last Hours" by Charles Sabin Taft, M.D., *Century Magazine,* February, 1893, p. 634.

Page 32. *Personal Reminiscences of Abraham Lincoln* by Smith Stimmel, p. 88 ff. "I am frequently asked, 'Where was Lincoln's bodyguard the night of his assassination; and how did it come that they let him be killed?' In reply I have to say that President Lincoln flatly refused to have a military guard with him when he went to places of entertainment or to church in the city. He said that when he went to such places he wanted to go as free and unencumbered as other people; and there was no military guard with him the night of the assassination."

William H. Crook explained the matter of a personal bodyguard in *Harper's Magazine*, December, 1906, "Lincoln as I Knew Him." "His friends had been begging him. . . Lamon and Stanton particularly. . . for protection. He hated being on his guard; and the fact that it was necessary to distrust his fellow Americans saddened him. He refused to be guarded as long as it was possible for a sane man to persist. Toward the end of 1864 he yielded." It was Crook's opposite number, John Parker, who was derelict in duty that fatal night. (Parker was never tried or punished for his failure).

Page 33. *From the Diary and Correspondence of Benjamin Brown French*, edited by grandson Amos Tuck French. Entries, April 15 and 16; and letter to sister Pamela, May 21, 1865. Library of Congress.

Page 36. The "assassin wanted" advertisement was widely reprinted following Lincoln's death as proof of the deliberate plot. Here it is:

ONE MILLION DOLLARS WANTED TO HAVE PEACE
BY THE FIRST OF MARCH

If the citizens of the Southern Confederacy will furnish us with the cash or good securities for the sum of One Million Dollars, I will cause the lives of Abraham Lincoln, William H. Seward and Andrew Johnson to be taken by the 1st of March next. This will give us peace and satisfy the world that cruel tyrants cannot live in a land of liberty! If this is not accomplished nothing will be claimed beyond the sum of fifty thousand dollars in advance, which is supposed to be necessary in order to reach and slaughter the three villains.

I will give, myself, one thousand dollars toward this patriotic purpose.

Everyone wishing to contribute will address Box X, Cahawba, Ala.

Footnote on final outcome is based on Otto Eisenschiml's "Did They Try to Kill Lincoln?" *The Lincoln Herald*, June, 1946.

Page 37. Stanton's remarks were published nationwide. In his "Report of the Secretary of War to the President, November 22, 1965," he said:

"This assassination appeared to be part of a deliberate comprehensive conspiracy to assassinate the President, Vice-President, Secretary of State, Lieutenant-General and other officers of the Government with a view to its disorganization. . . . The details are given in the 'Report of the Judge Advocate General.'" See *The War of the Rebellion: a Compilation of the Official Records of the Union and Confederate Armies,* Series III, vol. V, p. 508.

The Confederate captain almost mobbed at the White House was not named.

Page 38. The "rebel major-general" was Brigadier General William H. Payne, C.S.A. He enlisted as a private in the Fourth Virginia Cavalry and was wounded thrice. He was captured near his home in Warrenton, Virginia. After the war he moved to Washington and became general counsel of the Southern Railway. *Generals in Gray* by Ezra J. Warner.

Page 41. Former President Fillmore incident: *Buffalo* (N.Y.) *Commercial Advertiser,* April 29; and *Morning Express,* April 17.

Former President Pierce incident: *Concord* (N.H.) *Patriot,* April 19, excerpted in the press. *New York Times,* April 26.

Page 42. The wise general was George H. Gordon, commanding the District of Eastern Virginia. Reported in *New York Herald,* April 19.

Sixth Corps letter was written by an unnamed soldier of Sixty-ninth New York Volunteers to his father in Brooklyn: quoted in *Buffalo Express,* April 27.

Page 43. Publisher of *Philadelphia Press,* John W. Forney, also owned and edited *Washington Morning Chronicle* in which this report appeared April 18.

Theodore Gerrish's quotes are from his *Army Life: a Private's Reminiscences of the Civil War.* Private Gerrish was in front line of last assault at Appomattox when stopped by the first flag of truce from Longstreet's lines. After the war he became a Congregational minister. The first lieutenant colonel of the Twentieth Maine, Joshua L. Chamberlain, wounded five times and awarded the medal of honor, rose to brigadier general and took the surrender of Confederate troops on April 12. He tells the moving story in *The Passing of the Armies.* J. J. Pullen's *Twentieth Maine* relates that when Adalbert Ames, the

regiment's first colonel, saw the sorry lot of raw recruits ranged before him he exploded, "For God's sake men, stand up and draw in
your bowels."

Page 44. *The Seventy-ninth Highlanders, New York Volunteers in the
War of the Rebellion, 1861-1865* was authored by William Todd of
Albany although the regiment was mostly from New York City.

The History of the Ninty-sixth Regiment, Illinois Volunteer Infantry
by Charles A. Partridge, a sergeant major in the regiment who became
editor of *Waukegan Gazette.*

Page 46. Johnston's remark: Sherman's *Memoirs,* II, 349.

*The History of the Fourth Regiment of Minnesota Volunteers During
the Great Rebellion* by Alonzo L. Brown. The Fourth was the only
Minnesota outfit in Sherman's fabulous Fifteenth Corps. Brown advanced to captain of Company G, Fiftieth Regiment, U.S. Colored
Infantry.

Page 47. Townsend's dispatches from Richmond: *New York World,*
April 18. He also used the by-line "Gath."

Chapter 3

Page 52. Springfield events chronicled in *Illinois State Journal,* and
Illinois State Register. The *Washington National Intelligencer* reported Monday (April 17), "The committee of citizens from Illinois who
desire that the remains of President Lincoln may be removed to that
State, will call upon Mrs. Lincoln today and they confidently entertain
the belief that their earnest wish in this respect will meet her favor
and consent."

Page 53. Reports on embalming and undertaking were conflicting and
contradictory, the worst fraud being a Thomas H. Holmes who had
come to the nation's capital at the outbreak of war and set himself up
as a "Dr." He advertised as "Father of Embalming—America's Pioneer
Embalmer." He claimed to have embalmed the remains of President
Lincoln by the improved methods the President had ordered him to
develop four years before. Holmes made a fortune embalming officers'
bodies. Not one of his grandiose claims can be substantiated. R. W.
Habenstein and W. M. Lamers in *The History of American Funeral
Directing* published under the auspices of the American Funeral

Directors Association straightened out the fraudulent Holmes (which other works have not), and provide an objective report of American embalming practice. Modern embalming got its start during the Civil War and has had its greatest development in the United States.

Gideon Welles' *Diary* said Mrs. Welles stayed all day with Mrs. Lincoln. He went over to the Executive Mansion after breakfast and met his wife in the library. Attorney General Speed came in and left with him. "As we were descending the stairs, Tad, who was looking from the window at the foot, turned, and seeing us cried aloud in his tears, 'O, Mr. Welles, who killed my father?' Neither Speed nor I could restrain our tears nor give the boy a satisfactory answer."

Page 54. Mrs. Elizabeth Keckley told of her service with Mrs. Lincoln in *Behind the Scenes.* She said that as soon as she could leave for a few minutes she asked permission to enter the guest room across the hall where the President's remains were temporarily laid. "Never did I enter the solemn chamber of death with such palpitating heart and trembling footsteps as I entered it that day," she wrote. "No common mortal had died. What a noble soul was his! The Moses of my people had fallen in the hour of his triumph."

New York Herald, April 17, said Mrs. Lincoln was under doctor's care attended only by her sons and the two cousins who had come to the obsequies; and that she would only see Secretary Stanton "who had an interview with her this afternoon to ascertain her wishes in regard to the funeral arrangements." All accounts vary in details.

Footnote: Dr. Henry, physician and Whig politician, had been appointed by Lincoln Surveyor General of Washington Territory. His wife remained there when he came east to see the President about getting an appointment in Washington City. He wrote her he "followed the hearse in the funeral procession in the third carriage as one of the family," and was "seated in the East Room with the mourners when the ceremony was performed." Typewritten transcript, "Nicolay Papers," Library of Congress.

Page 55. "Kiss me, Emilie . . ." was recorded by her daughter, Katherine Helm, in *The True Story of Mary, Wife of Lincoln* which recounted the mother's recollections. Further information in Ruth P. Randall's *Mary Lincoln; Biography of a Marriage.*

Mrs. Lincoln's remark to her husband, "What will Miss Harris think?" was occasioned by the presence in the box of their theater guests, Clara H. Harris, daughter of New York Senator Ira Harris, and her escort and fiancé, Major Henry R. Rathbone. The likelihood was that the two guests, later married, were too engrossed in each other to notice what the Lincolns were doing. (The Major tried to stop the assassin and got his arm severely slashed.)

Page 56. Nicolay and Hay, *Abraham Lincoln: a History*, X, 319.
Commissioner French's letter and resolution are in the "Elihu B. Washburne Papers," Library of Congress. The letter is addressed to Hon. Samuel Foot, chairman, Public Grounds Committee, Thirty-ninth Congress.

James River churchyard episode was related by Isaac N. Arnold, a close and valued friend, in *The Life of Abraham Lincoln*. "Mrs. Lincoln told this incident to the author," he says in a footnote to p. 435, "in 1874. Some of his friends had desired him to be buried in town but she said she preferred Oak Ridge and related the above as stating his own wishes on the subject."

Page 57. Numerous versions of Mary's decisions are reported. Browning said (*Diary*, II, 22) that "we all think the body should be taken to Springfield for interment but Mrs. Lincoln is vehemently opposed to it." Mary declined to see Browning when he called—as she did almost everyone. Perhaps he felt miffed since he considered himself to be a special friend. But Mary was in no condition for social visits or to entertain a parade of condolences.

Stanton's appointment of Brough and Garrett was confirmed by letter, April 18. Letterbook, War Department, IV, 94, "Stanton Papers," Library of Congress.

Page 58. Train schedule appeared in the press nationwide. Quote is from *Intelligencer*, April 19. Next day the *Star* carried the complete arrangements per Stanton's request, headlined on p. 1, "Transportation of President Lincoln's Remains." Included in the press release were General Orders 66 and 67 announcing to the armies the death of the President and assuming of office by the Vice-President, *AGO 1865, General Orders 1 to 97*, Army and Air Corps Branch, National Archives.

Page 59. The AGO order validating and implementing the Brough-Garrett recommendations was neither numbered nor printed in

General Orders, although indexed. (Probably so handled since it did not directly concern a military subject.) Nor do any army orders on the subject appear in *Official Records, op. cit.* However, the complete schedule and transportation instructions were printed in a four-page, black-bordered folder that was given wide distribution. *1522-W-1865, AGO, encl. 2,* National Archives.

Page 60. The bitter charges against Stanton are given a thorough going-over in Otto Eisenschiml's *Why Was Lincoln Murdered?* Conclusion: "An indictment against Stanton cannot be sustained for lack of evidence." Thurlow Weed wrote: "The truth is that the first and paramount design of secession leaders was to obtain on or before the 4th of March by *coup d'etat,* possession of the capital with the sanction of the government. That design was thwarted by Mr. Stanton." *Life of Thurlow Weed,* II, 331. (See Chap. 10, p. 158, further on Weed.)

For "betrayal" of their cherished scheme to usurp the government by connivance, Stanton was never forgiven by former political associates. Their charges against him amount to nothing more than outright political quackery. The recent careful study of *Stanton, the Life and Times of Lincoln's Secretary of War* by Benjamin P. Thomas (an able Lincoln biographer) and H. M. Hyman finds that Stanton was unduly maligned, and that Lincoln himself knew this; telling a journalistic friend that the Secretary of War "was utterly misjudged . . . the man's public character is a public mistake."

Footnote: Shelby M. Cullom, *Fifty Years of Public Service,* p. 107. He was one of the Illinois delegation on the train and traveled, he says, from Harrisburg to Springfield.

Page 62. Private secretaries quote: Nicolay and Hay, *op. cit.,* X, 319.

Page 63. Government control over railroads was a war measure (U.S. Statutes at Large, XII, 334-5) and was incorporated into a military order, General Order #10, AGO. The single rail line into Washington, the Baltimore and Ohio Railroad, was placed under War Department control although it continued to operate as a private enterprise throughout the war. The law never had to be invoked against a loyal railway. However, from the lines captured in Confederate territory a system of U.S. Military Railroads grew up. See *Reports of Bvt. Brig. Genl. D. C. McCallum.*

Chapter 4

Page 65. When Seward had been incapacitated by a carriage accident, son Frederick assumed charge as Assistant Secretary of State. Now both had been almost assassinated and their condition was serious. The able chief clerk, William Hunter, took over as Acting Secretary. He addressed his notice of the White House ceremonies "To the People of the United States." *Official Records, op. cit.,* Series III, Vol. IV, p. 1275.

Page 66. Edward Everett Hale: "The funeral service of the 19th of April, 1865, was the most impressive religious service ever held in this country. By one impulse, the people of the land thronged the churches which at the hour of the funeral of the President were everywhere open," stated this former chaplain of the Senate and author of the famed "Man Without a Country." From "The President's Words," Boston, 1865.

AGO General Order No. 66 had Grant's instructions incorporated into it. Stanton's part began: "The distressing duty has devolved upon the Secretary of War to announce to the Armies of the United States that at twenty-two minutes after seven o'clock on the morning of Saturday, the 15th day of April, 1865, Abraham Lincoln, President of the United States, died of a mortal wound inflicted upon him by an assassin. . ." Order was issued Sunday the sixteenth. Instructions to close down for ceremonies on the nineteenth, fly flags at half-staff, and so on, was AGO No. 69, April 17. *AGO 1865, General Orders 1 to 97,* National Archives.

Page 69. *New York World,* April 20, reported the press was represented in East Room by "Mr. Canzaran of the *Chronicle,* Mr. Tracy of *Republican,* Mr. Fiske of *New York Herald,* Major Benjamin Perley Poore of *Boston Journal,* Mr. Gobright of Associated Press, Mr. Painter of *Philadelphia Inquirer,* Mr. Mataran of *Philadelphia Press,* Mr. Crounse of *New York Times,* Messrs. Bonwell and Crane of Frank Leslie's paper, A. H. Byington of *New York Tribune,* Mr. Ward of *Harper's,* and Mr. Reid of *Cincinnati Gazette";* and not forgetting the *World's* correspondent who reported this, George Alfred Townsend. Their dispatches form the basis for this chapter.

Page 71. Veterans Reserve Corps was first known as Invalid Corps.
Confusion exists regarding "Bucktail." The Bucktail Brigade of

which the One Hundred Fiftieth Regiment was a part was not the only Pennsylvania outfit using that prefix. First was a regiment from northwestern part of the state variously listed on official rolls but calling themselves "Pennsylvania Bucktails." Their service is recounted in *History of the Bucktails* by O. R. H. Thompson, and more recently by E. A. Glover in *Bucktailed Wildcats*. The Bucktail Brigade was mostly made up of Philadelphians, but the One Hundred Fiftieth and particularly Companies D and K were from the mountains and forests of northwestern counties. Both companies were detailed for guard duty at the summer White House (a cottage at Soldier's Home now preserved as a Lincoln memorial). Captain Henry W. Crotzer of D Company shared with Derrickson of K the regard of the Lincolns, often dined with the President, and said that one of the most pleasing memories of his men was the unvarying kindness of Mrs. Lincoln who arranged midnight lunches for guards on duty.

K Company knew by heart the President's letter:

Executive Mansion,
Washington, Nov. 1, 1862.

To Whom It May Concern:
Capt. Derrickson, with his company, has been for sometime, keeping guard at my residence, now at the Soldier's Retreat. He, and his Company, are very agreeable to me; and while it is deemed proper for any guard to remain, none would be more satisfactory to me than Capt. D. and his company.

A. Lincoln.

The President's letter had been prompted by the keen desire of the men to join the regiment in active service (Company D did). Lincoln desired that Company K stay on. *History of the One Hundred and Fiftieth Regiment, Pennsylvania Volunteers* by Thomas Chamberlin.

Page 72. The East Room ceremony was fully covered in the press. Mr. Gurley's eulogy and other quotes are from *Washington Chronicle*, April 20.

Chapter 5

Page 80. *Baltimore Sun*, April 20, reported the horse was the celebrated "Dave Gordon" belonging to Captain G. H. Tompkins, assistant quartermaster, whom he had ridden in the early part of the war and to whom the President had taken a liking. The working guard of honor and the honorary Guard of Honor both mounted guard in shifts around the clock.

Officers and men of the working guard were awarded Medals of Honor by the Secretary of War "in testimony of faithful and exemplary conduct as one of the escort." President Lincoln himself had signed the Medal of Honor Act, July 12, 1862. The Army Re-organization Bill of June 3, 1916, authorized a Board of Review and 911 Medals of Honor were withdrawn including those of the Lincoln escort (*AGO-2411162, Feb. 2, 1917*). Purpose was to make the Medal represent the highest honor of the government for actual combat "distinguished by conspicuous gallantry or intrepidity at the risk of life above and beyond the call of duty." Today this is what the Medal of Honor stands for. See *The Medal of Honor of the United States Army.*

Page 81. Twenty-second Regiment, U.S. Colored Infantry, was organized at Camp William Penn near Philadelphia, January, 1864. Took part in battles around Richmond and Petersburg from June, 1864, to April 2, 1865. April 3, occupied Richmond (related in Chap. 1). After Lincoln obsequies sent to Maryland's eastern shore and lower Potomac to help capture assassins. Then to Texas border to mop up Confederate hold-outs and guard against troops of the French puppet Emperor of Mexico. Mustered out October, 1865.

Page 82. Regimental flag of Treasury Guards, the volunteer organization of Treasury employees, can be seen today at Lincoln Museum (formerly Ford's Theater), Tenth Street, Washington.

The special dirge by Marine Band was composed by Major General John G. Barnard, Chief Engineer of Armies in the Field. Barnard was deaf.

"We have shown today the neatest and most soldierly troops, the most splendid military equipment, a galaxy of the most illustrious faces ever known in a single nation, and a civilian display which was not more suggestive of the spirit of our nationality than it was overwhelming, reliant, temperate, and respectful. The day of the panic has gone by. . . . We regret that man but we feel the country is eternal." "Gath," *New York World,* April 20.

Page 83. Mr. Gurley's prayer: *Chronicle,* April 20.

"At the time of the funeral, the Union Light Guard together with the company of infantry attended without arms as mourners, occupying the Blue Room," related Robert W. McBride, a member of the troop, in *Personal Recollections of Abraham Lincoln.* p. 74. "The two companies marched behind the hearse to the Capitol and encircled the coffin in the center of the great rotunda while the final family funeral service was conducted by Rev. Dr. Gurley. The only persons within the circle thus formed were the officiating clergy, Robert T. Lincoln, members of the Cabinet, and a few general officers."

Page 84. Extracts from General Meigs' pocket diaries which he carried with him during the war: "April 20—Lying-in-state in Capitol—The body is embalmed and well preserved. The discoloration of the eyes is gone and swelling reduced. Placed in charge by Secretary Stanton. I visited Capitol several times during the day. April 21—At 6 A.M. at the Capitol. The Cabinet, Gen'l Grant, etc. and myself removed to the railroad depot, placed it in a funeral car with that of his son, Willie Lincoln. At 8 A.M. The last of our great and good President left the city. He will live in history with Washington. The one connects his name with Republican Liberty; the other with Personal Liberty and Emancipation." "M. C. Meigs Collection," Library of Congress.

Page 85. Newsman in the gallery was Noah Brooks, *Washington in Lincoln's Time, op. cit.,* p. 236.

Page 87. Transportation Division of Smithsonian Institution, Howard I. Chapelle, Curator, and John H. White, Jr., Curator of Land Transportation.

Page 88. Girder-and-rivited-plate construction was described by president of Union Pacific Railroad Company, Carl R. Gray, in a speech before American Branch of Newcomen Society, New York, 1937. U. P. was the first private owner. One of the actual builders, W. H. H. Price, foreman of car shop of the U.S. Military Railroad at Alexandria, Virginia, did not mention this special design in his letter to *Locomotive Engineering,* September, 1893. He indicated regular construction. After using for trips by officials, U. P. sold the car and it was exhibited at St. Louis World's Fair in 1904 and at various fairs around the country. Bought by Thomas M. Lowry of Minneapolis and placed on exhibition, surrounded by a "crate," the car was destroyed in a prairie grass fire March 18, 1911. Ashes were combed by souvenir hunters.

At Union Pacific Museum, Omaha, Nebraska, are displayed original lounge-beds, silver service, oil paintings, and other paraphernalia of the car, including a scale model. (Open to public weekdays.)

Page 89. Flag that draped the casket: "The flag was obtained new from
the Quartermaster Department and was used throughout the entire
route to Springfield to drape President Lincoln's casket and whenever
it was moved from the car to the halls where the remains lay in state.
In the halls the casket was opened down to the waist so as to display
the face and bust to the view of the people," wrote General Townsend
on May 17, 1889, in response to a request from Secretary of War
Redfield Proctor. "When the last rites were concluded I brought the
flag away." Was encased and placed in Secretary of War's Office. *401A
(AGO) 1865, National Archives.* Flag is now at Lincoln Museum
(Ford's Theater), Tenth Street, Washington.

Family pastor's final words. *National Intelligencer,* April 22.

Page 91. General Townsend's authority: *Letter of Instructions,* April 20,
from Secretary of War, "Official duties prevent the Secretary of War
from gratifying his desire to accompany the remains of the late beloved and distinguished President, Abraham Lincoln, and therefore
Assistant Adjutant-General Townsend is specially assigned to represent the Secretary of War and to give all necessary orders in the name
of the Secretary of War as if he were present." Stanton listed eight
specific items for Townsend to follow. *1522-W-1865, AGO, encl. 9,
National Archives.*

AGO General Order No. 72, April 20, appointed ten general officers
as Guard of Honor; but there were last minutes changes. QM. Genl.
Montgomery C. Meigs was assigned to accompany Genl. Grant to
resume hostilities in North Carolina. The final group—appearing in
Washington, Philadelphia, and New York dailies—included afore-
mentioned Genl. Townsend; Bvt. Brig. Genl. James A. Ekin, in charge
of purchase and inspection of horses; Brig. Genl. A. D. Eaton, Com-
missary Genl.; Bvt. Maj. Genl. J. G. Barnard, Chief Engineer of
Armies in the Field; Brig. Genl. Geo. D. Ramsay, Chief of Ordnance;
Brig. Genl. A. P. Howe, Inspector of Artillery; Brig. Genl. Charles
Thomas, Ass't. QM. Genl.; Brig. Genl. D. C. McCallum, Supt. of
Military Railroads; Brig. Genl. J. C. Caldwell, president of commission
for examination of officers reported for dismissal; and Maj. Genl.
David Hunter, unassigned. Secretary of the Navy appointed Rear
Adm. Charles H. Davis to represent him, with aides Capt. W. R.
Taylor, U.S. Navy; and Maj. T. II. Field, Marine Corps.

Footnote: *The Collected Works of Abraham Lincoln* (Rutgers edition), VIII, 422.

Chapter 6

Page 97. News quotes: *New York Herald*, April 22.

Page 99. Comment on Lincoln: *Baltimore Sun*, April 22.

Page 100. The *Sun*, April 22, reported Governor Bradford and staff, along with General Tyler who represented the district military commander (General "Lew" Wallace) and staff, proceeded to Annapolis Junction and met the cortege, escorting it to Baltimore.

Page 101. Telegraphic advices from the War Department to the governors and district commanders were sent April 19. These were published in leading newspapers as were the governors' proclamations.

The timetable and program mentioned in the War Department telegram referred to the four-page black-bordered folder noted in Chap. 3, p. 59, explanatory note.

Page 103. *Pennsylvania Daily Telegraph*, April 22.

Page 104. Nicolay and Hay, *op. cit.*, X, 349.

Point Lookout dispatch: *Telegraph*, April 22.

"The one all-absorbing subject of conversation": *New York Herald*, April 22.

Harrisburg was a staging area for Union troops throughout the war; called "The Rendezvous of the North." Sent more men enlisted in more ways than any other Union camp—three-month men, three-year men, duration men, Pennsylvania Reserves, draftees, nine-month and hundred-day volunteers; a total of 300,000 from every loyal state. See *Northern Rendezvous—Harrisburg During the Civil War*, by Janet M. Book.

Page 105. Secretary of War's 1865 summary: *Official Records, op. cit.* Series III, Vol. V, p. 511.

Page 107. *Abraham Lincoln and the Sleeping Sentinel*, the Vermont Historical Society account by W. F. Glover. The Scotts were Scotch;

the father, Thomas, arrived in America in 1825. Five sons were in the
Union army including William. Three died in service and one soon
after returning home. William enlisted at Montpelier July 10, 1861;
arrived in Washington July 26. A month later, August 31, the officer
of the guard found him asleep at his post. The President pardoned him
September 9. Killed April 16, 1862, at Lee's Mill, Warwick, Virginia.

Page 108. Lincoln made the comment to C. H. Philbrick, White House
clerk from Griggsville, Illinois, substituting for Nicolay; to whom he
wrote the circumstances October 28, 1864. "Nicolay Papers," Library
of Congress.

Wm. F. Zornow's "Lincoln Voters Among the Boys in Blue," *The
Lincoln Herald,* Fall, 1952, concludes, "The soldier vote was not
decisive in the 1864 election." See also T. Harry Williams' "Voters
in Blue, the Citizen Soldiers of the Civil War," *Mississippi Valley
Historical Review,* September, 1944.

Page 109. Lincoln's comment to McClure: *Our Presidents, and How
We Make Them* by Alexander K. McClure, p. 184.

"This government must be preserved . . .": Remarks to the One
Hundred Forty-eighth Ohio Regiment, August 31, 1864.

Chapter 7

Page 111. "American Hotel, Philadelphia, Sunday, April 23, 1865. Dear
General Butler: 'The Beloved Remains' are knocking the machinery
of social life here into a cocked hat. I could not get a bed at any hotel
last night—had to sleep in my shawl on some chairs—fought for my
breakfast and am inexorably parted from my luggage." Letter from
Samuel Wilkeson in *Private and Official Correspondence of General
Benjamin F. Butler.* (Wilkeson had been a judge in Buffalo. Moved to
Washington to edit American Colonization Society publications.
Governed Negro colony of Liberia. Well acquainted with Lincoln.
Headed *New York Tribune* Washington bureau.)

Page 112. Union League: Despite the massiveness of Lincolniana and
Civil War literature there is need for a comprehensive work on the
Union League movement—this patriotic uprising of civilians during
the war that upheld Lincoln and the Union like Job's sons upheld

his arms. An excellent beginning is Guy J. Gibson's doctoral disserta-
tion, "Lincoln's League—the Union League Movement During the
Civil War." One of the greatest untold stories of Lincoln and the
American people.

Page 113. News quote: April 22, *North American and United States
Gazette*; "No common bereavement could have evoked such an extraordinary demonstration. . . . His inanimate remains go back in a
funeral pageant unequalled for its prodigious length and immense
preparations. . . . Those who have questioned why the funeral should
traverse such a route may see in this its appropriateness—that it is
exactly that traveled by our lamented chief on his way to the capital
to be inaugurated."

The motto on the Liberty Bell is from Lev. 25:10.

Page 114. Lincoln's address in Independence Hall: February 22, 1861.

Allan Pinkerton and Frederick Seward both published accounts of
the Baltimore plot. President Lincoln also presented his version. Chap.
22 and 23 *Lincoln's Journey to Greatness* by this author.

Page 115. News quote: *Philadelphia Inquirer,* April 24.

News quote *Philadelphia News,* April 24.

Page 117. Mrs. Olmsted's letter: Lincoln Collection, Lincoln Memorial
University, Harrogate, Tenn.

"Reminiscences of Abraham Lincoln" by Grace Greenwood in the
New York Independent, April 4, 1895.

Page 118. Loyal Legion. *Historical Address, the Military Order of the
Loyal Legion of Maine, Fiftieth Anniversary,* by Major H. S. Burrage.
"We halt for a backward look tonight. One of those memories carries
us back to that saddest of all sad days. . . April 15, 1865. Three officers
who had served in the Union Army during the war. . . while conferring
together concerning the thoughts in all hearts and upon all lips, the
suggestion was borne in upon them of an organization of officers of
the army and navy similar to the Society of Cincinnatus of the
Revolution that would perpetuate the companionships and experiences of the War of the Rebellion."

Maj. Genl. George Cadwallader of Philadelphia was elected first commander of the Pennsylvania Commandery on Nov. 8, 1865, the first to be organized. See *Ceremonies in Commemoration of Abraham Lincoln.*

Page 119. News quote: *Philadelphia Telegraph,* April 25.

Page 120. Judge Kelley's speech: *Telegraph,* April 26.

Page 123. Verse reporting Jersey City reception (*New York Herald,* April 25) was introduced thusly: "No deeper reverence and no more profound respect was ever paid to the living or dead of mortal men. He was received. . ."

Chapter 8

Page 126. Squeezing anecdote: *New York News,* April 25. Irish woman, *New York Tribune,* April 25.

Page 127. Woodsman and elderly lady anecdotes: *New York Tribune,* April 25.

Page 128. *New York Herald* quote: April 27.

A book could be devoted to describing the community decorations and especially the mottoes and expressions of grief that appeared everywhere; their originality and variety were remarkable. The many quotes from literary sources revealed widespread familiarity with classical literature. The biblical references were particularly numerous. Americans were clearly seen as an educated people. This was true not only of Manhattan and adjacent communities but all along the route.

Page 130. Of City Hall rotunda the *Herald,* April 25, said: "There is no trace of interior architecture. From dome to base there is a wall of crape, relieved by shrouded ensigns and semi-circular folds of black paramatta; all these are arched by festoons which fall gracefully over the combined display of flags and mourning, the symbols of the life of the Republic and the death of its ruler."

The photographer was Jeremiah Gurney, Jr. of J. Gurney and Son, 707 Broadway.

Exclusive photographing right had been granted by city authorities since the lying-in-state was on city property, permission having been given also by General Townsend (who was in the picture). Late Tuesday evening Stanton wired Townsend: "I see by the New York papers this evening that a photograph of the corpse of President Lincoln was allowed to be taken yesterday. . . I cannot sufficiently express my surprise and disapproval of such an act. . ." The Secretary ordered all plates and prints seized and demanded a full report. Townsend replied from Albany where the wire reached him that he was responsible; to which Stanton responded, "Having no other officer of the Adjutant General's Department that can relieve you, you will continue. . . The taking of the photograph was expressly forbidden by Mrs. Lincoln." Townsend, along with others in the entourage, believed the photograph was justified as showing "a grand view of what thousands saw but thousands could not see." He was right but so was Mrs. Lincoln, who abhorred this public display of her dear one's corpse. It all depended on the point of view. Beecher, Bryant, Raymond, and others supported the general, and he sent a print to the Secretary to support his position. Somehow this print escaped destruction over the years and turned up in the "Nicolay Papers" at the Illinois Historical Society, Springfield.

Interchange of telegrams between Stanton and Townsend: *Official Records, op. cit.,* Series I, Vol. XLVI, Part III, p. 952, *op. cit.*

Page 131. "Common-looking fellow": Nicolay and Hay, *op. cit.,* X, 347. "He was a great and powerful lover of mankind, especially those not favored by fortune," say his secretaries in introducing this anecdote, and note that because "Lincoln kept himself in such constant sympathy with the common people he was rewarded by a reverence and love hardly ever given to a human being."

Page 132. *Lincoln in Photographs* by Charles Hamilton and Lloyd Ostendorf, p. ix. *The Photographs of Lincoln* by Frederick H. Meserve and Carl Sandburg.

Herndon quote: *Abraham Lincoln; the True Story of a Great Life* by William H. Herndon and Jesse W. Weik, generally known as *Herndon's Lincoln,* III, 587. Without Herndon we would not know Lincoln as a person. Here is Herndon to Truman Bartlett (a Boston sculptor): "He seemed to have no blood in his frame; his flesh was dark and wrinkled and folded; it looked leathery and dry, tough and everlasting," from *The Hidden Lincoln* by Emanuel Hertz, p. 185. Again on p.

198: "The flesh was coarse, dry, hard, heavily-wrinkled, saffron-brown, with no blood seemingly in it."

Donn Piatt: *Memories of Men Who Saved the Union,* p. 30.

Page 133. Ward Lamon: *The Life of Abraham Lincoln,* p. 469.

General Sherman: *Memoirs, op. cit.,* p. 328.

Marquis de Chambrun: "Personal Recollections of Mr. Lincoln," *op. cit.,* p. 32.

"Art speaks in ways words never can": In his letter to *New York Independent,* April 26, F. B. Carpenter noted that it was the business of his life to study the human face "and I say now, as I have said repeatedly to my friends, that Mr. Lincoln had the saddest face I ever painted." (For more on Carpenter see p. 173.)

Isaac N. Arnold: "easily caricatured," *The History of Abraham Lincoln and the Overthrow of Slavery,* p. 675; "tenderness of heart," *The Life of Abraham Lincoln,* p. 442.

Page 135. "Observer" quotes: *New York Times,* April 25.

Co-publisher of Bryant's *New York Evening Post* was Parke Godwin.

Page 136. *The Report of Special Committee on Volunteering of the County of New York, Document #12, August 15, 1866.* "Documents, Board of Supervisors," vol. II, part 2, p. 9 shows that "expenditures from Public Funds" totaled $20,632,265. This figure included $9 million for bounties, $6 million for relief of volunteer families during the war, $1½ million for riot damages, $1½ million for interest on borrowed money and for other items furnished such as equipment, rations, etc.

Determining the number of men furnished the armed forces looks easy but is difficult owing to multiple enlistments—30-day men, 3-month men, 100-day men, 3-year men, volunteers from other states, and the disloyal bounty jumpers. In his *New York in the War of the Rebellion,* (I, 69), Bvt. Maj. Genl. Frederick Phisterer sets up a formula based on population. His careful compilations show that about 400,000 men were furnished and this represented 10.30 per cent of the total state population. Applying this ratio to New York City's population of 814,000 (1860 federal census) would result in 82,000. But others claim New York state furnished closer to half a million. So our figure of 90,000 for Manhattan (which then comprised New York City) would seem to be about right. Sources from New York Public Library.

Page 138. Gen. E. D. Townsend, *Anecdotes of the Civil War*, p. 233.

Page 139, 140. News quotes: *New York Post*, April 24, 25, 26.

Page 141. Bancroft's speech: *Post*, April 26. Exercises at Union Square: *Times*, April 26.

Page 142. Bryant's other poem: *Post*, April 26, titled "Thou Hast Put All Things Under His Feet" was not germane to Lincoln.

Chapter 9

Page 146. News quotes: *Times* and *Post*, April 15, *World*, April 17.

Page 147. McCulloch's letter April 16 to Stewart: "McCulloch Papers," Library of Congress.

Stewart's letter: *ibid.*

Page 148: *Herald* quote: April 18.

Footnote: *Men and Measures of Half a Century* by Hugh McCulloch (Secretary of the Treasury under Lincoln, Johnson and Arthur), p. 226.

Page 149. *Times* quote: April 26.

Table of bond purchases and Horace Greeley quotes: *Tribune*, April 28.

Page 150. Lincoln to Kennedy: *Lincoln's Journey to Greatness, op. cit.*, p. 187.

Rev. Hitchcock quote: *Post*, April 26.

Page 151. Raymond on Petigru: *Times*, April 17. Raymond was founder and editor of the *Times*.

Carpenter's letters: *Post*, April 18 and 22.

Page 153. *Harper's Weekly*, April 29.

Page 154. Railroad time table published in most New York papers; this quote from *Herald*, April 25.

Page 156. Depew quote: Speech at *Centennial Celebration of Birth of Abraham Lincoln* held by the G.A.R. Dept. of New York at Seventy-first Regiment Armory.

Page 157. "Observer" quote: *New York World*, April 27.

Chapter 10

Page 158. *Life of Thurlow Weed*, 2 vols., the first volume edited by favorite daughter, Harriet, called *Autobiography* and second volume, called *Memoirs*, edited by grandson Thurlow Weed Barnes, son of Emily, another daughter.

Page 159. Tweed: *"Boss" Tweed: the Story of a Grim Generation* by Denis T. Lynch; and *Tiger in the Streets* by Wm. A. Bales. Both have bibliographies for further study.

Tweed's son, W. M. Jr., acted as aide to Second Division Marshal in Tuesday's farewell procession. This division comprised city, county, state, and federal officials. *New York News*, April 24.

Page 163. Santayana remark: *The Philosophy of Santayana*, p. 666.

Page 164. Footnote: *Personal Recollections of Early Decatur and Abraham Lincoln* by (Mrs.) Jane Martin Johns, p. 15.

Senator Albert J. Beveridge commented in his *Abraham Lincoln, 1809-1858*, I, 177, that "this legislature (1836) was remarkable not only in what was done but in the quality of its members."

Page 165. "To be able to raise a cause": Lincoln's response to query of T. W. S. Kidd, Springfield's court crier, cited by Carl Sandburg, *The Prairie Years*, II, 115.

Lincoln's temperance speech: To Washingtonian Temperance Society in Springfield, February 22, 1842.

"The human instrumentalities": From his "Meditations on the Divine Will" quoted in full at close of Chap. 14.

"Every foul bird comes abroad": From letter to Chas. D. Drake and others of a Kansas-Missouri delegation who called on him October 5, 1863.

Page 166. "Where there is no vision": Prov. 29:18.

Herndon's quotes: *Herndon's Lincoln*, III, 606.

Footnote: Nicolay and Hay, *op. cit.*, X, 355.

Page 167. Absalom and King David: II Sam. 15.

Page 168. *Recollections of the Civil War* by Charles A. Dana, p. 175.

Page 169. The one-hundred-gun salvo on Capitol Hill was not the only way Lincoln was apprised of the outcome. A military telegraph ran from the Capitol to the War Department, maintained by the latter. Private Secretary Nicolay was on the scene and wired the President: "Constitutional amendment just passed by 119 for 56 votes against." "Nicolay Papers," Library of Congress.

Lincoln to Rollins: Told by Rollins in *The Lincoln Memorial*, O. H. Oldroyd (ed.), p. 493.

Page 170. Footnote. Federal bureaucracy: *Lincoln and the Patronage* by H. J. Carman and R. H. Luthin, p. 331. Today: *Congressional Record*, "Annual Report of the Senate Committee on Nonessential Federal Expenditures," Senator Harry F. Byrd (Va.), Chairman.

Chapter 11
Page 172. Albany speech to legislature: February 18, 1861.

Page 174. A more direct precedent was the return, thirteen years earlier, of another notable Kentuckian, the great Henry Clay, Lincoln's "beau ideal." The Sage of Ashland died in Washington, not long after making his immortal speech in the Senate, "This Union is my country." His remains were brought back to Lexington by way of Baltimore, Philadelphia, New York, Buffalo, Cleveland, Cincinnati, and Louisville; and it was the most impressive cortege up to that of Lincoln's overwhelming journey.

Nicolay to Therena Bates: "Nicolay Papers." Library of Congress.

Lincoln to Massachusetts' governor: February 7, 1861.

Page 175. Secretaries quote: Nicolay and Hay, *op. cit.*, III, 289.

Herndon quotes: *Herndon's Lincoln, op. cit.*, III, 479.

Page 176. Greeley quote: *New York Tribune*, February 19, 1861.

Page 177. "When a first class mind": "Lincoln, the Constitutional Lawyer," by John M. Zane, *Abraham Lincoln Association Papers* (Springfield, 1933). His father, Charles S., was associated with Lincoln from 1856 to 1861 and became Herndon's partner after Lincoln went to Washington. He ended a long and honorable legal career as first Chief Justice of Utah Supreme Court. Family name still lives as Zanesville, Ohio. The son was a prominent Chicago attorney and author. He remarked that "the objection to the statements of such original sources as Herndon, Lamon, Whitney, Swett, even Judge Davis and many others, is that they strongly tint Lincoln's mentality with their own." He is right but unfortunately there is no other way hermeneutists can carry on; that is why history must be continually revised and reevaluated. Zane suggested the subject speak for himself; and this we have tried to do herein.

Page 178. *Cincinnati Commercial* quote: February 15, 1861.

New York Herald quote: February 14, 1861.

Lincoln's letter accepting nomination: May 23, 1860.

New York Times quote: February 16, 1861.

Page 180. Davis quote: Letter February 8, 1861, to Simon Cameron, "Cameron Papers," Library of Congress.

Lincoln's expositions of his "House Divided" concept were presented in various speeches during the campaign with Douglas; for example, July 10, 1858, speech at Chicago.

Page 181. Fort Sumter: Probably Lincoln's most difficult and certainly his most fateful decision. A great deal of partisan writing has gone into this turning point of American history. Browning in his *Diary* (July 24, 1862—over a year after the event) wrote that Lincoln "was sustained by only two members of his Cabinet, Blair and Chase, and that when he determined to give the rebels notice of his purpose the entire Cabinet was against him although they all now admitted he was right." Browning had only part of the story. When the alternative of evacuating the fort or provisioning it was put to the Cabinet on March 15, five members advised withdrawal; Chase gave an ambiguous reply; Blair alone stood for it; and when their opinions were canvassed two weeks later, Blair, Chase, and Wells unequivocally favored the provisioning expedition, the others still opposed. The Navy maintained the fort could be taken. The army (General Scott) said that to do so would require 20,000 trained men and then would be problematical. The pulling and hauling to which Lincoln was subjected was something fierce. His determination had to be made against confusion compounded.

Page 182. Hay to Herndon: September 5, 1866, *The Hidden Lincoln, op. cit.*, p. 307-8.

Page 183. Seward's response to serenade: *Seward at Washington* by Frederick W. Seward, III, 249.

Page 185. "The Knickerbockers of Albany": *New York Tribune*, April 27, 1865.

Page 186. *Rochester Union* comment quoted in *Buffalo Express*, May 1.

Page 187. *Buffalo Express* quotes: April 28. The editor rode with Lincoln on the inaugural journey as chairman of Buffalo delegation. He was a staunch supporter. Lincoln appointed him postmaster.

Page 188. Townsend quote: *Anecdotes of the Civil War, op. cit.*, p. 235.

Chapter 12

Page 190. Demarcation of juridical jurisdiction between civil and military is not easy in a democracy during civil conflict. General Townsend in *Anecdotes of the Civil War, op. cit.*, Chap. 35, offers clear exposition of the "Origins of Military Commissions." He points out on p. 163 that Washington was a garrisoned town having in and around it several thousand soldiers to protect public officials and public property. "The President was Commander-in-Chief of the Army and his murder was adjudged to be clearly within the statutes."

Additionally, the day before the deed AGO General Order No. 64

stated, "The Headquarters of the Armies of the United States are established at Washington, D.C." With Commander-in-Chief and Chief-of-the-Armies both in a city encircled by forts manned by troops and war still going on, the military *had* to assume adjudication of the crime against its head. There was no alternative.

Page 191. Jefferson Davis to Jacob Thompson: *Official Records*, Series IV, vol. III, p. 332.

Page 195. *Confederate Operations in New York and Canada* by John W. Headley details his personal operations in sabotage and espionage against the Union.

Page 197. Felix Stidger relates his undercover experiences in *Treason History of the Sons of Liberty*.

Page 198. See *The Pinkerton Story* by J. E. Horan and Howard Swiggett, p. 120 ff.

Page 199. "The fire in the rear": Bibliographies on undercover activities are in *The Hidden Civil War* by Wood Gray; *Abraham Lincoln and the Fifth Column* by G. F. Milton; *Confederate Agent* by James D. Horan; and the conspirators plottings are detailed in Theodore Roscoe's *The Web of Conspiracy*.

In *Secret Missions of the Civil War* P. V. D. Stern concludes: "There is every reason to believe unseen backers were aiding him [the assassin] but their identity is shrouded in mystery."

A seldom mentioned powerful force, that of orthodox religion and its allies, is discussed in Emmett McLoughlin's *An Inquiry into the Assassination of Abraham Lincoln*. A hundred years ago the United States of America was viewed by the reigning monarchs of the Old World as the Russian experiment is being viewed by the "free" world today—radical. America, and its doctrine of government by the people, was considered by them a threat to world peace and so orthodoxy wanted the nation destroyed that said all men are created equal; hoping and helping it to consume itself in fratricide. Only now do we begin to recognize how close to the brink we came, and how much we owe to Abraham Lincoln for preserving our ideals. See *Lincoln and the Emperors* by A. R. Tyrner-Turnauer.

A singular fact thus takes on added significance. No coroner's inquest was ever held over Lincoln's body; no legal evidence on the manner of his death was ever assembled; and not a single person accused of connection with the crime was ever brought into a court of law. Not to this day are there any legal facts on his murder, the cause of it, or who killed him.

Page 202. "Among the people of the Southern States": First Inaugural Address.

"How *sound* and *strong* we are": Response to Serenade, November 10, 1864.

Chapter 13
Page 203. Townsend: *Anecdotes of the Civil War, op. cit.,* 225.

Page 204. Grace Bedell's letter, at this writing, reposes in the vault of the Delphos State Bank, the bank founded by her husband now run by their grandson, Rodger Billings.

Page 208. Campbell quotes: Letter to Daniel Chandler (brother-in-law) December 4, 1860, *Southern Historical Society Papers,* XLII, 24, Library of Congress.

Page 210. "Slavery is grounded in selfishness": Peoria Speech, October 16, 1854.

"This is a world of compensation": Letter to Henry L. Pierce and others April 6, 1859, given wide circulation in the press.

Page 211. "Those who deny freedom to others": Letter to Henry L. Pierce, *ibid.*

Page 212. Horace Greeley in *New York Tribune:* " 'Buy Louisiana for us!' said the slaveholders. 'With pleasure.' 'Now Florida!' 'Certainly.' Next, 'Violate your treaties with the Creeks and Cherokees and expel those tribes from the lands they have held from time immemorial so as to let us expand our plantations.' 'So said, so done.' 'Now for Texas!' 'You have it.' 'Next, a third more of Mexico!' 'Yours it is.' 'Now break the Missouri Compact and let Slavery wrestle with Free Labor for this vast region consecrated by the Compact to Freedom.' 'Very good. What next?' 'Buy Cuba for 150 millions.' 'We have tried but

Spain refuses to sell.' 'Then wrest it from her at all costs!' And all this time, while slavery was using the Union as her catspaw, dragging the Republic into iniquitous wars and enormous expenditures, and grasping empire after empire thereby, the Northern men (or more accurately men at the North) were constantly asking why people living in the Free States would not leave Slavery alone." Quoted in Greeley's *The American Conflict*, I, 354-55.

Page 213. Wilmot Proviso: In his Peoria Speech Lincoln remarked, "I think I may venture to say I voted for it at least forty times during the short term I was there."

Page 215. Lincoln's two slave cases: The Nance case (Bailey vs. Cromwell) was heard at Tremont Circuit Court, Tazewell County, July 23, 1841. Lincoln lost. He appealed to the state Supreme Court and won. He established as basic principles that "the presumption of law in Illinois is that every person is free without regard to color," and that "the sale of a free person is illegal." His second case heard at Coles County Circuit Court, Charleston, October 16, 1847, involved the runaway slaves of Robert Matson who put them in jail before trying to take them back to Kentucky. Lincoln represented the slave-owner in what some biographers characterize as "one of the oddest anomalies in the life of this man of paradoxes." The Court, on a writ of habeas corpus, ordered the slaves discharged from sheriff's custody. Lincoln's next case on the docket (Watson vs. Gill) he won. A week later he and the family left Springfield for Washington to serve his term in Congress.

Page 216. *Uncle Tom's Cabin:* Everybody knows this book written by Harriet Beecher Stowe to whom Lincoln said, when she came to see him at the White House, "So you're the little woman who wrote the book that made this great war." Few people know she wrote a supplementary book, *A Key to Uncle Tom's Cabin; Presenting the Original Facts and Documents upon Which the Story Is Founded. Together with Corroborative Statements Verifying the Work.*

The Impending Crisis by Hinton R. Helper is less known today; but it had such a powerful effect that its author, a North Carolinian, had to flee to New York for his safety. Helper wrote facts and figures that produced a devastating picture.

"We find ourselves": Address, "The Perpetuation of Our Political Institutions," January 27, 1838.

Page 217. Twice defeated for senator; Senators were then elected by the state legislature, not by popular vote as now.

"In giving freedom to the slave"; Message to Congress, December 1, 1862.

Chapter 14

Page 219. "While at Columbus I rec'd a note from a lady accompanying a little cross made of wild violets. The note said the writer's little girls had gone to the woods in the early morning and gathered the flowers with which they had wrought the cross. They desired it might be laid on little Willie's coffin, 'they felt so sorry for him' ": Townsend, *Anecdotes of the Civil War, op. cit.,* p. 237.

Footnote: Walt Whitman's lecture, "Death of Abraham Lincoln," appears in *Complete Writings of Walt Whitman.* His four poems on Lincoln appeared originally in *Sequel to Drum Taps.* Oddly, Whitman's composition for which he is most widely known, "O Captain, my Captain," is least like him; it has meter and rhyme.

Page 220. State senator from Chillicothe district was Job E. Stevenson, an outstanding orator.

Ohio State Journal quote: May 1.

Page 222. Footnote: An advertisement April 20, *Cincinnati Gazette:* "As Played with Great Applause by Menter's Band—Hess' *Funeral March in Memory of President Lincoln.* Price 40 cents, post free. Published by A. C. Peters & Bros., Pike's Opera Bldg., Cincinnati, O."

The marble bust was sculpted from life in a Springfield hotel room while the President-elect composed his journey speeches. Statue now stands at head of stairway outside Senate chamber in State House at Columbus. Sculptor Thomas D. Jones was an Ohioan. See his *Memories of Lincoln.*

Page 226. Letter to Mrs. Gurney: September 4, 1864.

Remarks made to a delegation of "Progressive Friends": June 20, 1862.

Response to emancipation proposal of a group of Chicago clergymen representing various religious denominations: September 13, 1862.

Page 227. His two-and-a-half-hour Lewistown speech, August 17, four days before first debate with Douglas at Ottawa, was not reported in full by the press. *Chicago Press and Tribune* reporter set down a summary of "Mr. Lincoln's noble and impressive apostrophe to the Declaration of Independence." He asked Lincoln to check it over. Lincoln did, saying, "Well, those are my views . . . but not nearly so well as that is said." However, so well did others think of his views they were reprinted in 1860 campaign literature, titled "Lincoln on the Declaration of Independence."

Page 228. "Don't kneel to me": Admiral D. D. Porter, "President Lincoln's Entry into Richmond," *Belford's Magazine,* September and October, 1890, p. 590. Wrote the admiral, "Mr. Lincoln looked on the poor creatures at his feet; he was much embarrassed at his position. . . 'You must kneel only to God,' he said, 'I am but God's humble instrument.' "

"As your Father in Heaven": July 10, 1858, speech. King James Version, Matt. 5:48 reads: "Be ye therefore perfect, even as your Father which is in Heaven is perfect."

Page 229. Footnote: Lincoln to Choate, December 19, 1864.

Page 232. Lincoln's "Meditation on the Divine Will": Actual date of composition is not known. Nicolay and Hay, *op. cit.,* VI, 341, say, "It is a paper which Mr. Lincoln wrote in September, 1862"; and then in their *Complete Works* (Gettysburg-Tandy edition) question that date.

Chapter 15

Page 235. The three railroads taking the train from Indianapolis to Chicago operated under agreed-upon regulations as follows:

RULES AND REGULATIONS.

1. The figures in Table represent the time upon which the Pilot Engine is to be run; and the FUNERAL TRAIN will follow, leaving each Station ten minutes behind the figures of this Table.
2. The Funeral Train will pass Stations at a speed not exceeding five miles an hour, the Engineman tolling his bell as the Train passes through the Station and Town.
3. Telegraph Offices upon the entire route will be kept open during the

passage of the Funeral Train, and as soon as the Train has passed a Station, the operator will at once give notice to that effect to the next Telegraph Station.

4. The Pilot Engine will pass no Telegraph Station without first getting information of Funeral Train having passed the last preceding Telegraph Station, coming to a full stop for that information, if necessary.

5. Upon the entire route a Safety Signal will be shown at each Switch and Bridge, and at entrance upon each curve, indicating that all is safe for the passage of Pilot and Train—each man in charge of a signal knowing personally such to be the case, so far as his foresight can provide for it. The signal from Indianapolis until reaching broad daylight to be a White Light, and from that point to Chicago, a White Flag, draped.

6. The Engineman in charge of Pilot Engine will carry two red lights in the night, and an American flag, draped, during daylight, at head of Engine, indicating that a Train is following; and will also provide themselves with proper red lights, flags and extra men, to give immediate notice to the Funeral Train in case of meeting with anything on the route causing delay or detention.

7. The Engineman in charge of the Funeral Train will keep a sharp look out for the Pilot Engine and its signals.

8. The Pilot and Funeral Train will have entire right to the line during its passage, and all Engines and Trains of every description will be kept out of the way.

9. Each Road forming the route will run its Train upon its own standard time.

W. F. REYNOLDS,	B. F. MASTEN,	R. N. RICE,
Pres. L. & I. R. R.	Sup't. L., N. A. & C. R. R.	Gen. Sup't. M. C. R. R.

Page 238. *Tribune* quote: May 2. "Behold how they loved him" is a paraphrase of John 11:36.

Page 239. "Conquered the hearts of his countrymen": Lincoln has become America's greatest national figure. A survey by the American Institute of Public Opinion (Gallup poll) asking which was the greater gave Lincoln a 2 to 1 margin over Washington; the principal reasons being that Lincoln "was a greater humanitarian, more down to earth, more of a people's president . . . he was a self-made man." James Russell Lowell wrote in his "Commemorative Ode": "Here was a type of the true older race/ And one of Plutarch's men talked with us face to face. . . The kindly, earnest, brave, forseeing man/ New birth from our new soil, The First American."

Townsend quote: *Anecdotes of the Civil War, op. cit.*, p. 239.

"Here I have lived a quarter of a century . . .": From his never-to-be-forgotten "The Farewell to Springfield," February 11, 1861.

Page 240. Coming of the railroad into Logan County prompted platting of the town "named after I was." The naming took place in Lincoln's law office as he drew up power of attorney for the three landowners who were personal friends; he acting as their counsel, preparing deeds for sale of lots, etc. Several names were advanced and rejected and finally the principal owner proposed naming for their attorney who replied, "You better had not for I never knew anything named Lincoln that amounted to much." *History of Logan County* by Lawrence B. Stringer, I, 568.

On the gala lot-selling day (August 29, 1853) Lincoln came over, and it being typical corn-growing weather, bought two watermelons to cool off. Inviting his clients to share them he said, "Now we will christen the new town."

1654 miles: Itinerary and mileage on facing page.

Page 241. *Illinois State Journal* quotes: *April 26, op. cit.*

Crowded city: *Chicago Tribune,* May 4.

The *Journal* noted that a twenty-wagon emigrant train had arrived on its way to Oregon Territory.

At a meeting of the Sub-committee on Burial, the *Journal* reported that the offer of Jared P. Irwin to erect a vault free of charge had been accepted. The vault was partly constructed on the selected downtown site (where the state capitol now stands) before Mrs. Lincoln decided interment would be at Oak Ridge.

Page 242. "The whole community wearing widow's weeds": Total cost of the Lincoln obsequies to the federal government was only $30,000. Railroads furnished equipment and transportation without charge. Local communities paid expenses at their own stopovers—states paying a share at state capitals. The bulk of federal expenditure went for local Washington purposes; decorating public buildings, the hearse, catafalque, mourners' apparel, carriage hire, etc. The casket cost $1500 and was built of walnut not mahogany as most accounts have it. Embalming cost $100. Accounts were kept by Commissioner of Public Buildings French and are preserved at National Archives: *Records of the Office of the Secretary of Interior* (RG48), "Ledger containing a/c of expenditures for Lincoln funeral."

ITINERARY AND MILEAGE

First day—Friday, April 21
Washington to Baltimore, 38 miles, Baltimore and Ohio R.R.
Baltimore to Harrisburg, 85 miles, Northern Central R.R.

Second day—Saturday, April 22
Harrisburg to Philadelphia, 106 miles, Pennsylvania R.R.

Third day—Sunday, April 23
At Independence Hall, Philadelphia

Fourth day—Monday, April 24
Philadelphia to New York, 86 miles, from Kensington Station via Philadelphia
and Trenton R.R., Camden and Amboy R.R., New Jersey Transportation Co.,
and ferryboat across Hudson River from Jersey City to New York

Fifth day—Tuesday, April 25
New York City to Albany, 141 miles, Hudson River R.R. from 30th St. Station
to East Albany and by ferryboat across Hudson River to Albany

Sixth day—Wednesday, April 26
Albany to Buffalo, 298 miles, New York Central R.R.

Seventh day—Thursday, April 27
Buffalo to Cleveland, 183 miles, Buffalo and State Line R.R., Erie and
Northeast R.R. and Cleveland, Painesville and Ashtabula R.R. to Euclid
Ave. Station of Cleveland and Pittsburgh R.R.

Eighth day—Friday, April 28
Cleveland to Columbus, 135 miles, Cleveland, Columbus and Cincinnati Rwy.

Ninth day—Saturday, April 29
Columbus to Indianapolis, 187 miles, Columbus and Indianapolis Rwy. and
Indiana Central R.R.

Tenth day—Sunday, April 30
Indianapolis to Chicago, 210 miles, Indianapolis and Lafayette R.R., Louisville,
New Albany and Chicago R.R., Michigan Central R.R. and Illinois Central
R.R.

Eleventh day—May 1
At Cook County Courthouse, Chicago

Twelfth day—May 2
Chicago to Springfield, 184 miles, St. Louis, Alton and Chicago R.R.

Total Travel Time, 12 days
Total Mileage, 1,654 miles

Page 243. Herndon quote: *Herndon's Lincoln, op. cit.,* III, 573.

Quotes on appearance: *Chicago Tribune* and *Illinois State Journal,* May 4.

Contrariwise: "The face had considerably withered, the flesh adhering closely to the bone and the skin had turned dark. This might have been owing to the exposure since it was unprotected from the atmosphere all the way to Springfield," wrote L. A. Gobright, Chief of Washington Bureau of Associated Press in *Recollections of Men and Things at Washington,* p. 361.

Gobright, whose dispatches appeared in all AP members papers and who went the entire distance, said that although most of the traveling was at night no matter what hour crowds gathered "whenever we halted flowers were brought into the funeral car and placed on the coffin by the delicate hands which had culled them for this purpose." He concluded his recollection, *"It would have been impossible to render greater honors to any mortal remains."*

Page 244. "All America was in town": *Illinois State Register* reported through its editor: "The columns of marchers reached from curb to curb and in close order. . . The cortege was of such great numbers and so great a length that the head of the procession reached Oak Ridge before more than one-half of it was in line." *Transactions of the Illinois State Historical Society,* 1909, p. 182.

Page 245. "We have followed the remains": Dr. Adonis, *Chicago Tribune,* May 5.

Soldier's lament: "O, Wrap the Flag Around Me, Boys!" Words and music by Robert S. Taylor, Ft. Wayne, Indiana, written late 1861 or early 1862, purports to be the words of a dying soldier; and was an immediate hit. Third stanza: "But though my body moulder, boys,/ My spirit will be free./ And every comrade's honor, boys,/ Will still be dear to me./ There in the thick and bloody fight,/ Ne'er let your ardor lag,/ For I'll be there, still hov'ring near,/ Above the dear old flag." The One Hundred Forty-sixth Illinois Volunteer regimental band rendered the stirring ballad at the head of the procession from depot to State House; and again next day from State House to Oak Ridge. *Lincoln Lore 99,* Lincoln National Life Foundation, Ft. Wayne, Indiana.

Page 247. "As When Thy Cross Was Bleeding": This was a most appropriate hymn at this point in the program since it was first sung following President Lincoln's reading of his Second Inaugural Address.
Here it again followed his immortal words. G. F. Wright wrote the
lyrics. He also wrote those of the next hymn, "Over the Valley the
Angels Smile," especially for this occasion. His first hymn was set to
a familiar tune by Otto; the latter to a composition of Storch.

A dozen or more original hymns and dirges were published immedi-
ately following Lincoln's demise. Three have been mentioned, one in
Indianapolis and two in Chicago. Others include: "A Nation Weeps"
by J. W. Turner (Boston), "The Nation Is Weeping" by Louise S.
Upham (Providence), "President Lincoln's Funeral March" by
E. Mock (Philadelphia), "Abraham Lincoln's Funeral March " by W. J.
Robjohn (Detroit), "Our Noble Chief Has Passed Away" by George
Cooper and J. R. Thomas (New York). The Smithsonian Institution,
Division of Political History, Herbert R. Collins, Assistant Curator,
enriched by the Becker Collection of Political Americana, has originals
of the sheet music, a field of Lincolniana little explored.

Another little-explored field of Lincolniana is the poetry evoked in
his honor. That appearing at the time of his untimely end was tremendous. A representative collection was issued by J. B. Lippincott
and Company of Philadelphia (1865), *Poetical Tributes to the Memory
of Abraham Lincoln,* The next year Francis Janvier (of Sleeping
Sentinel fame) brought out *Patriotic Poems.* Other volumes have
appeared over the years such as O. H. Oldroyd's compilation *The
Poets' Lincoln,* and Archie D. Williams' *The Praise of Lincoln; an
Anthology.*

So huge was the output of poetry, the press threw up its hands
and closed its columns to the flood. Nor were the journals themselves
immune from rhymed emotion. The *National Republican,* the day after
the White House ceremonies, opened its lead editorial: "O, Earth, all
bathed in blood and tears, yet never/ Hast thou ceased putting forth
thy fruits and flowers"; and went on to ask if there was no pity left
for mankind. Shakespeare had a field day. Even public officials joined
in, and Comr. French concluded his account of the last day's events,
"Unveil thy bosom, sacred tomb/ Take this new treasure to thy trust/
And give these sacred relics room/ To slumber in the dust."

The *Chicago Tribune* announced (May 1) they were suffering from
a "severe attack of poetry. . . and an accurate inventory of the wind-

falls of the past three days discloses 45 poems which open 'Toll, toll, ye mournful bells, With saddening cadence toll'; and 115 gave the corresponding direction, 'Mourn, mourn, ye tolling bells, With cadent sadness mourn.'" The subject warrants further exploration since it is a little-known facet of Americana.

So also are the editorials that appeared in virtually every newspaper the country over. Regardless of their partisanship they offered a heartwarming aspect of American life at this trying period; not only expressing regret and sorrow but in many different ways telling of his high value to the nation. A representative collection is long overdue.

Of the ten thousand or more sermons delivered on this "Black Easter" Sunday and subsequent Sundays, many appeared in full or were excerpted in the press. Some have been preserved through the then widespread custom of congregations printing noteworthy sermons as tokens of appreciation to the pastor and distributing copies to all interested parties. Hundreds of these printings are scattered across the country in public libraries, historical societies, church repositories, and in collectors' files. No modern survey of them exists although several early compilations were made: *Sermons Preached in Boston on the Death of Abraham Lincoln* (1865) and *Our Martyr President, Abraham Lincoln* (1865).

Tribute poured in from around the globe, from heads of state, and from just plain people, many gathered in groups to express their condolences. The collection was printed in a folio volume of a thousand pages authorized by Joint Resolution of Congress (March 2, 1867) titled, *Tributes of the Nations to Abraham Lincoln*. Many cities issued commemorative volumes in which were included the ceremonial programs, eulogies, expressions of bereavement from prominent individuals and from many kinds of organizations. "Memorials" were issued also by cities along the homeward route such as New York, Troy, Indianapolis, and so on as well by outlying communities like Boston, Omaha, and San Francisco.

All and altogether, the memorabilia of Lincoln's passing—the badges, pamphlets, posters, books, special newspaper editions, magazine features, sketches, engravings, photographs and other souvenirs—is beyond belief. Here we can do no more than recommend further study. Nothing like it has been witnessed before or since. Thus did the American people demonstrate their understanding of "The People's President" and his contributions to the national welfare.

Chapter 16

Page 249. General Townsend's summary: *Anecdotes of the Civil War,
op. cit.,* Townsend has been frequently quoted herein since he was
the only member of the official escort, commissioned or enlisted, to
make a comprehensive report. He also reported daily by telegraph
to the Secretary of War and these are published in *Official Records,*
Series I, Vol. XLVI, Part III, p. 886 ff. *op. cit.*

Page 251. "My paramount object in this struggle": Letter on August 22,
1862, replying to Horace Greeley's "open letter." Lincoln ended his
letter, "I have here stated my purpose according to my view of *official*
duty; and I intend no modification of my oft-expressed *personal* wish
that all men everywhere could be free."

Page 252. "The whole galaxy of patriots": In this connection Lincoln's
retort was noteworthy when a delegation from Baltimore, where
federal troops passing through en route to Washington had been fired
on, came to see the President on April 22, 1861, and demanded he stop
the bloodshed forthwith and make peace on any terms. He exploded:
"There is no Washington in that—no Jackson in that—no manhood or
honor in that!"

Page 254. The voice of God speaks through the people: A similar concept is stated in Matt. 18:20: "Where two or three are gathered in my
name, there am I in the midst of them."

"The almost chosen people": Speech to the New Jersey Senate,
February 21, 1861. "I shall be most happy," he said, "if I shall be an
humble instrument in the hands of the Almighty, and of this, his
almost chosen people, for perpetuating the object of that great struggle." (He was referring to the struggle for American independence
many battles of which took place in New Jersey.)

"That form of government whose leading object is to elevate . . .":
Message to Congress, July 4, 1861.

Page 255. "Thanks to all" Letter to James C. Conkling, August 26, 1863.

Was the unprecedented outpouring of people only for Lincoln?
Were the long processions and immense throngs for him alone? Or
did thousands upon thousands of mothers, fathers, sisters, brothers,

aunts, uncles, cousins, wives, sweethearts, widows, orphans, friends
and neighbors hold this to be a vicarious ceremony for their lost loved
ones? Was not the memorial journey a national obsequy?

That conclusion did not escape the more perceptive. The Honorable
George Bancroft told a Joint Session of Congress on Lincoln's Birthday, 1866, that "though the hand of Lincoln raised the flag the
American people was the hero of the war." Lincoln would have so
viewed it himself, asserted his private secretaries, saying, "He would
have seen the pageantry and the processions as a collective ceremony
for the half-million fellow-citizens who died to keep their country free."

And an unnamed newsman, suffocating in the mass of mourners
and spectators watching the flag-draped casket escorted by hosts of
marchers, pleaded—

> O, countrymen, our deep regret
> Is wasted here; arise and pay
> To Freedom and to him your debt
> By following where he led the way.

BIBLIOGRAPHY

Following the closing scene depicted in the narrative, memorial books were quickly published that gained wide circulation. *The Memorial Record of the Nation's Tribute to Abraham Lincoln,* compiled by Benjamin F. Morris, was similar to J. D. G. Shea's *The Lincoln Memorial —a Record of the Life, Assassination and Obsequies of the Martyred President.* Both volumes devoted much space to eulogies, their descriptions of the journey excerpted from newspaper accounts. Morris issued another edition in 1867 adding foreign tributes. The editor of the *Ohio State Journal,* W. T. Coggeshall, compiled *The Journeys of Abraham Lincoln,* also published in 1865, from dispatches that appeared in his pages and covered both inaugural and memorial journeys. When the Lincoln tomb in Springfield was opened to the public in 1872, its first custodian, John C. Power, published details of its design and construction and told how it was financed by the American people. He recounted the homeward trip and titled his book *Abraham Lincoln, His Great Funeral Cortege and Description of the National Monument.* On the centennial anniversary of Lincoln's birth in 1909, F. W. Z. Barrett issued a souvenir book, *Mourning for Lincoln.* These five titles comprise the bibliography of the return journey. (Most full-length biographies end at Ford's Theater where his physical life ended.)

Since then almost five thousand separate titles of books about him have been published. The tremendous output demonstrates that his memory has been a continuing one and has increased with the passage of time. The fact that more books and magazine articles and newspaper pieces have been printed, and more speeches and sermons and poems have been uttered, concerning The Gentle Man of the Civil War evidences the high esteem he is held by his fellow countrymen. Yet the Lincoln theme has not been exhausted. New things are being discovered at this seemingly late date and old things are being retold in the light of modern knowledge and research. The present volume is an example: It represents the first book treatment of his last days from White House to Oak Ridge.

This volume was researched and written in Washington, D.C. The historic scenes of the Lincoln presidency were experienced firsthand. The writer was provided study facilities in what is probably the largest literary repository in the world, the Library of Congress. Manifestly it is not possible to list here the immense number of books, magazines, newspapers, pamphlets, manuscript collections, diaries, letters, congressional documents, presidential papers, doctoral dissertations, and official publications that were consulted to make this volume authentic. The writer devoted seven years full time in Washington to researching and writing about Lincoln and the Civil War.

The Library of Congress is a fabulous institution that would be better appreciated if known as the national library. The Rare Book Division with its priceless collections—in the present instance the Toner and Stern Collections—is a treasure-house of American memorabilia. The Manuscript Division houses the greatest assemblage of Lincoln documents to be found anywhere and includes the basic R. T. Lincoln Collection (known popularly as The Lincoln Papers) without which no work on the sixteenth President can be properly researched. The Newspaper and Periodical Division contains a comprehensive assembly of American journals, and the rare issues are being put on microfilm for permanent protection.

The Library's knowledgeable personnel is enhanced by three Lincoln savants: D. C. Mearns, chief, Manuscript Division, author of *The Lincoln Papers;* Roy P. Basler, chief reference librarian, editor (Rutgers edition), *The Collected Works of Abraham Lincoln;* and Dr. C. P. Powell, cataloger of the Lincoln Papers and former research director of the Lincoln Sesquicentennial Commission that sponsored *Lincoln Day by Day.*

With this said, the scope of the sources behind this work can be better appreciated.

At each stopover the local press served as the prime reference source. Metropolitan newspapers—Philadelphia, New York, Chicago—were also consulted since local journals, limited in size, were limited in their coverage of the event. Big city papers had correspondents traveling with the cortege; some went all the way as did the chief of the Associated Press Washington bureau. Altogether the press coverage of the Lincoln assassination and aftermath was without parallel in journalistic history.

Newspapers of the United States and where they can be seen are cataloged in *Union List of Newspapers, 1821-1937,* supplemented by *Newspapers on Microfilm.* Magazines and periodicals are listed in *Union List of Serials* and supplement, and in *New Serial Titles, 1950-1960.* Hometown journals can generally be found in public and university libraries, historical societies, and publishers' offices. Magazine articles for seventy-five years are cataloged by subject in *Reader's Guide to Periodical Literature.* The articles quoted or cited in this narrative are identified in the notes.

Lincoln books, 3,943 separate titles, are cataloged in *Lincoln Bibliography, 1839-1939,* by Jay Monaghan—a monumental job. (Note this goes only to 1939, since when many more titles have been published.) "100 Best Lincoln Books" are offered as a supplement in *Lincoln's Education* by M. L. Houser. In the outstanding one-volume full-length biography, *Abraham Lincoln,* Benjamin Thomas provides expert analysis (in the appendix) of Lincoln literature. *Lincoln the President,* volume 2, by James G. Randall, contains an excellent bibliography on this phase of his career. A recent comprehensive bibliography covering his whole life is embodied in the annotations of Reinhard H. Luthin's *The Real Abraham Lincoln,* but as it is not arranged alphabetically the references must be extracted as the narrative progresses.

A valuable bibliography is appended to the Lincoln Sesquicentennial Commission's landmark work, *Lincoln Day by Day,* volume 3, although it does not include books published after 1957. The reference source on up-to-date Lincoln books is, of course, *Subject Guide to Books in Print,* the latest year. General reference sources include *Bibliographies in American History* and *Writings on American History.*

All quotes attributed to Lincoln in the text are identified in the notes. His words (over a million) should be the object of study and understanding by every American; for here is American literature at the grassroots level offering some of the finest compositions in the English tongue. Here is the man himself. There are several anthologies beginning with Nicolay and Hay's *The Complete Works of Abraham Lincoln.* Most recent is the Rutgers edition of *The Collected Works of Abraham Lincoln.*

The vastness of Lincoln literature indicates it is impossible to offer a "complete" bibliography. Only the vastness of the holdings of the Library of Congress and other governmental repositories—National Archives, National Library of Medicine, Smithsonian Institution, and departmental libraries—make it possible to adequately tap the voluminous prime sources; and even then special collections must be consulted such as at the Illinois Historical Society, Brown University, New York Public Library, and others including private collections. Following are books quoted or cited in narrative and notes.

ARNOLD, ISAAC N. *The History of Abraham Lincoln, and the Overthrow of Slavery.* Chicago: Clarke and Co., 1866.

————. *The Life of Abraham Lincoln.* Chicago: Jansen, McClurg & Co., 1885.

BADEAU, ADAM. *Military History of Ulysses S. Grant.* 3 vols. New York: D. Appleton & Co., 1868-81.

BALES, WILLIAM A. *Tiger in the Streets.* New York: Dodd, Mead & Co., 1962.

BANCROFT, GEORGE. *History of the United States.* 10 vols. Boston: Little, Brown & Company, 1834-75.

BARRETT, FRANK W. Z. *Mourning for Lincoln.* Philadelphia: John C. Winston Co., 1909.

BATES, DAVID H. *Lincoln in the Telegraph Office.* New York: The Century Co., 1907.

BATES, EDWARD. *Diary of.* Edited by Howard K. Beale. (Vol. IV, Annual Report American Historical Association.) Washington: Government Printing Office, 1933.

Battles and Leaders of the Civil War. Edited by R. U. Johnson and C. C. Buel. 4 vols. New York: The Century Co., 1887-88.

BEERS, HENRY P. *Bibliographies in American History.* New York: H. W. Wilson Company, 1938.

BENTON, JOSIAH H. *Voting in the Field.* Boston: Privately Printed, 1915.

BEVERIDGE, ALBERT J. *Abraham Lincoln, 1809-1858.* 2 vols. Boston: Houghton Mifflin Company, 1928.

BOOK, JANET M. *Northern Rendezvous—Harrisburg During the Civil War.* Harrisburg: Telegraph Press, 1951.

BROOKS, NOAH. *Washington in Lincoln's Time.* New York: The Century Co., 1895.

BROWN, ALONZO L. *The History of the Fourth Regiment of Minnesota Infantry During the Great Rebellion.* St. Paul: The Pioneer Press Company, 1892.

BROWNING, ORVILLE HICKMAN. *Diary of.* Edited by Theodore C. Pease and James G. Randall. 2 vols. (Illinois State Historical Library Collections, vols. XX, XXII, 1925-33.) Springfield, Ill.: The Trustees of the Illinois State Historical Library.

BURRAGE, HENRY S. *Historical Address, Fiftieth Anniversary.* Portland, Me.: The Military Order of the Loyal Legion, Maine Commandery, 1917.

BUTLER, BENJAMIN F. *Private and Official Correspondence of.* Edited by Jessie A. Marshall. 5 vols. Norwich, Mass.: The Plimpton Press, 1917.

CARMAN, HARRY J. and LUTHIN, REINHARD H. *Lincoln and the Patronage.* New York: Columbia University Press, 1943.

CARPENTER, FRANCIS B. *Six Months at the White House with A. Lincoln.* New York: Hurd and Houghton, 1866.

Ceremonies in Commemoration of Abraham Lincoln. Philadelphia: The Military Order of the Loyal Legion, Pennsylvania Commandery, 1909.

CHAMBERLAIN, JOSHUA L. *The Passing of the Armies.* New York: G. P. Putnam's Sons, 1915.

CHAMBERLIN, THOMAS. *History of the One Hundred and Fiftieth Regiment, Pennsylvania Volunteers.* Philadelphia: Press of F. McManus, Jr., 1905.

CHAMBRUN, [MARQUIS] C. ADOLPHE DE P. DE. *Impressions of Lincoln and the Civil War.* Translated from the French by Aldebert de Chambrun. New York: Random House, 1952.

CHASE, SALMON P. *Inside Lincoln's Cabinet: the Civil War Diaries of.* Edited by David Donald. New York: Longmans, Green & Co., 1954.

COGGESHALL, WILLIAM T. *The Journeys of Abraham Lincoln.* Columbus: Ohio State Journal, 1865.

COLFAX, SCHUYLER. *Life and Principles of Abraham Lincoln.* Philadelphia: J. B. Rodgers, 1865.

CONNOR, HENRY G. *John Archibald Campbell.* Boston: Houghton Mifflin Company, 1920.

CRÈVECOEUR, MICHEL G. ST. J. DE. *Letters from an American Farmer.* London: Printed for T. Davies, 1782.

CROOK, WILLIAM H. *Through Five Administrations.* Compiled and edited by Margarita S. Gerry. New York: Harper & Bros., 1910.

CULLOM, SHELBY M. *Fifty Years of Public Service.* Chicago: A. C. McClurg & Co., 1911.

DANA, CHARLES A. *Recollections of the Civil War.* New York: D. Appleton & Co., 1898.

DU BOSE, JOHN W. *General Joseph Wheeler and the Army of the Tennessee.* New York: The Neale Publishing Co., 1912.

EISENSCHIML, OTTO. *Why Was Lincoln Murdered?* Boston: Little, Brown & Company, 1937.

GERRISH, THEODORE. *Army Life: a Private's Reminiscences of the Civil War.* Portland, Me.: Hoyt, Fogg & Donham, 1882.

GIBSON, GUY J. "Lincoln's League—the Union League Movement During the Civil War." Unpublished Ph.D. dissertation, University of Illinois, 1957.

GLOVER, EDWIN A. *Bucktailed Wildcats—a Regiment of Civil War Volunteers.* New York: Thomas Yoseloff, 1960.

GLOVER, WALDO F. *Abraham Lincoln and the Sleeping Sentinel.* Montpelier: The Vermont Historical Society, 1936.

GOBRIGHT, L. A. *Recollection of Men and Things at Washington.* Philadelphia: Claxton, Remsen & Haffelfinger; Washington: W. H. & O. H. Morrison, 1869.

GRANT, ULYSSES S. *Personal Memoirs of.* 2 vols. New York: C. L. Webster & Co., 1885-86.

GRAY, CARL R. *The Lincoln Car on the Union Pacific.* Princeton: Printed at the Princeton University Press, 1937.

GRAY, WOOD. *The Hidden Civil War.* New York: The Viking Press, 1942.

GREELEY, HORACE. *The American Conflict.* 2 vols. Hartford: O. D. Case & Company; Chicago: G. & C. W. Sherwood, 1864-66.

————.*Greely on Lincoln.* Edited by Joel Benton. New York: The Baker & Taylor Co., 1893.

HABENSTEIN, ROBERT W., and LAMERS, WILLIAM M. *The History of American Funeral Directing.* Milwaukee: Bulfin Printers, 1955.

HALE, EDWARD EVERETT. *Memories of a Hundred Years.* 2 vols. New York: The Macmillan Company, 1902.

HAMILTON, CHARLES, and OSTENDORF, LLOYD. *Lincoln in Photographs.* Norman: University of Oklahoma Press, 1963.

HELM, KATHERINE. *The True Story of Mary, Wife of Lincoln.* New York: Harper & Bros., 1928.

HELPER, HINTON R. *The Impending Crisis.* New York: Burdick Bros., 1857.

HERNDON, WILLIAM H., and WEIK, JESSE W. 3 vols. *Abraham Lincoln, the True Story of a Great Life.* Chicago: Belford, Clarke & Co., 1889.

HERTZ, EMANUEL, editor. *The Hidden Lincoln.* New York: The Viking Press, 1938.

HORAN, JAMES D., and SWIGGETT, HOWARD. *The Pinkerton Story.* New York: G. P. Putnam's Sons, 1951.

HOUSER, MARTIN L. *Lincoln's Education, and Other Essays.* New York: Bookman Associates, 1957.

HOWELLS, WILLIAM D. *Life of Abraham Lincoln.* (Facsimile of 1860 biography corrected by Lincoln himself.) Bloomington: Indiana University Press, 1960.

JANVIER, FRANCIS DE H. *Patriotic Poems.* Philadelphia: J. B. Lippincott & Co., 1866.

JOHNS (MRS.) JANE M. *Personal Recollections of Early Decatur.* Decatur, Ill.: Decatur Chapter, Daughters of the American Revolution, 1912.

JONES, THOMAS D. *Memories of Lincoln.* New York: The Press of the Pioneers, 1934.

KECKLEY, ELIZABETH. *Behind the Scenes; or Thirty Years a Slave and Four Years in the White House.* New York: G. W. Carleton & Co., 1868.

LAMON, WARD HILL. *The Life of Abraham Lincoln.* Boston: James R. Osgood & Co., 1872.

——. *Recollections of Abraham Lincoln, 1847-1865.* Edited by Dorothy Lamon Teillard. Chicago: A. C. McClurg & Co., 1895.

LEALE, CHARLES A. *Lincoln's Last Hours.* New York: Military Order of the Loyal Legion, New York Commandery, 1909.

LINCOLN, ABRAHAM. *The Collected Works of.* 9 vols. Edited by Roy P. Basler *et. al.* New Brunswick: Rutgers University Press, 1953-55.

————. *The Complete Works of.* Edited by John G. Nicolay and John Hay. 2 vols. New York: The Century Co., 1894. Rev. edition, 12 vols. New York: F. D. Tandy Company, 1905.

Lincoln Day by Day. 3 vols. Washington: Lincoln Sesquicentennial Commission, Government Printing Office, 1960.

Lincoln Talks. Edited by Emanuel Hertz. New York: The Viking Press, 1939.

LINCOLN, WALDO. *History of the Lincoln Family.* Worcester: Commonwealth Press, 1923.

Lincoln's Springfield, a Guide Book and Brief History. Springfield, Ill.: The Abraham Lincoln Association, 1938.

LUTHIN, REINHARD H. *The Real Abraham Lincoln.* Englewood Cliffs: Prentice-Hall, 1960.

LYNCH, DENIS T. *"Boss" Tweed: the Story of a Grim Generation.* New York: Boni and Liveright, 1927.

McBRIDE, ROBERT W. *Personal Recollections of Abraham Lincoln.* Indianapolis: The Bobbs-Merrill Company, 1926.

McCALLUM, D. C. *U.S. Military Railroad Dept.; Reports of Bvt. Brig. Gen. D. C. McCallum.* 2 vols. Washington: Government Printing Office, 1866.

McCLURE, ALEXANDER K. *Our Presidents, and How We Make Them.* New York: Harper & Bros., 1900.

McCULLOCH, HUGH. *Men and Measures of Half a Century.* New York: Charles Scribner's Sons, 1888.

McLOUGHLIN, EMMETT. *An Inquiry into the Assassination of Abraham Lincoln.* New York: Lyle Stuart, 1963.

Magazines. See *Union List of Serials, New Serial Titles*, and *Reader's Guide to Periodical Literature.*

MEARNS, DAVID C. *The Lincoln Papers; the Story of a Collection.* 2 vols. Garden City: Doubleday & Company, 1948.

Medal of Honor of United States Army. Washington: Government Printing Office, 1948.

The Medical and Surgical History of the War of the Rebellion, 1861-1865. 3 vols. Washington: Office of the Surgeon General, 1870.

MESERVE, FREDERICK H., and SANDBURG, CARL. *The Photographs of Abraham Lincoln.* New York: Harcourt, Brace & Company, 1944.

MILTON, GEORGE F. *Abraham Lincoln and the Fifth Column.* New York: The Vanguard Press, 1942.

MONAGHAN, JAY. *Lincoln Bibliography, 1839-1939.* Springfield: Illinois State Historical Library, 1943 and 1945. Vols. XXXI and XXXII.

MORRIS, BENJAMIN F., editor. *The Memorial Record of the Nation's Tribute to Abraham Lincoln.* Washington: W. H. & O. H. Morrison, 1865.

New Serial Titles, 1950-60. 2 vols. Washington: Library of Congress, 1961.

Newspapers. See *Union List of Newspapers.*

Newspapers on Microfilm. Washington: Library of Congress, 1961.

NICOLAY, JOHN G., and HAY, JOHN. *Abraham Lincoln: a History.* 10 vols. New York: The Century Co., 1890.

Official Records: See title, *The War of the Rebellion; a Compilation of the Official Records* . . .

OLDROYD, OSBORN H. *The Lincoln Memorial: Album—Immortelles.* New York: G. W. Carleton & Co., 1882.

————. *The Poets' Lincoln; Tributes in Verse to the Martyred Lincoln.* Washington: O. H. Oldroyd, 1915.

Our Martyr President, Abraham Lincoln. New York: Tibbals and Whiting, 1865.

PARTRIDGE, CHARLES A. *History of the Ninety-sixth Regiment, Illinois Volunteer Infantry.* Chicago: Brown, Pettibone & Co., 1887.

PATRICK, REMBERT W. *The Fall of Richmond.* Baton Rouge: Louisiana State University Press, 1960.

PHISTERER, FREDERICK. *New York in the War of the Rebellion.* 3rd edition, 6 vols. Albany: J. B. Lyon Company, State Printers, 1912.

PIATT, DONN. *Memories of Men Who Saved the Union.* Chicago: Belford, Clarke & Co., 1887.

PITMAN, BENN, compiler. *The Assassination of President Lincoln and the Trial of the Conspirators.* Cincinnati: Moore, Wilstach & Baldwin, 1864.

Poetical Tributes to the Memory of Abraham Lincoln. Philadelphia: J. B. Lippincott & Co., 1865.

PORTER, DAVID D. *Incidents and Anecdotes of the Civil War.* New York: D. Appleton & Co., 1885.

PORTER, HORACE. *Campaigning with Grant.* New York: The Century Co., 1887.

POWER, John C. *Abraham Lincoln, His Great Funeral Cortege and Decription of the National Monument.* Springfield: np. 1872.

PULLEN, JOHN J. *The Twentieth Maine: a Volunteer Regiment in the Civil War.* Philadelphia: J. B. Lippincott & Co., 1957.

QUARLES, BENJAMIN. *Lincoln and the Negro.* New York: Oxford University Press, 1962.

RANDALL, JAMES G. *Lincoln, the President.* 4 vols. New York: Dodd, Mead & Co., 1945-55.

RANDALL, RUTH P. *Mary Lincoln; Biography of a Marriage.* Boston: Little, Brown & Company, 1953.

RAYMOND, HENRY J. *Lincoln, His Life and Times.* 2 vols. New York: Hurst & Co., 1891.

Reader's Guide to Periodical Literature. New York: The H. W. Wilson Co., 1890—.

ROEHRENBECK, WILLIAM J. *The Regiment That Saved the Capital.* New York: Thomas Yoseloff, 1961.

ROSCOE, THEODORE. *The Web of Conspiracy.* Englewood Cliffs: Prentice-Hall, 1959.

SANDBURG, CARL. *Abraham Lincoln: the Prairie Years.* 2 vols. New York: Harcourt, Brace & Company, 1926.

Santayana, The Philosophy of. Edited by Irwin Edman. New York: Charles Scribner's Sons, 1953.

Scotia's Bards. New York: R. Carter & Bros., 1854.

SEARCHER, VICTOR. *Lincoln's Journey to Greatness.* New York: Holt, Rinehart and Winston, 1960.

Sermons Preached in Boston on the Death of Abraham Lincoln. Boston: J. E. Tilton & Co., 1865.

SEWARD, FREDERICK W. *Seward at Washington: a Memoir of His Life with Selections from His Letters.* New York: Derby & Miller, 1891. Vols. 2 and 3.

SEWARD, WILLIAM H. *Autobiography of* (vol. 1 of above). New York: D. Appleton & Co., 1877.

SHEA, J. D. G., editor, *The Lincoln Memorial.* New York: Bunce & Huntington, 1865.

SHERIDAN, PHILIP H. *Personal Memoirs of.* 2 vols. New York: C. L. Webster & Co., 1888.

SHERMAN, WILLIAM TECUMSEH. *Memoirs of, By Himself.* 2 vols. New York: D. Appleton & Co., 1875.

STERN, PHILLIP VAN D. *Secret Missions of the Civil War.* Chicago: Rand McNally & Co., 1959.

STIDGER, FELIX G. *Treason History of the Order of Sons of Liberty.* Chicago: Felix G. Stidger, 1903.

STIMMEL, SMITH. *Personal Reminiscences of Abraham Lincoln.* Minneapolis: W. H. M. Adams, 1928.

STOWE, HARRIET BEECHER. *A Key to Uncle Tom's Cabin.* Boston: J. P. Jewett & Co.; Cleveland: Jewett, Proctor & Worthington, 1853.

――――. *Uncle Tom's Cabin.* Same as above, 1852.

STRINGER, LAWRENCE B., editor. *History of Logan County.* 2 vols. Chicago: Pioneer Publishing Co., 1911.

Subject Guide to Books in Print. New York: R. R. Bowker & Co., 1963.

THOMAS, BENJAMIN P. *Abraham Lincoln, a Biography.* New York: Alfred A. Knopf, 1952.

――――, and HYMAN, HAROLD M. *Stanton: the Life and Times of Lincoln's Secretary of War.* New York: Alfred A. Knopf, 1962.

THOMSON, O. R. HOWARD, and RAUCH, WILLIAM H. *History of the "Bucktails."* Philadelphia: Electric Printing Co., 1906.

TODD, WILLIAM. *The Seventy-ninth Highlanders, New York Volunteers in the War of the Rebellion, 1861-1865.* Albany: Brandow, Barton & Co., 1886.

TOWNSEND, EDWARD D. *Anecdotes of the Civil War.* New York: D. Appleton & Co., 1884.

Tributes of the Nations to Abraham Lincoln. Washington: Government Printing Office, 1867.

Tributes: Abraham Lincoln. New York: Tibbals & Whiting, 1865.

TYRNER-TURNAUER, A. R. *Lincoln and the Emperors.* New York: Harcourt, Brace & World, 1962.

Union List of Newspapers. New York: The H. W. Wilson Co., 1937.

Union List of Serials. New York: The H. W. Wilson Co., 1943.

——, *Supplement to, 1944-1949.* Same as above.

United States Government. *Census, 1860, Preliminary Report.* Washington: Government Printing Office, 1860.

——. *Census, 1860.* Washington: Government Printing Office, 1861.

——. *Medal of Honor of United States Army.* See under title.

——. *Official Register. 1861-65.* Washington: Government Printing Office, 1861-65.

——. Surgeon General's Report. See title *The Medical and Surgical History of the War of the Rebellion.*

——. *Tributes of the Nations to Abraham Lincoln.* See under title.

The War of the Rebellion: a Compilation of the Official Records of the Union and Confederate Armies. 128 vols. Washington: Government Printing Office, 1880-1901.

WARNER, EZRA J. *Generals in Gray.* Baton Rouge: Louisiana State University Press, 1959.

WEED, THURLOW. *Life of, Including his Autobiography and a Memoir.* 2 vols. Boston: Houghton, Mifflin and Co., 1883-84.

WELLES, GIDEON. *Diary of.* 3 vols. (Amended Edition) New York: W. W. Norton & Co., 1960.

WHITMAN, WALT. *The Complete Writings of.* 10 vols. New York: G. P. Putnam's Sons, 1902.

——. *Sequel to Drum Taps.* Camden: Walt Whitman, 1866.

WILLIAMS, ARCHIE D. *The Praise of Lincoln; an Anthology.* Indianapolis: The Bobbs-Merrill Company, 1911.

Writings on American History. Annual Reports of the American Historical Association. Washington: Government Printing Office, 1920—.

INDEX

311

802 809 9